The Future of Glo

With today's social and geopolitical order in significant flux this project offers vital insight into the future global order by comparatively charting national media perceptions regarding the future of global competition, through the lens of Ontological Security (OS).

The authors employ a mixed-method approach to analyze 620 news articles from 47 Russian, Chinese, Venezuelan, and Iranian news sources over a five-year period (2014–19), quantitatively comparing the drivers of their visions while providing in-depth qualitative case studies for each nation. Not only do these narratives reveal how these four nations understand the current global order, but also point to their (in)flexibility and agentic capacity for reflection in adapting, even shaping the future order, and their identity-roles within it, around an economic and diplomatic battleground. The authors argue these narratives create trajectories with inertial effects grounded in their OS needs, providing enduring insights into their behavior and interests moving into the future.

The Future of Global Competition will help readers understand how influential nations typical aligned in opposition to the USA, envision the drivers of global competition and the make-up of the future international system. Those engaged in the study of media, global politics, international relations, and communication will find this book to be a critical source.

Robert S. Hinck is an assistant professor at Air University part of the US Air Force's educational system. He has previously co-authored *Global Media and Strategic Narratives of Contested Democracy: Chinese, Russian, and Arabic Media Narratives of the US Presidential Election* (2019). His expertise is in rhetoric, strategic narrative, and political communication.

Sara R. Kitsch is an assistant professor at Air University part of the US Air Force's educational system. Her research revolves around rhetorical theory and criticism, communication, strategic narratives, women's and gender studies, and citizenship. She has published articles in *Communication Quarterly, Southern Communication Journal*, and *Rhetoric and Public Affairs.*

Asya Cooley is an assistant professor of Strategic Communications in the School of Media and Strategic Communications, at Oklahoma State University. Her research revolves around nonprofit communications and management, higher education management, and philanthropy.

Skye C. Cooley is an assistant professor in the School of Media and Strategic Communications at Oklahoma State University. His research centers on Russian political communication, global media and digital democracy, as well as developing and testing platforms for civic deliberation online. In 2019 he was a co-author of *Global Media and Strategic Narratives of Contested Democracy: Chinese, Russian, and Arabic Media Narratives of the US Presidential Election* (2019).

Routledge Studies in Global Information, Politics and Society
Edited by Kenneth Rogerson, Duke University and Laura Roselle, Elon University

International communication encompasses everything from one-to-one cross-cultural interactions to the global reach of a broad range of information and communications technologies and processes. *Routledge Studies in Global Information, Politics and Society* celebrates – and embraces – this depth and breadth. To completely understand communication, it must be studied in concert with many factors, since, most often, it is the foundational principle on which other subjects rest. This series provides a publishing space for scholarship in the expansive, yet intersecting, categories of communication and information processes and other disciplines.

16. The Media and the Public Sphere
A Deliberative Model of Democracy
Thomas Häussler

17. Internet and Democracy in the Network Society
Jan A.G.M. van Dijk and Kenneth L. Hacker

18. Global Media and Strategic Narratives of Contested Democracy:
Chinese, Russian, and Arabic Media Narratives of the US Presidential Election
Robert S. Hinck, Skye C. Cooley, Randolph Kluver

19. Post-truth, Fake news and Democracy
Mapping the Politics of Falsehood
Johan Farkas and Jannick Schou

20. Infrastructure Communication in International Relations
Carolijn van Noort

21. The Future of Global Competition
Ontological Security and Narratives in Chinese, Iranian, Russian, and Venezuelan Media
Robert S. Hinck, Asya Cooley, Skye C. Cooley, Sara Kitsch

"In this vivid study, Robert Hinck, Asya Cooley, Skye Cooley and Sara Kitsch provide a mixed-methods illustration of the origins, and operation, of narratives in four crucial contemporary case settings. This well-organized, carefully and superbly written book provides a masterful blueprint for analyzing the dynamics of status, ontological security, and strategic narratives in a potentially emergent post-liberal world order."

Brent Steele, *The University of Utah*

The Future of Global Competition

Ontological Security Narratives in Chinese, Russian, Venezuelan, and Iranian Media

Robert S. Hinck, Sara R. Kitsch, Asya Cooley and Skye C. Cooley

NEW YORK AND LONDON

First published 2022
by Routledge
605 Third Avenue, New York, NY 10158

and by Routledge
2 Park Square, Milton Park, Abingdon, Oxon OX14 4RN

Routledge is an imprint of the Taylor & Francis Group, an informa business

Library of Congress Cataloging-in-Publication Data
A catalog record for this title has been requested

ISBN: 978-1-032-05417-9 (hbk)
ISBN: 978-1-032-05418-6 (pbk)
ISBN: 978-1-003-19747-8 (ebk)

DOI: 10.4324/9781003197478

Typeset in Times New Roman
by Taylor & Francis Books

Dedicated To Hugo and Indiana

Contents

Figures

Tables

Tables

1 The Future of Global Competition

Ontological Security and Narratives in Chinese, Iranian, Russian, and Venezuelan Media

Introduction

Amid a world in flux—with societies flooded by fake news, foreign propaganda and misinformation, rising uncertainty and distrust in political leaders, and changing social values—how is it that nations, as political collectives, mobilize their populace to meet the challenges of the future global order? The answer is not obviously clear, evident not only by America's recent vacillation between isolationism and globalism, but by its competitors' policy responses as well. For instance, prior to 2013 observers of China hoped Xi Jinping's tenure in office would usher in a new wave of economic and political reform. And yet, faced with a slowing economy with doubts over China's ability to escape the middle income trap and lingering concerns over US policy in the Pacific, in addition to internal political competition, under Xi's leadership the Chinese Communist Party has doubled down on its authoritarian practices. Perhaps, more troublesome, when in 2014 Ukraine elected a Western, pro-democratic president, Russia surprised the world by sending "volunteer" troops into Eastern Ukraine and retaking control of Crimea despite costly Western economic sanctions, widespread international condemnation, and limited strategic benefit all while Russia's economy experienced already insipid growth.

In both cases Western audiences might interpret such actions as disconcerting with China and Russia carving a distinct, anti-Western camp akin to a new Cold War. And yet, by invoking such a metaphor this explanation might do more to assuage Western fears of the unfamiliar or "cultural outsiders" than describe the motivating force behind such actions. Indeed, a feeling of Western decline permeates political elites in the US and Western Europe and has done so for some time. As a result, it is easy to view nearly any action taken by China or Russia as a harbinger of a new world order.

But if one steps out of this narrative of threat, we see both Chinese and Russian officials having called too, at various times, for greater global governance, even affirming various aspects of the international architecture built by the US after World War II. Indeed, during 2016–20 China did more than the US in making explicit calls to uphold the neo-liberal global order

DOI: 10.4324/9781003197478-1

while Russia repeatedly invoked the values embedded within it to admonish US behavior. This is not say that neither nation wants a greater voice or place in global affairs or desires some revision to the global order moving forward. It merely cautions observers of international affairs from making simple, clear-cut explanations portending dramatic shifts in the international landscape, especially when such interpretations arise from feelings of self-anxiety and decline.

To some extent, such a call is a tall order. Anxiety is a fundamental element of the human condition with humans necessarily formulating mental shortcuts to cognitively order a chaotic world. But in accepting one's inability to know or control everything and recognizing that all actors share such a position, we can begin to better understand the role of those anxieties as springboards for action but also self-imposed constraints to change, for both our and others' actions. Thus, as all nations seek their own space in global affairs, understanding how they situate themselves within an anxious global order is both an intellectually worthy pursuit and one with very real material ramifications. As such, for this project, we examine how four nations—China, Russia, Iran, and Venezuela—widely viewed as in contention with the US, envision the nature of global competition amid an increasingly anxious global order.

In doing so, we argue that the manner in which these countries narratively understand who they and others are, in addition to the nature of the international environment they operate within, are driven by their domestic anxieties which impact their ability to adapt and shape the global system. Identifying the narrative roles states encapsulate themselves in not only provides a more nuanced understanding of the drivers of state behavior, but also entry points for international cooperation, with the potential to mitigate misunderstandings fueling further conflict. Indeed, as our findings demonstrates, Chinese, Russian, Iranian, and Venezuelan societies are more concerned with the economic and diplomatic dimensions of global competition than its military aspects. Nonetheless, these nations differ in their levels of reflexivity with some trapped to previously held identities and beliefs inhibiting their ability to provide material prosperity and cognitive security for their populace. Others, however, appear more optimistic, and thus poised to have a greater impact on the future order. To make our argument, this chapter begins by tracing the contours of global anxiety before discussing elements of global order. We then turn to how states manage anxiety through the lens of Ontological Security (OS) with specific attention placed to the role of narratives in doing so.

The Global Age of Anxiety

Today's social and geopolitical order is in significant flux with rising global anxiety over the challenges of the future. As a recent Pew study explains, "anger at political elites, economic dissatisfaction and anxiety about rapid social changes have fueled political upheaval in regions around the world in recent years" (Wike et al., 2019, para. 1). Growing economic concerns abound with economists reporting a sharp increase in trade uncertainty for the first time in over 20 years as the global economy transitions from a robust, synchronized expansion to widespread slowdown amid rising trade tensions between the US and China, the aftermath of Brexit, and idiosyncratic stresses in emerging economies (Ahir et al., 2019; Bobasu et al., 2020).

Although the impacts of globalization have been debated for decades, events over the last five years show the social transformations unfurled by globalization shaking the political core of the very countries who originally championed it. The Covid-19 pandemic is a case in point, with global supply chains disrupted to such an extent that even the US found itself unable to provide essential medical products (Prasad, 2020). Ideological cracks too are present with politicians in the US and UK successfully campaigning on "country first" rhetoric while retreating from global trade pacts.

While economic globalization has benefited some, global inequality continues to rise with trust in societal institutions on the decline (Alvaredo et al., 2017). According to the 2020 Edelman Trust Barometer report, 73 percent of the global population supports change in the current system of global capitalism while none of the four societal institutions measured (government, business, non-governmental organizations, and media) are trusted (Edelman, 2019). Causes for this include growing cynicism around capitalism, doubts regarding the fairness of the current economic system, declining trust in elites, and deep-seated fears about the future. More specifically, workers are afraid of being left behind, owing to advances in technology—including automation—and fears of foreign competition with immigrants willing to work for less. All this leads to pessimism with national leaders perceived as ill equipped to address future challenges.

Reflective of these concerns, Pew found rising dissatisfaction with democracy linked to beliefs that elected officials do not care what people think, with some even doubting whether their government is being ran for the better of all (Connaughton et al., 2020). Although core ideas of liberal democracy remain popular among some global publics, commitment to democracy remains weak with international perceptions on the performance of democratic systems "decidedly negative" (Wike et al., 2019, para. 2). Thus, anti-establishment parties and populist movements have gained significant traction on both the left and right side of the political spectrum.

Some might argue that the global commitment to liberal democracy has been on the decline for years. Indeed, Freedom House reported in 2018 that democracy was in retreat, recording the 13th consecutive year of decline in global freedom scores across every region of the globe (Freedom House, 2019). However, a qualitative shift can be seen in its 2020 report whereby growing numbers of leaders in Central and Eastern Europe have dropped even the pretense of playing by the rules of democracy with Central and Eastern European leaders beginning to openly attack democratic institutions. As such, today, there are fewer democracies in the region than at any point since Freedom House launched their annual report back in 1995 (Csaky, 2020).

Freedom House's 2020 report argues that the fraying global order is significantly contributing to these events. The post-Cold War consensus has now given way to great-power competition and the pursuit of self-interest (Csaky, 2020). The rise of authoritarian powers, including Russia, China, and Turkey have exacerbated the situation while democratizing forces have declined with even the US increasingly focused on backroom deals and deemphasizing any shared commitment to democracy. Likewise, the European Union (EU) has proven ineffective in addressing its own member states' failure to tackle rule-of-law violations, with Poland and Hungary facing little repercussions for authoritarian power grabs and erosion of rights for migrants and asylum seekers. Thus, not only are fissures emerging within the economic pillar of our current global order, but so too is its democratic façade.

The depiction of the global order discussed above is not intended to ring the alarm bell foretelling its collapse. Indeed, as Eilstrup-Sangiovanni and Hofmann (2020) note, distress over the fate of the contemporary global order is a leitmotif among international relations (IR) scholars. Yet, profound changes do appear to be manifesting themselves in important and impactful ways for both democratic and nondemocratic nations alike. As Öniş (2017) argues, we are in an "age of anxiety" characterized by relative economic stagnation and inequality coupled with shocks from mass migration and terrorist attacks. While Eilstrup-Sangiovanni and Hofmann (2020) maintain that what we are currently witnessing is not so much a profound or definitive crisis of the existing order, they do conclude that the system is undergoing a transformation from within into a broader, more inclusive system of governance reflecting the need to accommodate new actors and problems. How countries perceive these new problems and their ability to successfully compete in this future global order is the concern of this project.

We argue that central to understanding the challenges of the future global competition is examining the role of anxiety in motivating, and in some cases incapacitating, societies as they attempt to define who they are and how they can ensure a sense of agency within a system in flux. As Reus-Smit (2018) argues, anxiety over the future of international order is rife, with concerns ranging from its economic foundations, the effects of transnationalism, the decline of the West, and shifting balances of power, among other destabilizing challenges; underlining all of these concerns is growing angst regarding cultural diversity and identity. Indeed, the rapid social transformations brought forth by globalization and post-colonialism has provided a strong motivational force for minority and majority groups to seek out and reaffirm their self and collective identities (Kinnvall, 2004). Thus, some of the greatest challenges people are facing is not physical security but a sense of unease and concern over their daily lives and whether their leaders are able to answer the challenges of the twenty-first century (Kinevall et al., 2018).

This is not to say that great power politics has no role in how states come to define themselves or the tools needed to compete in tomorrow's global order. Not only do notions of "great power" status confer in themselves a form of identity and grandeur, but also implicate how states manage their security dilemmas (Mitzen, 2006a; Roselle, 2017; Miskimmon & O'Loughlin, 2017; Pu, 2019). However, the motivations for such status often arise from feelings of insecurity and are fueled by domestic anxieties over changes in one's environment. As research shows, the more domestically insecure a country is the more likely its leaders are to signal high international status to boost domestic legitimacy (Pu, 2019). This is especially true for rapidly ascending states with domestic calculations often taking precedent over international ones as swift economic development leads to social and political dislocations leaving national leaders to confront mounting internal pressures, including: rising domestic expectations, heightened nationalism, and fears of economic stagnation. For these reasons, Pu (2019) argues for the need to bring back domestic politics to determine the sources of insecurity driving nations' status signaling behavior. His claim further affirms the need for research examining how nations discuss their identities and roles in the global order as well as their instruments of power ensuring their competitive success; particularly those countries perceived as actively challenging it.

Argument

To capture the tools by which countries deal with this anxiety, we propose to examine Chinese, Russian, Iranian, and Venezuelan media narratives discussing the future of global competition from the perspective of OS. While multiple theoretical perspectives help explain the changes of today's evolving global order, we focus on OS as it is premised on the idea that social collectives, much like individuals and including states, face underlining, ineradicable anxiety and must manage it to develop a sense of agency. Accordingly, to manage this anxiety they must form a sense of cognitive stability allowing them to impose order on their environment through the creation of a stable sense of self identity and routination of their relationships with others, often through narratives. Taken together, these form the actor's basic trust system, which regularizes social life, making it and the "self" knowable thereby providing the capacity to act (Giddens, 1991; Mitzen, 2006a); allowing us to explore how these four nations make sense of the evolving global order and the means by which they seek to influence it.

Understanding how these four nations grapple with their OS concerns, then, weaves a larger lens by which we can see how the future order might unfold by those most often in contention with it, including key elements of competition among its material, ideational, institutional, and normative dimensions. Unlike IR theories treating the state as a unified actor, our perspective takes into account the constitutive and fraying dynamics by which social collectives coalesce; including the domestic and sociological fears nations face (Giddens, 1991), the cultural means by which nations imagine what binds their communities together (Anderson, 2006), and the strategic ways in which they communicate their identities and mobilize public support (Miskimmon et al., 2013). More specifically, this narrative approach enables us to identify how nations make sense of the changes in the global order and the problems, solutions, allies, and contenders embedded in these narratives as they seek to compete, revise, or do without it and the implications of the trajectories of these narratives depicting the future of global competition.

Therefore, we argue that, as support for a global order requires a belief in its legitimacy (Kissinger, 2014; Acharya, 2018), actors must come to see its effectiveness in affording them with the ability to provide for their populace. Consideration, then, of global order draws first upon domestic political legitimacy before international. Both of which, however, comes from the expression of political communities to form some level of agreement regarding who they are at a specific moment in time and what they collectively desire to move towards, especially when grappling with anxiety present in an ever changing world (Arendt, 1972; Crick, 2014; Berenskötter, 2020; Hom & Steele, 2020).

Accordingly, we argue that state media discourse constitutes a nation's capacity to coordinate shared meanings within its citizenry, and in doing so, not only provides OS for their population but also builds capacity for common action. Embedded in a state's media discourse are narratives propagated by the state and drawn from the constructs of society, which functions as an attempt to reassure its populace regarding who the nation is by looking to the future by connecting elements of its past and current situation. As such, narratives set the stage for understanding while also posing constraints on the imaginable and actionable. As MacIntyre (1984) argues, it is through narrative that we are able to discern what a standard of good action is with Burke (1969) arguing that narratives furnish us with motives for action.

However, not all states are equally positioned to build such capacity for coordinated action. We contend that confidence and optimism are key variables embedded in a nation's media discourse that enable a country to actualize a productive sense of self; that is a narrative whereby the state can move forward and adapt to its environment in contrast to retrenchment or paralysis. Importantly, the narrative resources available to states to construct a productive sense of self when facing changes within the global order are dependent upon both how they view their relationships with others, including international organizations, but also the coherence of their domestic situation. In the latter case, this coherence reflects the extent to which a nation's domestic material realities align with their discursive values and beliefs of who they are. In other words, when a state's domestic realities appear bleak, this is turn inhibits its capacity for collective sense making and future oriented action. In cases where the domestic realities are particularly unraveled, the political community becomes stuck with a fractured sense of self preventing their ability to collectively come together to shape and influence their international environment.

Our study provides both theoretical and empirical contributions to understanding the importance of OS in international affairs as well as insights regarding how nations adapt to a changing global environment. First, whereas the body of research on OS has grown over the past decades, with at least four special issues dedicated to the topic, little comparative research has been done to understand similarities and differences in how states are able to achieve a sense of self and security. Furthermore, our project's emphasis on non-Western countries, especially those less aligned with the US, helps to further the study of OS beyond EU and Western media.

Second, while much has been written on the role of autobiographical narratives in the creation of political communities' construction of OS, the focus tends to be on historical cases or first and second image analysis (Hom & Steele, 2020). Our project advances the theoretical payoff of OS by emphasizing the future oriented direction of a state's narratives by examining how the nation's media constructs the challenges of future global competition, including areas of vulnerability and strength. In this sense, we extend research not only regarding how nations narrate their own insecurity but also the manner in which they situate themselves within an ontologically *in*secure global order—including how they seek to contribute, or not, to restoring or reshaping that order. This focus helps address the "status quo bias" in OS (Mitzen & Kinnvall, 2020) by examining how positive change and identity adaption is possible—although difficult, as well as extending OS research into third image considerations regarding the construction of the international order as a collective project in its own right (Hom & Steele, 2020).

Third, whereas the emphasis on narrative within recent OS studies provides ample qualitative studies examining the discursive elements and deconstruction of referent symbols used to promote ontological *in*security, our project's comparative, mixed-method design allows for more generalizable findings regarding how nations function as OS suppliers by including quantitative measures providing insight into the driver of these narratives. Finally, and in relation to the future oriented emphasis of our study, we advance research theorizing the implications of nation's narrative trajectories in conjunction to a state's capacity for narrative reflection and agency.

The rest of this chapter lays out the theoretical lens by which we examine national discourses regarding the future of global competition. We begin with a discussion of global order and agency. We then provide an overview of OS before turning to the role of national media systems as a site for understanding narrative constructions of global perceptions. Finally, we end with an overview of the book and a summary of the chapters.

Global order and agency

According to Acharya (2018), the meaning of order in world politics is much disputed with its definitions being situational or descriptive, as well as normative. Thus, IR realists or scholars of diplomatic history, when sharing assumptions of an anarchical world, focus on global distributions of power at specific moments of time as defining various international systems (Kissinger, 1994; Mearsheimer, 2001; Gilpin, 1981; Allison, 2017). Alternatively, liberal-institutionalists focus on the emergence of common interests and values created by international society bounded by common rules working towards promoting common institutions (Bull, 1977; Keohane, 2005). A third view comes from constructivists contending that shared ideas, perceptions, and beliefs provide our social world structure, order, and stability (Wendt, 1999; Finnemore & Sikkin, 1998; Checkel, 1998). Regardless of which camp one gravitates towards, two elements appear central to notions of global order: power and legitimacy.

As Kissinger (2014) explains, any system of order requires a set of commonly accepted rules and a balance of power to enforce restraint when these rules break down. Power, however, can extend beyond its material manifestations to include control of thought or belief and practiced by those with various levels of influence. As Crick (2014) states, "power is a capacity to act in concert through communicative understanding, using available resources, technologies, and mediums, to overcome resistance in pursuit of an imagined good" (p. 6). His definition highlights communication as the realm by which individuals come together to exert collective influence for coordinated action and draws upon philosophers such as Michel Foucault (1982) who see power as "relationships between partners" (p. 135) and Hannah Arendt's (1970) claim that power is the ability "not just to act but to act in concert" (p. 46). As Arendt (1972) explains, "power needs no justification" but "what it does need is legitimacy" (p. 151).

This view of power supports Acharya's (2018) call for examining the normative dimension of global order, placing the question of legitimacy as its central concern. Drawing from Barnett (2008), he argues that while traditional IR scholarship credits powerful actors with order-creation, maintenance, and change, global order is "created and sustained not only by great power preferences but also by changing understanding of what constitutes a legitimate international order" (p. 168). Thus, Acharya's (2018) contribution to studies on global order is that legitimacy depends on representation and participation of not just established powers but emerging regional and global players, the latter of which he argues will likely drive the impetus for change.

Global order, then, consists of the rules for international action—including visions and buy-in regarding what actions are (in)appropriate and imaginable. Incorporated within it are the ideational, material, and institutional realms of international interaction. Importantly, conceptualizations of global order are not universal, nor do they necessarily exclude consideration of regional orders. Indeed, both Kissinger (2014) and Acharya (2018) highlight the importance of regional or local understandings of legitimacy. Kissinger (2014) specifically locates conceptualization of order within regional imaginaries, stating: "world order describes the concept held by a region or civilization about the nature of just arrangements and the distribution of power thought to be applicable to the entire world" (p. 9). For Kissinger (2014), the difference between regional and global visions of order comes from the extent to which these beliefs are applied to a substantial part of the world to the point of impacting the global balance of power. Acharya (2018), however, goes further to argue that such conceptualizations can influence "not just the global balance of power, but also global interdependence, normative structures, and institutions of cooperation" (pp. 9–10).

Of concern for this project, is Acharya's (2018) statement regarding legitimacy as predicated on actors' belief in the *effectiveness* of a given global order. Here regional and global players could have different understandings of what constitutes a legitimate world order, but their support and participation within it rests on its ability to provide support for their interests, broadly defined. In Arendt's (1972) terms, power is tied up with legitimacy, lying in the expression of political communities, and is transformed and adapted to new circumstances in response to the opinions and needs of its citizens. As a result, "All political institutions are manifestations and materializations of power; they petrify and decay as soon as the living power of the people ceases to uphold them" (p. 140). Thus, we understand concerns over the "effectiveness" of global order as the extent to which political communities perceive and discuss their ability to acquire the economic wealth and freedom of action to meet their society's needs and sense of security. In other words, it lies in how their nations communicate their (in)capacity to compete with others to reach their goals and define their own sense of self within the global system.

Importantly, competition does not have to be a zero-sum game—it depends on how societies, and the nations that lead them, define their interests, which could differ, based on their position and alignment within the global system. Thus, we define competition broadly, encompassing physical security, economic attainment, cultural understandings, and diplomatic influence. The question of what happens when actors come to see the global order as one where they are unable to pursue their interests and the actions in which they seek to change the global system brings into consideration the nature of agency.

Agency in global order

As Acharya (2018) notes, the question of agency is of central importance when considering how global order is constructed. He explains that traditional conceptualization of agency emphasize its instrumentality or the capacity of acting or exerting power. Situating agency within the context of IR scholarship, Buzan et al. (1993) offer a definition of agency as the "faculty or state of acting or exerting power" (p. 103). And yet, such definitions often leave murky understandings of what it exactly means to exercise agency, including who or what might do so (Wight, 2006) with IR tending to privilege material forms of power when discussing it (Acharya, 2018).

When considering what makes up agency in world politics, we, like Acharya (2018) accept Wight's (2006) multilayered view. Here agency refers to both individual and social predicates, which both reflects and combines individuals' freedom of subjectivity and the socio-cultural systems by which agents learn their roles as social actors or positioned-practiced places. However, we depart from Acharya in that, as he states, his analysis of global order stresses Bhaskar's (2013) association of agency with the ability to foster change in order to consider how actors reject or transform the normative conceptualization of order. We contend that this view of agency presumes an already coherent social actor with knowledge of what they want to exert agency towards. This becomes especially problematic when changes in one's sociological conditions, as well as the international system, leads to doubts or questions of past practices opening up discussions regarding new formulations of organizational and political life. Thus, to understand how, as Acharya (2018) argues, agency is exercised in world politics through the challenging of key ideas and offerings of alternatives, actors must first find an understanding of self, that is who they are, as well as their relationships to others. This, in turn provides them with an idea of what they stand for and desire, laying the foundation to act, of which the literature on OS seeks to understand.

Ontological security

Rather than focusing on physical safety, OS refers to one's "security of being" (Kinnvall & Mitzen, 2017) or the securing of the subjective sense of who one is (Mitzen, 2006a). Whether it be individuals, social collectives, or states, actors require a sense of being in order to act. That is, without a sense of who one is, actors are unable to articulate their interests and form the value systems necessary to make decisions. OS, then, is a prerequisite of agency and self-identity, which Giddens (1991) defines as "the self as reflexively understood by a person in terms of his or her biography" (p. 244). One develops this sense of self through their trust in routines and biographical narratives; and these are tied to one's interpersonal and organizational relationships in a particular time and space. Thus, when one's relationships and understandings are destabilized, their OS is threatened, and if unmanaged, leads to anxiety and paralysis, even violence (Kinnvall & Mitzen, 2017). As Mitzen (2006a) states, "where an actor has no idea what to expect, she cannot systematically relate ends to means, and it becomes unclear how to pursue her ends" (p. 342). Taken together, OS can be defined as the condition that one obtains when an actor has confidence in their identity and ordering of their environment allowing for clear expectations about the means-end relationships governing their social life. However, ontological *in*security is the deep, incapacitating state of not knowing one's interests and which dangers to confront and which to ignore (Mitzen, 2006a).

For Giddens (1991) modernity and globalization posed the fundamental challenges towards a person's OS, or elemental sense of safety in their world, as traditional locales and social relations were upended. As Kinnvall (2004) demonstrated, the structural changes brought about by globalization left individuals vulnerable to feelings of existential anxiety. However, studies on OS have also explored its impact in IR (Steele, 2008; Mitzen, 2006a; Delehanty & Steele, 2009; Zarakol, 2010; Gustafasson, 2014; Chacko, 2014; Curtis, 2016; Browning, 2018b). According to Chacko (2013), periods of power transition in international politics provoke similar OS challenges, as they too are times of destabilization and uncertainty. Thus, US rhetoric regarding China and India's rise come from not only material factors but also perceptions of "a generalized uncertainty and anxiety about the maintenance of a world order that facilitates the perpetuation of a US identity based on the idea of American exceptionalism" (p. 2). For revisionist powers, Behravesh (2018) argues their identification with other outside powers provides some source of OS, but by opposing the status quo, subjects themselves to geopolitical exclusion engendering feelings of insecurity.

For others, OS helps explain state conflict and behavior more broadly. Mitzen (2006a) argues that uncertainty can prevent states from escaping security dilemmas when their identities and routines become attached to conflict. Hansen (2016) finds this the case in demonstrating that while Russia's hostility towards the West leads to more conflictual relations it also provides greater OS security, thereby strengthening Russia's identity. Likewise, Firoozabadi (2011) argues Iranian foreign policy prioritizes its OS over physical security, being more concerned about preserving its own identity as an Islamic state, and Curtis (2016) uses OS as a lens to explain Chinese behavior in the South China Sea as driven by its need to maintain security of its national identity.

While the notion that states need to construct and maintain their collective identity to maintain social cohesion is well documented in the public memory and identity literature, the impacts of such imaginations on the global order has not been fully fleshed out, emphasizing the past rather than the future. As Eyerman et al. (2017) explain, "collective memory refers to the selective and cumulative process through which collectivities, from groups to nations, make use and meaningful sense of the past" (p. 14). Whereas public memory and OS share assumptions that social collectives require a sense of continuity to maintain social cohesion over time, with narratives and rituals forming crucial components to such constructions, OS emphasizes how these notions implicate agency, specifically the capacity to act through one's sense of self, including one's relations with others, not just imaginaries of their own communities. In considering how nations view the global order, we are concerned not just with societies' autobiographical narratives and memories of their past but more so in how these collective sensemaking processes situate and relate the state with others and within the competitive global landscape moving forward.

Therefore, we argue that OS is an ideal lens to understand how nations understand, contend, or support the *future* global order As noted in the introduction, today's global order is in significant flux fueling anxiety across a variety of dimensions, ranging from culture, economics, and politics with all three overlapping and impacting one's identity and emotional fears. From the perspective of OS, these stressors, and how societies manage them, have significant implications regarding not just who they were or currently are, but also who they might be based on their ability to respond to new challenges and whether such future visions of self are actualizable within the constraints placed upon them by the global system. While most of the research on OS examines individual security issues or challenges political communities face, we set out to explore, chart, and compare the broader discursive landscape in which nations, as social collectives, discuss and narrate these challenges—in other words, their ability to compete—which in turn influences their support or revision of the global order.

Doing so allows for the identifying of potential fault lines for conflict, but also possible changes, or transformation, of boundaries creating new potentialities of cooperation. Analyzing how different political communities talk and define themselves in relation to their perceived challenges within the global community provides for not only new theoretical insights into OS, but also practical and ethical benefits as an exercise in perspective sharing. In this case, understanding how others see themselves, and in turn ourselves, provides a lens for self-reflection and, hopefully, greater appreciation of where others are coming from when grappling with the dynamics of today's shifting global order.

As the literature on OS suggests, those capable of adapting and defining who they are in today's and tomorrow's future landscape will likely succeed in competing, perhaps even shaping the future order. However, those unable to do so, as Mitzen (2006a) explains, are likely to suffer a lack of agency with their energy consumed by meeting immediate needs and unable to plan for the future. Thus, a key question is how states manage their anxiety and for identities enabling action, which the next section addresses.

The formation of identity: OS and the management of anxiety

According to Kinnvall and Mitzen (2017), Gidden's articulation of OS views the formation of the subject fraught with underlying, ineradicable anxiety with social actors needing to manage this anxiety to develop a sense of agency. On a philosophical level, Berenskötter (2020) identifies three underlining drivers of such anxiety drawing upon Kierkegaard and Heidegger's existential phenomenology. The first being temporal, marking the contested nature of historical accounts and our inability to know what the future holds; the second, spatial, is our existence within an infinite cosmological space to which we know very little; and the third, social, speaks to the notion that we are unable to know how others think or feel. From this, Heidegger (1953) concludes that anxiety represents the foundational sentiment of the human condition upon which our desires—or wills—emerge in pursuit of a feeling of epistemological peace, or as Mitzen (2006a) puts it, the obtainment of cognitive and behavioral certainty. For Berenskötter (2020) the mechanisms, broadly speaking, for managing such anxiety include the temporal assignment of numbers—a sense of time or scale—onto which events become embedded, the establishment of routine practices emitting a familiarity of being through an established past carried into the present with predictive social interactions and experiences, and narratives enabling us to meaningfully situate ourselves in the past and into the future.

Like Berenskötter (2020), albeit moving from a philosophical standpoint to the context of IR, Mitzen's (2006a) OS framework lays out three means by which states manage uncertainty with an emphasis on how such mechanisms enable action. The first is identity, or securing a sense of who one is over time. Political actors require a sense of personal continuity as it underwrites their capacity for agency (Mitzen, 2006a). This is because knowledge of one's self, or identity, enables and motivates action and choice as it allows rational thought regarding one's interests and values. Not only do actors need knowledge of who they are, allowing them to identify their interests and desired goals, but they also need confidence regarding the stability of the environment to understand how their actions will take effect. Without this, and when confronting change or challenges, uncertainty can threaten one's identity and incapacitate the actor as they are unable to determine which dangers to confront and which ones to ignore.

Importantly, one's sense of "self" is not a permanent attribute, but does require a sense of stability. Identity is dynamic process from which action flows and in turn sustains identity; a crucial requirement of a stable self-understanding being one's actions can sustain it over time (Mitzen, 2006a). According to Combes (2017) identity is conceptualized as the practice of being-in-the-world with one's concept of "self" composed of situationally specific constellation of characteristics made meaningful through what they exclude. For Steele (2005, 2008) this continuity of "self" occurs in the telling of convincing stories through autobiographical narratives. Subotić (2016) adds that during times of great crisis and threats to state security, narratives provide the cognitive bridge between policy change resolving physical security while also preserving state OS by supplying autobiographical continuity, a sense of routine, familiarity, and calm.

Second, to manage uncertainty and strengthen self-identity actors create basic trust systems by developing routines. The purpose in doing so is the "drive to minimize hard uncertainty by imposing cognitive order on the environment" (Mitzen, 2006a, p. 346). Because actors cannot respond to all dangers at once, they develop "cognitive cocoons" to bracket the manifold possible events that could threaten their bodily or psychological integrity into more manageable questions; allowing for trust that their cognitive world will be reproduced. Generating this trust are routines which "regularizes social life, making it, and the self, knowable" (p. 346). Routines can be strictly personal, but social relationships also can be an importance source. By definition, routinized responses are unthinking or habitual. Unlike rational action, routines are not chosen, but taken-for-granted, suppressing reflection. By giving actors automatic responses to stimuli, routines pacify the cognitive environment, voiding the arena of deliberative choice, and provide individuals with ways of knowing the world and how to act. This in turn supports actors' agency-identity relationships by providing the certainty actors need to enable purposive choice while serving an emotional function of inoculating actors against the paralytic fear of chaos.

Examples of this include Mitzen's (2006b) study on the EU and Mälksoo's (2018) focus on North Atlantic Treaty Organization (NATO) fears related to hybrid warfare. As Mitzen (2006b) demonstrates, EU member states routinize relations with primary strategic partners to develop new identities non-dependent on discourses of danger. The publicity and deliberation inherent in these routines helps stabilize security relations among EU members and constitutes the collective aspirational identity of the EU. More recently, Mälksoo (2018) argues that the concept of hybrid warfare produces significant anxiety for NATO members as it overturns cognitive structures regarding what war is. To manage this threat, NATO pursued a routinization strategy turning fears over hybrid warfare into manageable certainties by identifying Russia as part of its strategy to combat hybrid warfare, thereby attaching routine relationships with that of its traditional antagonist.

Third, attachment and recognition provides individuals with a sense of agency and reinforces identities and routines (Mitzen, 2006a). Actors become attached to certain identities anchored in routines with significant others. Thus, in any given social environment, actors solidify identity and learn to be "agentic" through routinized relations, with recognition from powerful external actors helping determine how individual's intentional actions are received. From a platform of stable routines, aspiring agents come to know who they are, become recognized as such, and therefore can act; evident by Mitzen's (2006b) study on EU relations mentioned above. However, because recognition comes from others, self-conceptions that motivate intentional action are not always reinforced. Under these circumstances, actors could be forced to develop trust systems that support a less desired self, or second best identity; like in the case of Iranian identity as revisionist power allowing it to identify with outside powers, but also being excluded by status quo powers (Behravesh, 2018).

However, once actors become attached to certain identities or routines, it becomes hard to let go of these attachments, as doing so sacrifices a sense of agency. This can lead to the actors becoming attached to conflict, even if appearing irrational to do so (Mitzen, 2006a). Indeed, as Mälksoo (2018) demonstrated, NATO countries were quick to draw upon their routine relationships by attaching a conflictual identity to Russia. However, other sources of attachment can be included to define one's identity through narratives including a sense of home, past practices drawing upon emotional memories and symbols, and material representations. These narratives serve as key tools for elites to create borders and boundaries around constructions of collective identities (Cash & Kinnvall, 2017) and secure a sense of self by defining the "other" or "stranger" (Agius, 2017; Combes, 2017).

More recent OS scholarship has added additional specificity to Mitzen's (2006a) framework. Browning (2018a) lists six interconnected and reinforcing OS seeking mechanisms or practices, including: 1) the importance of biographical narratives with Solomon (2017) arguing that fractured or unclear biographical narratives could foster anxiety; and 2) routinization of everyday practices, adding that routines can reaffirm actors' sense of identity by reinforcing their identifications and bolstering their sense of purpose. Furthermore, citing Steele (2005), Browning notes that actors 3) "avoid actions that might potentially generate condemnation and shame at failing to live up to whom one claims to be" (p. 339), with additional mechanisms including: 4) vicariously identifying with broader communities or nations by enhancing one's sense of esteem by internalizing the community's achievements or warding of guilt; 5) refracting existential anxieties onto tangible objects of fear, especially in redirecting one's shortcomings by sanctifying essentialized claims of one's self-identity while securitizing the identities of others, and enemies; and 6) cultivating a sense of "home," whether lost or imagined, through an idealized place of roots and set of relationships allowing for a site of constancy upon which identities are constructed.

In sum, anxiety represents not only a condition which individuals grapple, but extends to the social and political communities they are members of. This in turn requires an understanding of at what level to examine the sources and management of OS destabilizing mechanisms.

States as OS providers

As research on OS has grown, scholars in IR have applied it in variety of ways, including focus on different referent objects (individual, society, group, state) and different political outcomes (cooperation, conflict, violence, stability or change), and draw from different methods, including quantitative, qualitative, and discursive approaches (Kinnvall & Mitzen, 2017). According to Kinnvall et al. (2018), there are two general approaches in studying OS in IR.

First is the exogenous approach (Mitzen 2006a, 2006b, Roe, 2008; Zarakol, 2010), which draws from Giddens' intersubjective notion of self where states, like individuals, are concerned with maintaining a consistent notion of self to enhance their OS in relations with other states. The exogenous approach focuses on states as unitary actors and explores their behavior with other states; it stresses the ways by which states secure their identity and sense of state distinctiveness (Mitzen, 2006a). While it provides a useful heuristic lens to understand state behavior, including state attachment to conflict with other states, Chacko (2014) argues it tends to treat the state as a monolithic actor, thereby overlooking the variability between and within states across space and time.

The second approach Kinnvall and Mitzen (2017) call the intra-subjective or endogenous perspective. Here emphasis is placed on the state as a provider of OS for its citizens whereby state representative tell convincing stories about the self through autobiographical narratives (Steele, 2005, 2008, 2012; Krolikowski, 2008, 2018; Chacko, 2014). Of note, this approach does not ignore state relations with others. As Krolikowski (2018) explains, states provide OS by ordering its social relations with foreign actors. However, this is just one part of the OS function of states, with the overarching purpose being to "supply individuals not only physical but also cognitive security and order" in which "States supply individuals with the sense that the world around them is knowable, rather than an overwhelming onslaught of unintelligible experiences" (p. 915). Drawing from Huysmans (1998), Krolikowski (2018) argues that modern nation-states derive part of their rationale and legitimacy from the ontological work they do. As Huysmans (1998) states "ultimately the legitimacy of the state rests on its capacity to provide order—not a particular content of order but the function of ordering, of making life intelligible" (p. 242).

Importantly, Chacko (2014) adds that the state agents play an influential role in providing OS for citizens by seeking to fulfill the self-identity requirements of their state as they conceptualize it (Kinnvall, 2007; Steele 2007; Krolikowski, 2008). They do so through the construction of a biographical narrative about the state, which helps them respond to contemporary systemic conditions in ways that mitigate anxiety over uncertainty. This biographical narrative could be "routinized" in a number of ways—through displays of nationalism at a societal level as well as through particular foreign policy positions and discourses. Emotion and values also come into play in states providing of order and identity for nations. As Steele (2008) argues, state agents favor "moral actions" in their foreign policy when they seek to cultivate "internal honor" to fulfill the OS needs of the states they represent. In the case of the United States, for instance, Steele finds internal honor linked to the discursive construction of American exceptionalism, as well notions of "strength," "will," and "manhood."

For the purpose of our study, we take the intra-subjective approach focusing on how narratives circulating in national media inform and attempt to provide OS for the nation as a social collective. We argue that the discourse present in national media when discussing the future of global competition and global order both depict the concerns or anxieties facing the nation, but also reveals the narrative visions of how to overcome them. In this sense, our focus is not only on how identity and agency can be challenged, but also evidence regarding how nations communicate and adapt these identities in order to build the capacity to act.

Ontological security: Stability vs change

So far discussion of OS has been focused on how actors prefer stable identities and relations to maintain agency during times of change; in Giddens (1991) terms, the need for "security of being." Indeed, as Browning and Joenniemi (2017) note, the general presupposition of most OS research is that actors prefer stability and certitude as change generates anxiety best avoided. In this sense, change is viewed as only having a disturbing, anxiety-inducing effect; with a focus on ontological *in*security, referring to a state of disruption whereby collectives have lost their stabilizing anchor, or sense of security (Kinnvall et al., 2018). As Browning and Joenniemi (2017) note while OS research exploring questions of identity-related stability have proven fruitful, too much emphasis is placed on securing this sense of self, and thus call for studies theorizing positive change.

Indeed, problems arise when states are unable to adapt their identities and routines. Not only can states become attached to irrational conflict (Mitzen, 2006a), but by responding to change by falling back on previously secured identities actors can engage in essentializing practices privileging narratives composed of hierarchical relationships in problematic ways (Agius, 2017). As Edenborg (2017) and Solomon (2015) suggest, violent cartographies of homogeneity and sovereignty could ultimately fail as they are internally contradictory and haunted by unruly elements and histories they seek to exclude.

Some research has attempted to address these concerns, moving away from Gidden's original view of "security in being" to "security of becoming." According to Kinnvall et al. (2018) the move towards security of becoming leads to social collectives to "accept the fragile nature of a constant becoming—of learning to live with a constitutive lack" (p. 531). Here actors become objects onto which fantasies of wholeness are projected to salvage the belief in core identities, and believe in an imagined, secure future relieving the individual from their present predicament. Collective emotions including hate, fear, disgust for the stranger or love for the nation, play central roles in narrative consolidation of these collective identities. Placing becoming over being recognizes the impossibility of any stable subjectivity even if this is the desired outcome. Thus, the privileging of a state narrative and its close relationships to an imagined sense of national identity involve emotional processes of imagination that define how individuals can act as a community (Berenskötter, 2014). Indeed, populist imaginaries of past, present, and future solutions can be applied to emotional anxieties and ontological *in*securities to provide powerful stories of who and what are to be blamed for a group or society's current predicaments while supplying convincing stories about a lost greatness.

Other attempts to reorient studies of OS to include explanations of change include separating OS and identity from that of physical insecurity. Rumelili (2011) argues that the conflation of ontological and physical security has generated an insufficient appreciation of how identity allows for possibilities regarding de-securitization. In this case, Rumelili creates a two-layered framework of security as both ontological and physical and separates how each produces certain identities over others. According to Rumelili (2011), although OS addresses questions of identity, primarily through the lens of oneself from "other," this does not necessitate a discourse of securitization of the "other" in defining it as a threat. Thus, Rumelili (2011) argues that studies on de-securitization need to incorporate processes of identity reconstruction and transformation.

In considering how states approach the future of global competition, the ability to adapt one's identity on face value seems to be a central concern. Whether and why states choose to retrench or reassert their identities could lead to greater capacity to act. A 'circle the wagon' mentality or appeal to previous past success can serve an important tool in combatting change. However, as the global landscape changes, with new technologies, increased communication and cultural flows, as well as rising powers seeking to revise the current order, state identities might need to evolve. In the context of a changing global order, new alliances, economic partnerships, or even failed policies all release potentialities for political communities to adapt and explore.

Thus, change is possible, albeit difficult, but perhaps ethically important to inquire into. As Kinnvall and Mitzen (2017) note, if actors gain OS through relations with others, then security dynamics could play a constitutive role for cooperative relations, forming a social glue enhancing the durability of cooperation (Browning & Joenniemi, 2013; Mitzen, 2006a). Likewise, Rumelili (2011) explain that ontological *in*security and anxiety can be a positive springboard for new forms of political resistance and agency. The question remains, where does this OS occur and how do nations connect these definitions of identity and agency to the individuals that constitute them?

National media discourses, narratives, and OS

We argue that examining national media discourse surrounding discussions of the future of global competition can provide insight to how nations such as China, Russia, Iran, and Venezuela conceptualize global order and the necessary tools to successfully shape and compete within it. Not only does national media discourse offer a site by which researchers can identify narratives of identity and OS, but more importantly, national media play a constitutive role connecting political elites to their citizenry. Although these narratives are flexible, subject to revision, adaptation, and change (Subotić, 2016), they are nonetheless constrained in that for them to be effective they must to some extent cohere with previous values, experiences, and identities (Fisher, 1985). This is not say that states form singular, monolithic storylines accepted by all or lead to consistent patterns of behavior (Lebow, 2016). As Kinnvall et al. (2018) argue, "any focus on ontological securities and insecurities proceeds from a view of identity and identifications as a process of becoming" (p. 253). Nonetheless, these stories, widely circulated and read, come to inform and define how actors make sense of specific issue, national identity, and international order (Miskimmon et al., 2013; 2017); and as we argue later, could produce an inertial force, or narrative trajectory, guiding state perceptions of the future global order.

Narratives in media discourse

Beyond functioning merely as a transmitter of information, Carey (2008) argues that media serve as a sort of cultural reservoir containing and circulating within it symbols, values, beliefs, stories, etc. that help bind people together in culture; with consumption of media functioning as a ritual where a particular world view is portrayed and confirmed. As such, members of a society habitually read the news and are provided with a presentation of reality at a particular moment in time comprising of generally repeating plotlines or moral lessons leaving the consumer with little new information learned. Nonetheless, the consumption of news media, as a ritual act, becomes part of a shared culture whereby meaning is sustained over time, providing a link among members of a community. Thus, Carey's perspective holds that media influences, contributes, and sustains the fabric of society, reflecting the ways in which we symbolically construct our reality.

Agius (2017) and Combes (2017) highlight this role of media in shaping OS by examining discourses of national identity that are tied to processes of defining and attaching meaning to "self" and "other." Agius (2017) explores how threats to OS are managed through narrative discourses used to reinforce a consistent sense of self when under threat by comparing Danish and Swedish responses to cartoons publishing images of the prophet Mohammad. In this case, Nordic values of tolerance and progressiveness were called into question leading to the need to construct the intolerant Muslim subject in contrast to the "right kind" of Muslim supporting Nordic identity and values. Similarly, Combes (2017) examines US media coverage of the Boston marathon bomber and the subsequent attempts to make sense of the threat of homegrown terrorism. Combes argues that the difficulties of distinguishing from "self" and "other" or friend and enemy, led US media to engage in a process of identity demarcation focusing on the "stranger." In both cases, media serve important discursive functions in ritualistically securing national identity through attaching identities of "outsideness."

Thus, we propose studying the discursive constructions of the future of global competition through analysis of national media. As Miskimmon et al. (2017) argue media ecologies are one system of discourse with enduring rules and roles that result in stable forms of news and political information that inform their audiences of visions of world order. These stable rules and roles can help contribute to how states act as OS providers with citizenry feeling secure with a stable sense of cognitive order on their world. As Hinck et al. (2019) argue, national identities and descriptions of relations between nations can be identified in national media, and in doing so, found comparisons of national and regional news reporting revealing perceptions of how nations view the global order, including definitions of themselves and others. The importance of national media as a cultural force is further seen by globalization resulting not in the homogenization of global media content, but strengthening the power of local, national, and regional media (Flew, Iosifidis, & Steemers, 2016). In this sense, communication technology has allowed states, and their media systems, to increase their power to pursue positive, or negative, regulatory interventions that help control and manage media narratives in ways that better shape the story nations want constructed on of a given event.

From the perspective of states as providers of OS, we contend that the narratives presented in national media make up an important vehicle whereby state policy is communicated, and at times contested. As Miskimmon et al. (2013) argue, strategic narratives are "a means for political actors to construct a shared meaning of the past, present and future of international politics to shape the behavior of domestic and international actors" (p. 2). The increased attempts at controlling media within nations such as China, Russia, Iran, and Venezuela suggests the state understands the importance of media as tool to inform and influence how their populations view of their domestic realities. Indeed, a significant body of research highlights how countries such as China and Russia employ narratives through their national media as a means to exercise soft power and reinforce collective identity (Hinck et al., 2016, 2017, 2018, 2019). In this case, narratives are a powerful tool by which states, through their media systems, are able to define the world, and their nation's place within it, to their populations.

This is not to say that such control is total. As Rozenas & Stukal (2019) argue despite being able to manipulate much of the news media, today's modern autocrat's ability to censor information is significantly more limited, as citizens are able to benchmark news against their own experiences and through exposure to outside information. According to Hagström & Gustafsson (2019) narratives become dominant only when a critical mass of social actors accepts it as common sense (Epstein, 2008; Krebs, 2015). Indeed, challenges arise when citizens are able to identity overt propaganda, leading to a loss of persuasive credibility for a state propagated narrative identified as such. Thus, for narratives to be effective they hinge on the public's acceptance of them (Schumacher, 2015) with elites and masses forming mutually constitutive interactions in constructing and receiving narratives within the cultural and discursive terrain in which they manifest (Liao, 2017).

In studying narratives and their persuasive impact, Miskimmon et al. (2013, 2017) suggest scholars look at how they are constructed, projected, and received and provide a spectrum of positions theorizing the role of communication in IR. At one end are those who take a system and set of actors as a given, studying the interaction and persuasion among them. Rationalist analysts providing thin accounts of communication take this position. At the other end of the spectrum are those studying how that system, and the identities and interests of actors there within form in the first place and how those conditions for interaction and persuasion are generated. Taking this perspective are those arguing for a poststructuralist view of communication, providing thick accounts exploring the discourses undergirding narrative understanding. For this study, we follow the "thick account" in that we seek to analyze how different narrative discourses are articulated by national media. Similar to Hinck et al.'s (2019) study of strategic narratives present in national media discourse, we are less concerned about who in particular is producing the narrative within a state's media ecology, other than its existence within a nation's national media system, than we are with what the final constructed narrative(s) tells us about the shared societal meaning presented regarding the country's understanding of the future of global competition. As Kinnvall and Mitzen (2017) state, "A focus on ontological security puts the emphasis on what goes into the stories or narratives we tell ourselves about ourselves and our relations to others" (p. 5).

Narrative trajectories

Finally, as sensemaking devices, narratives provide us with a temporal understanding of the present by connecting us to past and suggest some indication of future expectations, and possibly behavior. From the perspective of OS, the attributing of certain characteristics to actors within our narratives, both to ourselves and others, as well as the values, identities, and routines embedded within them, provide a sense of security and order. However, as discussed previously, revising or letting go of these attachments can become difficult. As such, we argue that narratives can have an inertial effect making change difficult. This inertial effect of narratives not only reveals how some nations could be unable to adapt to changes in the global environment, but also provides for some ability to project into the future the direction states could take in defining the global order and their actions or responses towards other actors. Indeed, Kinnvall and Mitzen (2017) argue that OS studies is important for IR in that narratives can result in certain pathways, leading to conflict, as states seek OS as much as physical security. In this sense, increased perceptions of ontological *in*security and uncertainty could deepen or worsen existing conflicts (Delehanty & Steele, 2009; Kinnvall & Nesbitt-Larking, 2011; Steele, 2012). This is especially noteworthy given the rising anxieties surrounding the future global order and competition within it.

If securing our sense of self is important for agency, as OS suggests, the ability for states to craft strong narratives uniting their nations in common purpose becomes central for successful competition. As Hagström and Gustafsson (2019) argue, narrative power is tied to the capacity of stories to produce effects by ascribing meaning and mobilizing collective action. As Homolar (2011) explains, narratives shape how actors think about policy challenges, enabling as well as constraining possibilities of policy shifts. Subotić (2016) summarizes the explanatory power of narratives as coming from its providing of cultural cognitive boundaries constraining the activities of political actors (Hart, 1992) which in turn makes action possible; this enables the pursuit of some practices and policies while foreclosing the possibility for others. Consequently, this process further reproduces and entrenches dominant policies while marginalizing alternative ones (Autesserre, 2012). Thus, narratives form social structures that create expectations, interests, and, ultimately, behaviors (Mattern, 2001) that create opportunities for action, as well as taboos that make certain actions unimaginable. From this, we can derive some broad expectations as to what guide state action into the future.

Even when revising one's narratives or adapting them to changes in the environment, Subotić (2016) maintains that the incorporation of new narrative elements nonetheless are done so by interpreting them in line with past narratives, thus preserving the continuity of how "before" and "after" is narratively maintained (Berenskoetter, 2014). Consequently, this can lead to previous, enduring larger narrative frameworks used in "unreflective, unanalytical, and unwitting manner" (Bartlett, 1995, p. 45 quoted in Wertsch, 2008, p.124) and are particularly prone to state control, production, and consumption. Indeed, over time, states can form national security cultures constructed in part by national mythologies of past events and relationships with historical friends or foes (Katzenstein, 1996; Berger, 1998; Soeya, Welch, & Tadokoro, 2011; Welch, 2002; Steele, 2017), highlighting how attachments are sustained. As Steele (2017) argues, the drive for OS can leave national elites even dependent upon particular organizational routines, habits, and inherited policies making change difficult; further suggesting a level of restriction regarding narrative construction and reception.

In addition to the enduring nature of certain narratives, within narratives the process of essentializing others and emotions as a means to secure one's sense of self can lead to inertial understanding of one's environment limiting nuance and inhibiting change. As Kay (2012) and Skey (2010) find, religious and nationalist narratives allow for collectives to create security as being through essentializing practices working at an emotional level. Furthermore, research focusing on social collectives emphasizing stability and routines as the crucial means to maintain their identity finds they do so by providing clear definitions of "self" versus "other", thereby ossifying social relations, with scholarship noting the occurrence of these rigid attachments to identity narratives as not only possible but dangerous (Kinnvall & Mitzen, 2017; Steele, 2008).

One more pathway of narrative trajectory arises from desire. As Subotić (2016) argues, social collectives need compelling stories addressing questions of what brings them together as a group and for what purpose. Autobiographical narratives supply these answers by explaining where "we" come from, how "we" came to be, and thus, who "we" are. Having a firm autobiographical narrative allows for sturdy feelings of one's past and history providing a sense of stability allowing the collective to move forward. In doing so, autobiographical narratives establish the foundation not only for what once was, but for what ought to be; therefore, carrying a desire for a particular social order and a particular set of social practices and policies.

However, actors can become attached to these objects of desire. In this case, fantasy narratives help guide a nation to some future aspiration, but can also create narrative closure making change difficult. According to Eberle (2019), a fantasy is a scenario through which subjects make sense of their ontological incompleteness. Eberle explains that fantasies connect subjects to social orders by arousing and channeling desire to socially constructed 'objects,' including commodities, partners, or ideological goals. Thus, fantasy narratives are movements towards an object of desire, but create black and white objectives in that one either obtains the object or not. As such, fantasies present only one type of 'resolution' to the 'problem' that is envisaged by the definition of narrative provided; consequently, there are only two possible versions of the future with no middle ground: either one recaptures the 'object' and they are safe or they fail and are ruined. Thus, fantasy narratives' affective pull is secured not only by the simple construction of the "object," but also by linking its achievement to dramatically simplified visions of the future. In this sense, the "object" in fantasies, and/or those preventing us from capturing it, attract desire with a particular force, because our very identity is portrayed as depending on this "object," thereby imposing a strong degree of closure on our narration of the world. Desire, then, is the engine of our life and the glue of social orders, since our attachment to socially available "objects" pushes us to engage in practices through which social orders are reproduced.

In sum, while autobiographical narratives and essentializing practices allowing for the defining of identity can secure one's sense of self and enable action, it can also prevent change. Thus, it appears that some level of narrative reflection is necessary to avoid the traps discussed above. The ability for actors to recognize change and self-reflect on their identity, relationship to others, and identification of healthy versus unhealthy routine behavior is an important factor to consider when dealing with change on a global scale. As Krolikowski (2008) argues, only when actors have stable basic trust systems are they afforded the ability to rationally deliberate and learn to adapt to changing circumstances. Consequently, those embroiled in conflict or uncertainty, with little trust in their control or understanding of their world, are unlikely to learn new behaviors with reduced capacity for creative reimagining of themselves and relations with others, thereby stuck repeating their rigid routines. As the global order evolves, new challenges collide with historical baggage and present concerns. How nations respond to these changes and balance their OS needs, whether through narrative continuity or reimagined identity roles, will have significant consequences on our future global order.

Summary of chapters

Having laid out the theoretical lens and aim of the project in Chapter 1, the rest of this project unfolds in the following manner. Chapter 2 discusses the role of media in international affairs, provides a justification of our four case studies, and details into our data collection procedures, operationalization of narratives, and data analysis methodology.

Chapter 3 examines Chinese narratives presenting the future of global competition. Our findings suggest that Chinese media present global competition as an economic battle centered on free trade and technological development. Rising nationalism and isolationist policies in Europe and the US are shown as undermining global stability with Chinese media presenting itself as a global leader supporting international institutions such as the United Nations and the World Trade Organization. Accordingly, successful competition requires promotion of diplomatic ties, domestic technological innovation, and continued reforms with China remaining optimistic in its ability to lead the world and manage a peaceful global order.

Chapter 4 shows Russian narratives presenting the future of global competition as one whereby Russia is in conflict with the Western-led global order. Chief Russian concerns include its perceived domestic economic and technological declines requiring Russia to develop greater Eurasian economic ties, especially with China, with Western information warfare causing societal disruptions and an unraveling of Russian national identity necessitating Russia to reinvest in the promotion and protection of its culture across key industries. Russia is seen as maintaining its great power status and aspiring to be a guarantor of security in a new global order while challenging US and EU backed institutions and establishing alternative multilateral partnerships to diminish US influence.

Chapter 5 shows Venezuelan narratives presenting the future of global competition in ideological terms where imperialist nations of all sorts, including the US, China, and Russia, compete for their own economic and political influence globally. Latin America, and Venezuela specifically, are seen as suffering the consequences of this competition, as the power brokers of the global order care little about the impacts of competition on the well-being of other nations. Thus, Venezuela sees itself as vulnerable to the outside across military, diplomatic, and economic domains, especially owing to its domestic turmoil and failed economic policies. Furthermore, authoritarian politics and corruption are viewed negatively and as undermining the nation's humanitarian needs. More specifically, Venezuela depicts itself as lacking capabilities to influence foreign nations.

Chapter 6 explores Iranian narratives. Here, Iranian media present the future of global competition through a regional lens whereby diplomatic and informational instruments of power are key for its ability to lead the Shia Crescent and combat the US attempts to isolate it. Iran is shown as under siege from an onslaught of US rhetoric and leveraging of the international community against Iran to which Iran argues that US actions are in violation of international law and norms. The US is thus seen as aiming to divide the Shia Crescent while Iran blames the US for its own internal weaknesses as well as for aiding in the militarization of the Middle East. To succeed in the future global order, Iran calls for greater regional unity within the Shia Crescent and greater diplomatic influence with the EU to balance against the US.

Chapter 7 synthesizes the quantitative findings from the four case studies. It examines the statistical drivers of positive and negative views toward the future of global order and competition, as well as how these four countries view the US and Western Europe (WE). We find that as countries' media report more favorably on their capacity to engage in economic and diplomatic capabilities, they view the future order more positively. Furthermore, as countries discuss vulnerabilities regarding their cultural strength and increases in their military capabilities, they see themselves as having a stronger role in the global order. All four nations view the US as an instigator of global conflict, but as competitors and descriptions of conflict management decreases, their views towards the US become more positive. Finally, all four countries end up viewing WE more positively when discussing alliances, suggesting that WE becomes a focal point for building cooperative relations and serves as a counterbalance to the US.

Chapter 8 summarizes our results across all four cases. It begins by comparing Chinese, Russian, Venezuelan, and Iranian narratives about themselves as international agents and their stories defining the international system. It then discusses how the global system becomes envisioned as collective project in its own right with attention placed on how this imagining ties into constructions of agency in an anxious global world. Finally, we detail the level of reflexivity in each nation's narratives and the implications of their trajectories as it relates to the future global order.

References

Acharya, A. (2018). *Constructing global order: Agency and change in world politics.* Cambridge University Press.

Agius, C. (2017). Drawing the discourses of ontological security: Immigration and identity in the Danish and Swedish cartoon crises. *Cooperation and Conflict*, 52 (1), 109–125.

Ahir, H., Bloom, N., & Furceri, D. (2019). New index tracks trade uncertainty across the globe. *IMF Blog*, September 9, 2019. https://blogs.imf.org/2019/09/09/new-index-tracks-trade-uncertainty-across-the-globe.

Allison, G. (2017). *Destined for war: Can America and China escape Thucydides's trap?*. Houghton Mifflin Harcourt.

Alvaredo, F., Chancel, L., Piketty, T., Saez, E., & Zucman, G. (2017). *World inequality report 2018*. https://wir2018.wid.world/files/download/wir2018-summary-english.pdf.

Anderson, B. (2006). *Imagined communities: Reflections on the origin and spread of nationalism*. Verso Books.

Arendt, H. (1970). *On violence*. Houghton Mifflin Harcourt.

Arendt, H. (1972). *Crises of the Republic: Lying in Politics; Civil Disobedience; On Violence; Thoughts on Politics and Revolution*. Harcourt Brace Jovanovich.

Autesserre, S. (2012). Dangerous tales: Dominant narratives on the Congo and their unintended consequences. *African Affairs*, 111(443), 202–222.

Barnett, M. (2008). Social Constructivism. In J. Baylis, S. Smith, & P. Owens (Eds), *The Globalization of World Politics* (4th ed.), pp. 160–173. Oxford University Press.

Bartlett, F. C. (1995). *Remembering: A study in experimental and social psychology.* Cambridge University Press.

Behravesh, M. (2018). State revisionism and ontological (in) security in international politics: The complicated case of Iran and its nuclear behavior. *Journal of International Relations and Development*, 21(4), 836–857.

Berenskötter, F. (2014). Parameters of a national biography. *European Journal of International Relations*, 20(1), 262–288.

Berenskötter, F. (2020). Anxiety, time, and agency. *International Theory*, 12(2), 273–290.

Berger, T. U. (1998). *Cultures of antimilitarism: National security in Germany and Japan*. John Hopkins University Press.

Bhaskar, R. (2013). *A realist theory of science*. Routledge.

Bobasu, A., Geis, A., Quaglietti, L., & Ricci, M. (2020). Tracking global economic uncertainty: Implications for global investment and trade. *European Central Bank*. www.ecb.europa.eu/pub/economic-bulletin/focus/2020/html/ecb.ebbox202001_01~b336806ed2.en.html.

Browning, C. S. & Joenniemi, P. (2017). Ontological security, self-articulation and the securitization of identity. *Cooperation and Conflict*, 52(1), 31–47.

Browning, C. S. (2018a). Brexit, existential anxiety and ontological (in) security. *European Security*, 27(3), 336–355.

Browning, C. S. (2018b). Geostrategies, geopolitics and ontological security in the Eastern neighbourhood: The European Union and the 'new Cold War'. *Political Geography*, 62, 106–115.

Bull, H. (1977). *The anarchical society: A study of order in world politics*. Columbia University Press.

Burke, K. (1969). *A grammar of motives*. University of California Press.

Buzan, B., Jones, C. A., Little, R., & Richard, L. (1993). *The logic of anarchy: Neorealism to structural realism*. Columbia University Press.

Carey, J. W. (2008). *Communication as culture, revised edition: Essays on media and society*. Routledge.

Cash, J., & Kinnvall, C. (2017). Postcolonial bordering and ontological insecurities. *Postcolonial Studies*, 20(3), 267–274.

Chacko, P. (2014). A new "special relationship"?: Power transitions, ontological security, and India–US relations. *International Studies Perspectives*, 15(3), 329–346.

Checkel, J. T. (1998). The constructivist turn in international relations theory. *World Politics*, 50(2), 324–348.

Chernobrov, D. (2016). Ontological security and public (mis) recognition of international crises: Uncertainty, political imagining, and the self. *Political Psychology*, 37(5), 581–596.

Combes, M. D. (2017). Encountering the stranger: Ontological security and the Boston Marathon bombing. *Cooperation and Conflict*, 52(1), 126–143.

Connaughton, A., Kent, N., & Schumacher, S. (2020). How people around the world see democracy in 8 charts. *Pew*, February 27, 2020. www.pewresearch.org/fact-tank/2020/02/27/how-people-around-the-world-see-democracy-in-8-charts.

Crick, N. (2014). *Rhetoric and power: The drama of classical Greece*. University of South Carolina Press.

Csaky, Z. (2020). Dropping the democratic façade in Europe and Eurasia. *Freedom House*. https://freedomhouse.org/report/nations-transit/2020/dropping-democratic-facade.

Curtis, H. (2016). Constructing cooperation: Chinese ontological security seeking in the South China Sea dispute. *Journal of Borderlands Studies*, 31(4), 537–549.

Delehanty, W. K. & Steele, B. J. (2009). Engaging the narrative in ontological (in) security theory: Insights from feminist IR. *Cambridge Review of International Affairs*, 22(3), 523–540.

Eberle, J. (2019). Narrative, desire, ontological security, transgression: Fantasy as a factor in international politics. *Journal of International Relations and Development*, 22(1), 243–268.

Edelman. (2019, January 19). *2020 Edelman Trust Barometer.* www.edelman.com/trustbarometer.

Edenborg, E. (2017). *Politics of Visibility and Belonging: From Russia's "Homosexual Propaganda" laws to the Ukraine War.* Taylor & Francis.

Eilstrup-Sangiovanni, M., & Hofmann, S. C. (2020). Of the contemporary global order, crisis, and change. *Journal of European Public Policy*, 27(7), 1077–1089.

Epstein, C. (2008). *The power of words in international relations: Birth of an anti-whaling discourse.* MIT Press.

Escalas, J. E. (2007). Self-referencing and persuasion: Narrative transportation versus analytical elaboration. *Journal of Consumer Research*, 33(4), 421–429.

Eyerman, R., Madigan, T., & Ring, M. (2017). Cultural trauma, collective memory and the Vietnam War. *Croatian Political Science Review*, 54(1–2), 11–31.

Finnemore, M. & Sikkink, K. (1998). International norm dynamics and political change. *International Organization*, 52(4), 887–917.

Firoozabadi, S. J. D. (2011). Ontological security and the foreign policy analysis of the Islamic Republic of Iran. *Institute for Strategic Research Journal*, 2, 31–60.

Fisher, W. R. (1985). The narrative paradigm: An elaboration. *Communication Monographs*, 52(4), 347–367.

Flew, T., Iosifidis, P., & Steemers, J. (Eds). (2016). *Global media and national policies: The return of the state.* Palgrave Macmillan.

Foucault, M. (1982). *Essential Foucault: Selections from the Essential Works of Foucault.* P. Rabinow & N. Rose (Eds).

Freedom House. (2019). *Democracy in retreat.* https://freedomhouse.org/report/freedom-world/2019/democracy-retreat.

Giddens, A. (1991). *Modernity and self-identity: Self and society in the late Modern Age.* Stanford University Press.

Gilpin, R. (1981). *War and change in world politics.* Cambridge University Press.

Gustafsson, K. (2014). Memory politics and ontological security in Sino-Japanese relations. *Asian Studies Review*, 38(1), 71–86.

Hagström, L. & Gustafsson, K. (2019). Narrative power: How storytelling shapes East Asian international politics. *Cambridge Review of International Affairs* 32(4), 387–406.

Hansen, F. S. (2016). Russia's relations with the West: Ontological security through conflict. *Contemporary Politics*, 22(3), 359–375.

Hart, J. (1992). Cracking the code: Narrative and political mobilization in the Greek resistance. *Social Science History*, 16(4), 631–668.

Heidegger M (1953). *Sein und Zeit.* Max Niemeyer Verlag.

Hinck, R. S., Chinn, J., Kluver, R., & Norris, W. (2016). Interpreting and shaping geopolitics in Chinese media: The discourse of the "New Style of Great Power Relations." *Asian Journal of Communication*, 26(5), 427–445.

Hinck, R. S., Kluver, R., Cooley, S. (2017). Russia re-envisions the world: Strategic narratives in Russian broadcast and news media during 2015. *Russian Journal of Communication*, 10(1), 21–37.

Hinck, R. S., Kluver, R., Norris, W., & Manly, J. (2018). Geopolitical dimensions of "The China Dream": Exploring strategic narratives of the Chinese Communist Party. *China Media Research.* 14(3), 99–110.

Hinck, R. S., Cooley, S., & Kluver, R. (2019). *Global media and strategic narratives of contested democracy: Chinese, Russian, and Arabic media narratives of the US presidential election.* Routledge.

Hom, A. R. & Steele, B. J. (2020). Anxiety, time, and ontological security's third-image potential. *International Theory*. 12(2), 322–336.

Homolar, A. (2011). Rebels without a conscience: The evolution of the rogue states narrative in US security policy. *European Journal of International Relations*. 17(4), 705–727.

Huysmans, J. (1998). Security! What do you mean? From concept to thick signifier. *European Journal of International Relations*. 4(2), 226–255.

Katzenstein, M. F. (1996). *The culture of national security: Norms and identity in world politics*. Columbia University Press.

Kay, S. (2012). Ontological security and peace-building in Northern Ireland. *Contemporary Security Policy*. 33(2), 236–263.

Keohane, R. O. (2005). *After hegemony: Cooperation and discord in the world political economy*. Princeton University Press.

Kinnvall, C. (2004). Globalization and religious nationalism: Self, identity, and the search for ontological security. *Political psychology*. 25(5), 741–767.

Kinnvall, C. (2007). *Globalization and religious nationalism in India: The search for ontological security*. Routledge.

Kinnvall, C., Manners, I., & Mitzen, J. (2018). Introduction to 2018 special issue of European Security: "Ontological (in)security in the European Union." *European Security*. 27(3), 249–265.

Kinnvall, C. & Mitzen, J. (2017). An introduction to the special issue: Ontological securities in world politics. *Cooperation and Conflict*, 52(1), 3–11.

Kinnvall, C., & Nesbitt-Larking, P. (2011). *The political psychology of globalization: Muslims in the West*. Oxford University Press.

Kissinger, H. (1994). *Diplomacy*. Simon and Schuster.

Kissinger, H. (2014). *World order*. Penguin Books.

Krebs, R. R. (2015). How dominant narratives rise and fall: Military conflict, politics, and the Cold War consensus. *International Organization*. 69(4), 809–845.

Krolikowski, A. (2008). State personhood in ontological security theories of international relations and Chinese nationalism: A sceptical view. *Chinese Journal of International Politics*. 2(1), 109–133.

Krolikowski, A. (2018). Shaking up and making up China: How the party-state compromises and creates ontological security for its subjects. *Journal of International Relations and Development*. 21(4), 909–933.

Lebow, R. N. (2016). *National identities and international relations*. Cambridge University Press.

Liao, N. (2017). The power of strategic narratives: The communicative dynamics of Chinese nationalism and foreign relations. In A. Miskimmon, B. O'Loughlin, & L. Roselle (Eds), *Forging the world: Strategic narratives and international relations*, 110–133. University of Michigan Press.

MacIntyre, A. (1984). *After virtue: A study in moral theory* (2nd ed.). University of Notre Dame Press.

Mälksoo, M. (2018). Countering hybrid warfare as ontological security management: The emerging practices of the EU and NATO. *European Security*. 27(3), 374–392.

Mattern, J. B. (2001). The power politics of identity. *European Journal of International Relations*. 7(3), 349–397.

Mearsheimer, J. J. (2001). *The tragedy of great power politics*. W. W. Norton & Company.

Miskimmon, A., O'Loughlin, B., & Roselle, L. (2014). *Strategic narratives: Communication power and the new world order.* Routledge.

Miskimmon, A., & O'Loughlin, B. (2015). Great power politics and strategic narratives of war. In B. De Graaf, G. Dimitriu, & J. Ringsmose (Eds), *Strategic narratives, public opinion and war*, pp. 85–106. Routledge.

Miskimmon, A., O'Loughlin, B., & Roselle, L. (2017). *Forging the world: Strategic narratives and international relations.* University of Michigan Press.

Mitzen, J. (2006b). Anchoring Europe's civilizing identity: Habits, capabilities and ontological security. *Journal of European Public Policy.* 13(2), 270–285.

Mitzen, J. (2006a). Ontological security in world politics: State identity and the security dilemma. *European Journal of International Relations.* 12(3), 341–370.

Öniş, Z. (2017). The age of anxiety: The crisis of liberal democracy in a post-hegemonic global order. *The International Spectator.* 52(3), 18–35.

Prasad, E. (2020, July 2). Hearing on supply chain resiliency. *Brookings.* www.brookings.edu/testimonies/hearing-on-supply-chain-resiliency.

Pu, X. (2019). *Rebranding China: Contested status signaling in the changing global order.* Stanford University Press.

Reus-Smit, C. (2018). Seeing Culture in World Politics. In G. Helmmann (Ed.), *Theorizing Global Order*, pp. 66–91. Cambridge University Press.

Roe, P. (2008). The 'value' of positive security. *Review of International Studies.* 34 (4), 777–794.

Roselle, L. (2017). *Strategic narratives and great power identity.* In A. Miskimmon, B. O'Loughlin, & L. Roselle (Eds), *Forging the world: Strategic narratives and international relations*, pp. 56–85. University of Michigan Press.

Rozenas, A. & Stukal, D. (2019). How autocrats manipulate economic news: Evidence from Russia's state-controlled television. *The Journal of Politics.* 81(3), 982–996.

Rumelili B. (2011). What Turks and Kurds 'make of' Europe: Subversion, negotiation and appropriation in the European periphery. In O. P. Richmond & A. Mitchell (Eds), *Hybrid Forms of Peace: From Everyday Agency to Post-Liberalism*, pp. 226–241. Palgrave Macmillan.

Schumacher, T. (2015). Uncertainty at the EU's borders: Narratives of EU external relations in the revised European Neighbourhood Policy towards the southern borderlands. *European Security.* 24(3), 381–401.

Skey, M. (2010). 'A sense of where you belong in the world': National belonging, ontological security and the status of the ethnic majority in England. *Nations and Nationalism.* 16(4), 715–733.

Soeya, Y., Welch, D. A., & Tadokoro, M. (Eds). (2011). *Japan as a 'normal Country'?: A nation in search of its place in the world.* University of Toronto Press.

Solomon, T. (2015). *The politics of subjectivity in American foreign policy discourses.* University of Michigan Press.

Solomon, T. (2017). Ontological security, circulations of affect, and the Arab Spring. *Journal of International Relations and Development.* 21(4), 934–958.

Steele, B. J. (2005). Ontological security and the power of self-identity: British neutrality and the American Civil War. *Review of international studies.* 31(3), 519–540.

Steele, B. J. (2007). Making words matter: The Asian tsunami, Darfur, and "reflexive discourse" in international politics. *International Studies Quarterly.* 51(4), 901–925.

Steele, B. J. (2008). *Ontological security in international relations: Self-identity and the IR state.* Routledge.

Steele, B. J. (2012). *Defacing power: The aesthetics of insecurity in global politics.* University of Michigan Press.

Steele, B. J. (2017). Organizational processes and ontological (in) security: Torture, the CIA and the United States. *Cooperation and Conflict.* 52(1), 69–89.

Subotić, J. (2016). Narrative, ontological security, and foreign policy change. *Foreign Policy Analysis.* 12(4), 610–627.

Welch, D. A. (2002). Culture and emotion as obstacles to good judgment: The case of Argentina's invasion of the Falklands/Malvinas. In S. A. Renshon & D. W. Larson (Eds), *Good judgement in foreign policy: Theory and application*, pp. 191–216. Rowman & Littlefield.

Wendt, A. (1999). *Social theory of international politics.* Cambridge University Press.

Wertsch, J. V. (2008). The narrative organization of collective memory. *Ethos.* 36 (1), 120–135.

Wight, C. (2006). *Agents, structures and international relations: politics as ontology.* Cambridge University Press.

Wike, R., Silver, L., & Castillo, A. (2019). Many across the globe are dissatisfied with how democracy is working. *Pew*, April 29, 2019. www.pewresearch.org/global/2019/04/29/many-across-the-globe-are-dissatisfied-with-how-democracy-is-working.

Zarakol, A. (2010). Ontological (in) security and state denial of historical crimes: Turkey and Japan. *International Relations.* 24(1), 3–23.

2 Research Design

Narrative Ordering and Contestation of Global Order

Introduction

Today's global landscape is changing as emerging economies take larger shares of global GDP and international trade as well as increases in military spending and troop deployments (Woetzel et al., 2018; SIPRI, 2019). While the physical manifestations of a transitioning world order away from US unipolarity are important to note, so too are the ways by which global populations make sense of them, specifically through media. This chapter justifies the decision for examining national media reporting as the site by which researchers can identify narratives of ontological security (OS) regarding the nature of future competition within the evolving global order. We began by briefly discussing the role of media in international affairs before justifying our selection of case studies, data collection procedures, operationalization of narratives, and data analysis methodology.

Global media and the shaping of international affairs

Whereas international relations (IR) research has typically shied away from examining the role of communication in relation to changes in the global order, preferring material sources of power, a significant body of research has argued that media influences world politics. This includes early mass media studies on propaganda (Lasswell, 1941; Schiller, 2008; Snow, 2002; Simpson, 1994) and more recent articulations of media-elite relationships serving to manufacture consent (Herman & Chomsky, 2010; Lang & Lang, 2004; Entman, 2008). Indeed, during the Cold War global order, this propaganda view took center stage in international statecraft as nuclear weapons prohibitively raised the cost of outright military conflict, leading to a new type of geopolitical contestation described by Taylor (2013) as: "a war on the mind, a contest of ideologies, a battle of nerves which...was to divide the planet into a bi-polar competition that was characterized more by a war of words and the threatened use of nuclear weapons" (p. 250). Thus, media became the key battleground for international influence requiring governments to both convince domestic and

DOI: 10.4324/9781003197478-2

international audiences that fears of the enemy were genuine, legitimate, and justified in order to signal their willingness to use nuclear weapons while maintaining support for their funding.

While the specter of nuclear war largely dissipated with the collapse of the Soviet Union, the importance of media in international affairs remained. As Price (2002) explains, the global media market that emerged throughout the 1990s led to a space by which "ideologies compete and forge allegiances that ultimately determine the persistence of governments and nations themselves, and an arena where imagery becomes a supplement or substitute for force" (p. 3). New communication technologies have made competition in this arena ever more present as global satellites and 24-hour news agencies reinforced the role of media agencies as actors constraining government's ability to maintain control over international events (Robinson, 2001; Gilboa, 2005a; Gilbao, 2005b; Thussu, 2018). Today the picture is even more complicated as social media provides new challenges by enabling greater speed and coordination by which disaffected populations can resist government rule (Lynch, 2011; White & McAllister, 2014; Bellin, 2012), albeit with governments developing new ways to maintain influence and control (Deibert, 2019; Bulovsky, 2019; Michaelsen, 2017; Xu, 2020).

Beyond concerns regarding the role of media in supporting government policy at home and abroad, global media flows impact our conceptions of global order and international security too. These flows not only shape international but also national cultures by itching the landscapes through which globalization occurs, including its financial, technological, and ideological dimensions (Appadurai, 1990). Transnational media and their relationship to globalization, sparked debates over whether the global community was pushing towards greater convergence or divergence of values (Samuel-Azran, 2009; Inglehart, 2020). While originally scholars optimistically pointed to these advances as leading to a new global civil society (Castells, 2008), more recent evidence points to its fracturing effects. Today, national media makes up an important cultural force strengthening the power of local, national, and regional media systems (Flew, Iosifidis, & Steemers, 2016; Flew, 2020) with countries such as China, Iran, and Russia engaging in media projects of cultural revivalism and revisionism (Thussu, 2018). As such, national media systems sustain and circulate a sense of shared culture reaffirming national world views (Carey, 2008; Anderson, 2006), including narrative logics providing a sense of who they are and how the world works (Miskimmon et al., 2014).

Recognizing the role of media in global affairs, a growing body of research within IR and international communication has focused on the impact of political actors strategically wielding narratives to construct world views in pursuit of political goals at home and abroad (Miskimmon et al., 2014, 2017). This includes their use as a form of soft power (Roselle et al., 2014) and studies examining strategic narratives within the context of national regional media systems (Hinck et al., 2019), as well as how narrative power operates and constitutes a form of power in itself within the international realm (Hagström & Gustafsson, 2019).

These narrative accounts of world order reflect research in OS in that they provide compelling narratives allowing states to provide OS for their citizens. In doing so, not only do these narratives define who the nation is through autobiographical accounts, but also help create cognitive order out of their relationships with others and their environment within a changing global landscape (Steele, 2008; Subotić, 2016). As Innes and Steele (2014) argue, states construct autobiographical identity narratives to make sense of their behavior in the international system and give meaning to their actions. Within the OS literature, emphasis thus tends to fall on states' (auto)biographical narrative construction, and, at its strongest, suggests that states "not only use biographical narratives to pursue certain policies, but that states are, in fact, biographical narratives themselves" (Subotić, 2016, p. 614; Berenskötter, 2014).

However, states' autobiographical narratives are not permanent. Subotić (2016) goes into detail describing the process by which state autobiographical narratives endure and change, arguing that narratives, as social constructs, are continuously activated and deactivated by political elites, cultural leaders, and the media; and are used strategically to justify policy shifts, promote collective values, and encourage a sense of "groupness and solidarity" (p. 612). This is not to suggest that a state's autobiographical narrative are always fundamentally altered, however. New events can be interpreted within certain elements of a specific narrative while deemphasizing other aspects. Even during times of great stress autobiographical accounts of the state can remain essentially the same while shifts in policy do occur, merely interpreted within a broader, pre-existing narrative template. For Berenskötter (2014) the process of maintaining such a narrative "or network of narratives" represents a form of governance and requires both agents with expertise and legitimacy capable of constructing and invoking authentic memories and visions, as well as those in possession of the resources to adopt and carry the narrative along, affirming it with tangible practices (p. 279). Importantly, the successful construction and dissemination of state's national narrative also depends on the structural-institutional configuration of the state (Tilly, 1994; Wight, 2004) with institutions not only lending the narrative the material infrastructure to sustain itself across generations, but also functioning to silence certain voices while rendering others dominant (Berenskötter, 2014).

For the purpose of this study, we focus on nation's national media systems as the site in which such narratives emerge and solidify. While elites and government leaders play important roles in providing definitions and visions for state policy, these policies still rely on media for their dissemination and support within the public (Hinck et al., 2019). Indeed, whether these attempts fail or succeed in reinforcing a country's domestic narrative depends on a country's media ecology (Chaban et al., 2017) with mainstream media functioning as both conduits and actors in themselves in voicing particular narratives (Arsenault, Hong, & Price, 2017). As both the strategic narrative and OS literature suggest, for narratives to be effective they rely on public acceptance, thereby limiting the room for narrative maneuverability by the degree to which they resonant within pre-existing societal narratives and cultural values (Schumacher, 2015; Subotić, 2016; Fisher 1985). Furthermore, while traditional national media are not the only actors narrating events in a global network society (Castells, 2008), national and international newspapers still serve as an important multiplier of crisis perceptions and resolutions (Cross, 2017). It is for these reasons that we examine national media discourse regarding coverage of the future of global cooperation and global order.

More specifically, we argue that national media discourse play a vital OS function. If OS is concerned about agency, or the capacity to act, with social collectives needing a stable sense of who one is within a given time and space in relationship to their environment, then it is through national media that nations are able to build the collective identities and shared world views to do so. Although globalization has disrupted the interpersonal and organizational relationships of global communities around the world (Giddens, 1991), it has also pushed social collectives closer together in search for a reaffirmation or strengthening of past identities (Kinnvall, 2004).

This is of particular significance in that governmental legitimacy is tied to the state's ability to provide order and OS for its populations (Krolikowski, 2008, 2018; Huysmans, 1998). In uncertain times the provision of narratives ordering the world and reaffirming a sense of self identity becomes especially important, requiring state leaders to assuage audiences of the nation's ability to endure and succeed in meeting future challenges (Subotić, 2016); including OS concerns over changing distribution of global power (Chacko, 2014; Behravesh, 2018; Steele, 2008), and anxiety over new threats facing the nation, such as hybrid warfare (Mälksoo, 2018), domestic terrorism (Combes, 2017), and immigration (Agius, 2017). Having laid out the argument for the importance of the role of media in understanding global politics and OS, the rest of this chapter is devoted to explaining the project's research design, including its selection of cases, data collection, and data analysis.

Research design

Since the end of the Cold War, the US-led international order has been preeminent. While Francis Fukuyama (2006) portended the "End of History" with US neo-liberal values marking the end point of global governance, China's neo-authoritarian rise and the formation of BRICS proves otherwise. Indeed, studies show a decline in liberal democratic countries with others reporting the spread of authoritarianism as a counter weight to democratic governance, thereby playing crucial roles in the future of global order by creating space for alternative political ideations (Ottaway, 2013; Diamond, Plattner, & Walker, 2016).

Thus, today, nations historically aligned in opposition to US interests, as well as emerging economies, form an important discursive pull away from Western values. No longer is the West the only socializing force in IR, with Pu (2011) arguing that BRICS nations too function as norm shapers; including messaging designed to challenge, unravel, or make space for alternative voices beyond the West's. Not only are these nations shifting the vision of the global order, making them pivotal to understand its future incarnation, but international communication scholarship has also been argued to be too Western-centric with calls for greater attention placed on how non-Western countries' perceive and impact the global order (Kluver et al, 2013; Hinck et al., 2019). For these reasons, we analyze four nations who have historically aligned themselves against US interests to chart their visions regarding both the future of global order and their anxieties and aspirations in depicting what competition looks like in this new age.

Case selection

Our project examines Chinese, Russian, Venezuelan, and Iranian media narratives regarding the future of global competition and the future world order. The selection of China and Russia likely comes to no surprise to those familiar with today's geopolitical competition; both nations self-ascribe themselves as "great powers" and actively challenge US-led norms in Europe and Asia, as well as in the Middle East, Africa, and South America. They also provide alternative models to Western democratic norms and express distrust, even feel threatened, by US pressures to democratize, in addition to serving as alternative economic models for other nations to emulate.

Although China and Russia represent two key power blocs with notable global influence, they also face significant challenges if they are to succeed in displacing US global influence. While Russia boasts one of the world's top military forces, including a vast nuclear arsenal, its economy remains relatively stagnate, overly dependent on oil prices, and susceptible to Western sanctions. Likewise, Russia finds itself relatively isolated diplomatically, concerned more with developing ties with China and maintaining its sphere of influence with former Soviet states.

China on the other hand represents the second, or by some measures the largest, economy. Nonetheless, it per capita terms, China ranks 67th within the world and holds significant trepidations regarding its ability to continue its economic transformation and escape the middle-income trap (IMF, 2019). As China experts notes, since the Tiananmen Square prodemocracy protests of 1989, the Chinese Communist Party's legitimacy has rested upon its ability to provide economic growth for its citizens, with Chinese leaders recognizing the importance of global trade to support its endeavors to move towards an economy capable of not just cheap manufacturing but capable of innovation. In support of its economic development, diplomatically China has actively sought to build new trade networks, most notably through its Belt and Road Initiative (BRI). Despite some successes, concerns about the efficacy of the BRI, in addition to general distrust about China's rise, place limitations on China's ability to displace US global influence. As Pew notes, global public opinion towards China remains mixed (Silver et al., 2019).

However, great powers are not the only influencers within the global order; regional actors too play important roles. As noted in Chapter 1, Kissinger (2014) includes regional actors in his defining of world order, stating that world order is a concept "held by a region or civilization about the nature of just arrangements and distribution of power believed to be applicable to the entire world" (p. 9). As Acharya (2018) argues, regional orders can affect the global balance of power as well as global interdependence, normative structures, and institutions of cooperation.

Thus, in addition to China and Russia, we also examine two regional powers through our inclusion of Iran and Venezuela. While both might lack the global influence China and Russia enjoy, they nonetheless claim to wield significant clout in their respective regions—the Middle East and Latin America respectfully, and use it to not only actively challenge US interests but also project alternative visions to the US-led neoliberal, democratic order more broadly. As influential regional actors, their articulations of appropriate and inappropriate international behavior, as well as their participation or resistance to the global order, pose important ideational sources for contestation.

First, we focus on Iran because of its revisionist, anti-US posturing. Although today, Iran and Saudi Arabia represent the two most influential nations in the Middle East projecting alternative, antagonistic visions of regional order through their competing views of Islam, Iran is one of the most active agents challenging not only US interests but also at heads with the international community. Iran's use of proxy forces, including support of Hezbollah, frustrate US goals and undermines the current international order's state-centric Westphalian system. Likewise, Iran's pursuit of nuclear weapons is perceived by US officials, and the international community more broadly, as critically destabilizing Middle East politics and fueling nuclear proliferation; with the Trump administration's pulling out of the Iran nuclear deal designed to pressure Iran economically, even induce regime change.

Beyond differences in foreign policy, Iran's cultural and economic resources provide additional sources of global influence. Iran's identity as defender of the Shia Crescent in addition to its historical past as a great

Persian power represent key OS resources to draw upon in defining its identity vis-à-vis the West as well as alternative civilizational views of world order (Kissinger, 2014). Likewise, Iran's geo-economic position, both as a large producer of oil but also its strategic location in the Gulf of Oman, specifically the Straits of Hormuz, provides it with weighty global economic influence, with the ability to threaten the global economy, evident in part by Iranian forces' recent threats and attacks on oil tankers in 2019. Nonetheless, Iran's weakening economy resulting from US sanctions, in addition to nations diplomatically aligned against it, such as Saudi Arabia and Israel—both US regional allies, showcases Iran's tenuous position.

Second, we select Venezuela as it too is a regional power with significant sway in Latin America and the Caribbean. Both historical, but also more recently, Venezuelan leaders have led the region in resistance against Western imperial powers. Most notably, since the 1990s with Hugo Chávez's rise to power, Venezuela challenged US influence in Latin America by establishing new regional organizations fueled by its oil revenues while also vociferously challenging US authority in the UN. Ideologically, Chavez promised a new form of socialist democratic governance aimed against its elites, technocrats, and the US, with his foreign policy vision directed towards the creation a new multipolar world order aligned against US global aspirations and supported by Venezuelan partnerships with Russia and China. Nonetheless, today's Venezuela looks dramatically different compared to Chavez's tenure in office. While the ideological commitments of the state, both domestically and with regards to foreign policy, remain the same, domestic turmoil resulting from a failed economy, a humanitarian crisis, and political instability has weakened the nation to such an extent that it prompted genuine concern over the very real possibility of foreign international intervention into the nation's domestic politics.

Taken together these four nations represent important agents in today and tomorrow's future global order. While they possess a variety of tools for economic, diplomatic, and even military competition they also enjoy considerable cultural prestige with a rich history implicating their national identities and autobiographical narratives. How these nations decide to invest and protect their instruments of power while also maintain their sense of cultural identity in the face of globalization are of significant concern both to each nation individually, but also the larger international order. Thus, all four nations share characteristics of regional or global influence and use that influence in opposition to the US. Additional similarities exist in their autocratic or authoritarian leanings, representing key alternative ideational models at odds with our current neoliberal, democratic order.

In this sense, our four cases can be further broken into two categories: global great powers and influential regional actors. The distinction between the two allows for determination into whether global influence and agency impact OS constructions of the world in similar or divergent ways. As Mitzen (2006) notes, agency is crucially tied to OS and so, one might imagine global powers to either possess or need to more actively articulate greater agency in world affairs relative to regional powers. Likewise, these four nations' positioning of themselves, in contrast to US-led narratives of global order, marks particularly rich areas for exploring OS. If global order, as Acharya (2018) conceptualizes it, is premised on representation and participation, then US attempts to ostracize, constrict, or define how China, Russia, Iran, and Venezuela are allowed to act implicates these nations own sense of agency. If done so to such a degree that these nations opt to reject our current order outright, the sustainability of our current system might increasingly become in doubt, especially as power shifts away from the West.

Although these nations are selected for their stark opposition to US interests, we believe scholars should avoid, as much as possible, falling into binaries defining the world into the "West" versus the "rest". Doing so ignores the nuance regarding the nature of today's global competition. Indeed, despite widespread criticism of our current order, even nations such China, Russia, Iran, and Venezuela enjoy some benefits of our current international institutional arrangement. While US narratives most certainly construct the global order in support of its own interests, including actively criticizing the nations under analysis for this project, focusing on US narratives not only robs voice to others but also lies outside of the scope of this study. This is not to say that counter messages to US narratives is not present in other nations. Instead, we choose to let such responses emerge organically from our cases' own media systems enabling a more nuanced understanding of how US actions or others influence our cases' conceptualizations of global competition, order, and agency.

Finally, we believe our selection of cases adds both novel and theoretical benefits to advancing our understanding of global competition within our current age of transition and anxiety. Although a multitude of studies have examined the strategic efforts by Russia and China to shape or revise the current world order, little comparative work has been done, let alone empirical studies determining how these efforts align or diverge from regional powers, like Iran and Venezuela. Likewise, a substantial amount of research on OS has been published over the past decade, but few studies attempt to quantify and compare OS providing practices among nations, especially those outside of Western European contexts.

National media and state-media relations

Before detailing our data collection and analysis procedures, we believe a brief discussion of these nations' media ecologies is in order. As noted above, a commonality of our cases is their relatively strong influence over their media ecologies. Indeed, although all four media systems vary in their degree of state-media involvement, none are considered free; according to Reporters without Border's 2020 World Press Freedom Index, out of 180 countries China ranks 177th, Iran 173rd, Russia 149th, and Venezuela 147th.

While this state-media partnership, or simply heavy-handed control, allows us to make stronger claims regarding their governments' OS performances, and expectations as shared by the state to their citizens via their media content, this is not to suggest that these nations' governments have complete control over their media systems; nor that the news coverage cultivated by their governments are universally accepted. No longer can authoritarian leaders rely on terrorizing or forcibly indoctrinating the population, but instead maintain their legitimacy by leading citizens to believe that they are competent and public-spirited (Guriev & Treisman, 2019). Thus, despite being able to manipulate much of the news media, today's autocrat's ability to censor information is significantly more limited, owing to the interconnectivity of our global communication environment resulting in new rhetorical styles employing softer forms of control (Rozenas & Stukal, 2019; Guriev & Treisman, 2019).

This new nature of our global communication ecology and authoritarian leading governments' reaction to it, by investing and strengthening their own control over their national communication systems, further highlights the importance of narratives in understanding how political actors, and political communities more broadly, create communicative power leading to coordinated action (Crick, 2014). While narratives can be persuasive resources for authoritarian-leaning systems to legitimate their rule, as well as insulate themselves from attacks arising from abroad (Cooley & Stokes, 2018), for these narratives to be persuasive, they must be credible and not appear as pure propaganda, accepted by their publics, and resonate with local political myths (Schumacher, 2015). In this sense, it's important to note that within a narrative context, credibility and factual accuracy are not one in the same. Narratives draw upon our socially experienced truths, those which "ring true" and resonate with our past experiences (Fisher, 1985. At any given time, multiple narratives circulate among various social institutions, including those created by media and governmental structures (Somers & Gibson, 1994) with narrative contestation ever present, even by elites (Subotić, 2016).

Therefore, it should be no surprise that nations such as China, Russia, Venezuela, and Iran have adapted their control over their media systems to maintain some public credibility. For instance, studies show how China, through its system of media control, has managed a new form of "authoritarian deliberation" allowing for criticism of state policy and citizen feedback, albeit within government sanctioned limits (He, 2014; He & Warren, 2011). Likewise, Chinese authorities strategically manage relations with critical journalists, even coopting them to aid state-driven policy (Repnikova, 2017). Other tactics include positive news framing (Stockmann & Luo, 2017) and ideotainment (Lagerkvist, 2010), both helping to circumvent critical reading of Chinese news. These tactics exist beyond

China as well; Diamond, Plattner, and Walker (2016) argue that authoritarian governments around the world are learning and adopting such practices developed by others.

An additional factor that supports state-led media narratives and credibility both at home and in protection from counter narratives from abroad is the politicization of news. Domestically, Chinese audiences view reporting as political—whether in support or against government policies (Repnikova, 2017). Likewise, Russians reject the idea of objectivity or balance in media reporting, consuming media through the lens of political players employed in the service of financial or political patrons (Oates, 2007). Internationally, foreign news media is labeled as biased and self-serving with China articulating narratives of Western reporting as propagating a "China threat theory" (Yang & Liu, 2012); Russia characterizing the US as intentionally undermining their economy (Cooley & Stokes, 2018); Iran claiming Western coverage presents factually incorrect information intended to support regime change and the presence of Iran-phobia in US foreign policy, including narratives of a "soft war" whereby foreign media attempts to undermine Iran's cutural norms and values (Rahim, 2015; Soleimanzadeh et al., 2018; Adegbola et al., 2020); and Venezuela viewing itself as under siege by imperialist nations (McCarthy-Jones & Turner, 2011), among other narratives claiming bias. Domestic audiences then face a choice regarding the extent to which they believe their own nation's news reporting versus that of the international Western press. As nations view the West in opposition to their own interests, attributions of bias are more likely with national media possessing an additional benefit in narrating issues resonant with local cultural beliefs and forms.

Therefore, while Western audiences are quick to critique news practices from authoritarian nations as mere propaganda, it is important to recognize that such readings are filtered through their own cultural and ideological biases. Indeed, it is worth pointing out that even in the US, consumers of news uncritically accept reporting supporting their political leanings. Our point is not to argue for complete relativism when considering culturally situated journalistic standards, but merely to note that nuance exists even within more authoritarian media systems. To that end, in the case study chapters we situate in greater detail each of the nation's unique media ecologies.

Data collection

Using a team of four academic researchers with cultural and/or linguistic knowledge of each nation, as well as with extensive experience analyzing media data for academic research, the study examined native language news reporting from China, Russia, Iran, and Venezuela. In total, 620 news articles from 47 Russian, Chinese, Venezuelan, and Iranian news sources were analyzed over a five-year period (see Appendix B). The initial data collection effort for this study began as part of a comprehensive project on Global Competition and Conflict for the Strategic Multilayer Assessment (SMA) with contributions to the USCENTCOM Assessments of Geopolitical Dynamics globally. The work builds upon comparative global media studies undertaken in previous work (Hinck et al., 2016, 2017, 2018, 2019, 2020).

Data for this project was gathered using the Dow Jones Factiva database, which offers a vast database of online news from 200 countries in 28 different languages. The comprehensiveness of the Factiva database earned it the CODiE award for "best business information or data delivery solution" in 2020. (Dow Jones, 2020). Factiva allows for country specific news media to be assessed across selected time windows, easily exported off platform for analyses. Because Factiva is oriented around global economic trade, source inclusion within each country is a careful consideration reflecting the ability of the source to accurately convey state and corporate intentions across commercial and military sectors. Thus, Factiva offers an "unrivaled selection of global news" as well as convenient tools to optimization search key terms such as word co-occurrences, sentiment analyses, and insightful visuals allowing researchers to better mine the vast trove of media data (Dow Jones, 2020).

The news media sources from each nation were accessed using the Factiva database made available through the Oklahoma State University library. The news sources selected for analysis were chosen from the provided Factiva listings based off of circulation size, availability, ownership, and political slant; although the more limited sources for Iranian and Venezuelan media provided some limitations in doing so (see Appendix B).

Factiva's data mining and co-occurrence tools were used to help generate country specific, native language, keywords relevant to global competition; these were then assessed by those researchers with relevant cultural or linguistic knowledge specific to the country of interest. Terms decided upon included "international order," "global order," "international competition," and "global competition," albeit with some subtle differences in how these terms and their relative meanings manifested themselves in native Russian, Chinese, Arabic/Farsi, and Spanish language (see Appendix C).

Articles were examined across a five year timeframe from January 1, 2014 to June 1, 2019. A systematic random sampling procedure was utilized at a 90% confidence level with a 5% margin of error using the aggregated articles across all keywords for each nation as a unique population during the five-year time period. Thus, four separate populations were sampled from in order to represent the articles from China, Iran, Venezuela, and Russia respectively, thereby making a manageable corpus of articles for which researchers both quantitatively and qualitatively code.

The time frame was chosen both out of convenience and recency, but also because 2014 represented a host of international events propelling international competition forward. Some of these events include: the

Russian Federation's annexation of Crimea and conflict in Ukraine, Islamic State's declared caliphate, Ebola outbreaks in West Africa, Prodemocracy protests in Hong Kong, and negotiations on an Iran nuclear deal (Lindsay, 2014). Within the five year time frame, large global shifts also transpired, including: changes to an US administration moving towards a more inward-looking, isolationist posture as well as shifting alliances internationally; US –DPRK negotiations over North Korea's nuclear program, as well as both a signed treaty over Iran's nuclear weapons followed by the US's subsequent pull out from the agreement; a trade war between the US and China; border crises resulting from Central American migration into the US, as well as widespread migration in Europe; and protests in Venezuela over a rigged election, among other important issues (Lindsay, 2019).

To some extent our cross-time analysis of the four cases represents a limitation in that it preferences an artificial timeline over exploration of individual momentous events. Indeed, the listing of events mentioned previously provides numerous case studies where one could dive deeper into the OS concerns of each country. Nonetheless, by lumping all these events together we argue to be able to identify the larger thematic patterns defining each country's notion of the evolving landscape of our global order and, more importantly, how they communicate their abilities to compete among a variety of issues and contexts. This approach does not negate the importance of specific momentous events—our systematic random sampling of articles across time means that if an event garners greater media attention more articles on the topic were included in the data set. If anything, our approach enables us to better identify more resonant narratives of self and the global order by unveiling how multiple events are stacked or stretched onto others within larger narrative structures. Beyond these conceptual benefits, we believe the practical considerations are worthy too in allowing for comparative analysis. Indeed, while numerous studies examine individual events driving specific OS concerns few, if any have attempted a comparative project like ours.

Data analysis

To uncover Chinese, Russian, Iranian, and Venezuelan media narratives depicting the future of global competition and global order, researchers employed a mixed methods design. After the identification of sources, search terms, and articles for investigation, the data was analyzed both quantitatively and qualitatively to reveal how each nation reported upon and narrated the topic of global or international order and global or international competition. This approach has been similarly applied to studies on strategic narratives in the IR literature (e.g. Krebs, 2015; Coticchia, 2016; Tsygankov, 2017), and large media studies comparing Chinese, Russian, and Arabic media coverage of the 2016 US election (Kluver et al., 2013; Hinck et al., 2019). As Krebs (2015) explains, the value of a mixed method approach comes from the quantitative content analysis aiding in the qualitative narrative analysis by identifying how discursive codes take narrative forms.

Operationalization of narrative

Conceptually, the focus on narrative analysis was driven by prior research on OS emphasizing the unique role of narratives in formulating a social collectives' sense of personal continuity, or OS. As Mitzen (2006) argues, identity is a dynamic process from which action flows, and in turn sustains it; making a stable self-understanding of one's self sustained over time a crucial requirement of OS formation. Although the literature on OS tends to examine (auto)biographical narratives, our operationalization of narrative comes from Miskimmon et al.'s (2014) strategic narrative framework which defines narratives as possessing "actors, an action, a goal or intention, a scene, and an instrument" (p. 5) with narratives operating on three levels: a) international system narratives describing how the world is structured; b) national narratives describing the story of the state, including its values and goals; and c) issue narratives describing why a certain policy is needed. This framework conceptually aligns with state autobiographical narratives in that national level narratives are those defining state identity with international level narratives as describing the international environment and a state's relationships with others. Thus, for this study's purposes, we argue that Miskimmon et al.'s (2014) broader conceptualization of narrative outside of just biographical accounts of state identity enables greater distinctions between identity (agents), one's environmental context (scene), and the tools, motivations, and the policies required for one's ability to compete in the global order.

Methodologically, the analysis of narrative is distinct from research examining media frames or discourse more broadly. As Miskimmon et al. (2014) explain narratives distinguish themselves through their inclusion of a temporal dimension and sense of movement. Specifically, discourses "do not feature a causal transformation that takes actors from one status quo to another, as narratives do" and frames, as analytical units, "lack the temporal and causal features narratives necessarily possess" (p. 7). Likewise, as Coticchia (2016) argues, frames are more tactical in nature, providing snapshots of events to serve short-term purposes of elites. Narratives, however, go beyond framing through their inclusion of temporality and are strategic in their focus on deeper, long-term sensemaking of events. Thus, while frames may serve as the bricks helping to compose a narrative, narratives help shape our understanding of the world, not merely reflecting it in the case of frames, by tying in questions of identity as well as latent social values and cultural myths emplotted over time (Hinck et al., 2019).

Oates et al. (2020) take a similar perspective, arguing that the difference between frames and narratives fall on their factual claims. Accordingly, frames operate within an organized view of reality selectively highlighting and emphasizing the material world whereas narratives represent a broader, particularized way of looking at the world. Thus, analysis of narratives within media reports begins with the reporting of a particular artifact—an individual, place, movement, quotation, etc.; and becomes connected to a news story or telling of a discrete event; which is then framed by selectively highlighting certain elements over others; with a narrative including a broader statement about life in general.

Quantitative analysis

Researchers began their analysis by conducting a quantitative content analysis of the data. According to Frey et al. (2000) quantitative coding analysis allows researchers to examine patterns of meaning found in textual data. The process includes five steps beginning with the selection of texts, determining the unit of analysis, development of content categories, coding of the data, and analysis of the data. Each article was determined as the unit of analysis with the content coding categories developed a priori to capture elements of global competition and order.

To determine how Chinese, Russian, Iranian, and Venezuelan media narrated the future of global competition researchers categorized issues related to competition across areas of diplomatic, informational, military, and economic (DIME) issues. This framework, while originating in US policy planning as a heuristic tool identifying state's instruments of power, nonetheless provides an overarching view on the instruments discussed related to global competition and allows for clearer comparative analyses than identifying each nation's unique conceptualization of power or influence within their own strategic doctrine. Thus, the DIME framework represents more of a holistic than solely military conceptualization of power and statecraft. This allows strategy to include financial, intelligence and law enforcement dynamics within the operational environment (Shehadey, 2013) with effective statecraft emerging from combinations of these instruments of power categorizable within the DIME framework providing insight into how nations broadly identify their strengths and weaknesses within an evolving global order.

More specifically, researchers coded reported elements of competition related to each country's DIME related vulnerabilities as separate from their reported DIME related capabilities. This separation was chosen to capture the arenas in which each country's national media deemed necessary for the state to compete within the geopolitical arena and global marketplace; here the separation of vulnerabilities and capabilities were designed to capture sources of competitive anxiety or weaknesses while also identifying places of opportunity, strength, or agency. For example, a media expression an informational vulnerability might cover threats such as cyber-attacks or foreign media propaganda. An Economic capability might be an expression of state-led economic growth in a specific market sector or the need for certain trade related alliances. A full description of all the DIME framework categories is provided in Appendix A.

In addition to the DIME framework, researchers included six additional broad categories intended to capture discussion related to global order. These categories included media expressions of conflict escalation, deterrence efforts, stated competitors and allies, and redlines to conflict; in addition to national perspectives and valence scores regarding the nation's role in the current global order and future global order, as well as valance scores regarding the US and Western Europe. Taken together, these categories provide comparative data to assess OS elements from each nation regarding their ability to act and shape the global order as well as their relationships and behaviors with other important actors on the global stage.

To reliably assess the quantitative portion of the study, multiple coder training sessions were conducted between the four researchers until an intercoder reliability score greater than.80 was obtained using Cohen's Kappa across all coding categories. This represents a substantive advancement relative to other studies quantifying narratives using only pair-wise percent agreement with levels of agreement as low as 70% (i.e. Krebs, 2015; Hinck et al., 2019). More specifically, coders began with an exploratory stage by familiarizing themselves with the content categories, piloting a small sample applying the categories to all four nations' media reports before discussing and revising the category definitions and identifying exemplars for each. Coders proceeded by conducting one further pilot study with the revised category definitions and discussed differences before completing a final ICR check based on a larger sample of the data.

Importantly, our quantitative approach is not intended to argue that OS narratives are objectively identifiable or fixed objects. Indeed, we recognize and largely agree with the tensions between quantitative analyses and measurement of OS—including concerns of "bracketing" how ontological *in*security could develop, as well as the subjective nature of narratives regarding the "self" and the "world." To mitigate these concerns we paid specific attention to include multiple coders in the coding process while using the quantitative analysis as a springboard for our qualitative approach. Our goal then for the quantitative portion of the study was simply to identify general patterns or trends among our four different case—aiding in the comparative analysis—while then focusing on the qualitative analysis to unveil the more subjective, nuanced narratives reported in each case; the process of which we discuss next.

Qualitative analysis

After completing the quantitative analysis, researchers then went back to the data to conduct their qualitative narrative analysis. Not only did this sequencing provide the coders time to familiarize themselves with the entire data set, but it also ensured objectivity and informed the qualitative analysis with the quantitative results providing some initial codes of the topical themes within the data (Krebs, 2015). The subsequent qualitative narrative analysis followed a grounded thematic approach (Strauss & Corbin, 1990), albeit with emphasis on the emerging narrative forms in which global order and competition emerged. This approach was chosen over a Critical Discourse Analysis for the reasons mentioned above distinguishing narrative and discourse analysis. It also follows the methodology from past studies examining narratives in large national media data sets (Hinck et al., 2019; Hinck & Cooley, 2020). Accordingly, coders began by reading through the qualitative data before rereading through it again and marking initial coding categories and themes before reading through the material and developing larger thematic categories identifying the narratives present. Coders met intermittingly to discuss their initial codes and work out disagreement among them regarding the narrative themes. To further validate the qualitative narrative analysis, researchers utilized a text-mining program (KH Coder). The program allowed the researchers to enter key terms, such as reoccurring topics or actions, references to nations, individuals, or institutions (agents), and other narrative elements. In doing so, the program allowed researchers to cross check additional key terms and identify the constellation of words constitutive of the narratives; as well as enabling researchers to quickly validate their findings through co-occurrence networking, parts of speech frequencies, and key word in context functions.

As part of this process, researchers specifically looked for emerging narrative themes related to global order and competition. Whereas researchers were granted more leeway in determining the narrative themes discussing the constitutive components of the international order within each data set, elements of competition were more limited with researchers focusing on identifying the qualitative components reflective of the DIME categories describing each nation's instruments of power, specifically depictions of DIME related vulnerabilities and capabilities. Nonetheless, in both areas these narrative articulations were driven by researchers isolating descriptions of the overarching scene of action, the actors involved, the instruments or tools being used, the act being done, and the purpose of the actions themselves, following Miskimmon et al.'s (2014) definition of narrative. The process allowed for common story patterns and anomalies in those patterns to be discussed and compared across case studies, as well as broader narrative articulations representing the key agents and institutions reported as making up the global order and competition.

References

Acharya, A. (2018). *Constructing Global Order: agency and change in world politics.* Cambridge University Press.

Adegbola, O., Gearhart, S., & Cho, J. (2020). Reporting Bias in Coverage of Iran Protests by Global News Agencies. *The International Journal of Press/Politics.* doi.org/10.1177/1940161220966948.

Agius, C. (2017). Drawing the discourses of ontological security: Immigration and identity in the Danish and Swedish cartoon crises. *Cooperation and conflict*. 52 (1), 109–125.

Anderson, B. (2006). *Imagined communities: Reflections on the origin and spread of nationalism*. Verso Books.

Appadurai, A. (1990). Disjuncture and difference in the global cultural economy. *Theory, Culture & Society*. 7(2–3), 295–310.

Arsenault, A., Hong, S. H., & Price, M. (2017). Strategic narratives of the Arab Spring and after. In A. Miskimmon, B. O'Loughlin, & L. Roselle (Eds), *Forging the world: Strategic narratives and international relations*. 190–217. University of Michigan Press.

Behravesh, M. (2018). State revisionism and ontological (in) security in international politics: the complicated case of Iran and its nuclear behavior. *Journal of International Relations and Development*. 21(4), 836–857.

Bellin, E. (2012). Reconsidering the robustness of authoritarianism in the Middle East: Lessons from the Arab Spring. *Comparative Politics*. 44(2), 127–149.

Berenskötter, F. (2014). Parameters of a national biography. *European Journal of International Relations*. 20(1), 262–288.

Bulovsky, A. (2019). Authoritarian communication on social media: The relationship between democracy and leaders' digital communicative practices. *International Communication Gazette*. 81(1), 20–45.

Carey, J. W. (2008). *Communication as culture, revised edition: Essays on media and society*. Routledge.

Castells, M. (2008). The new public sphere: Global civil society, communication networks, and global governance. *The ANNALS of the American academy of Political and Social Science*. 616(1), 78–93.

Chaban, N., Miskimmon, A., & O'Loughlin, B. (2017). The EU's peace and security narrative: Views from EU strategic partners in Asia. *JCMS: Journal of Common Market Studies*. 55(6), 1273–1289.

Chacko, P. (2014). A new "special relationship"?: Power transitions, ontological security, and India–US relations. *International Studies Perspectives*. 15(3), 329–346.

Combes, M. D. (2017). Encountering the stranger: Ontological security and the Boston Marathon bombing. *Cooperation and Conflict*. 52(1), 126–143.

Cooley, S. C. & Stokes, E. C. (2018). Manufacturing resilience: An analysis of broadcast and web-based news presentations of the 2014–2015 Russian economic downturn. *Global Media and Communication*. 14(1), 123–139.

Coticchia, F. (2016). A controversial warplane: Narratives, counternarratives, and the Italian debate on the F-35. *Alternatives*. 41(4), 194–213.

Crick, N. (2014). *Rhetoric and power: The drama of classical Greece*. University of South Carolina Press.

Cross, M. K. D. (2017). *The politics of crisis in Europe*. Cambridge University Press.

Diamond, L., Plattner, M. F., & Walker, C. (Eds.). (2016). *Authoritarianism goes global: The challenge to democracy*. John Hopkins University Press.

Deibert, R. J. (2019). The road to digital unfreedom: Three painful truths about social media. *Journal of Democracy*. 30(1), 25–39.

Dow Jones. (2020). *Welcome back to Factiva*. https://professional.dowjones.com/factiva.

Eberle, J. (2019). Narrative, desire, ontological security, transgression: Fantasy as a factor in international politics. *Journal of International Relations and Development*. 22(1), 243–268.
Entman, R. M. (2008). Theorizing mediated public diplomacy: The US case. *The International Journal of Press/Politics*. 13(2), 87–102.
Fisher, W. R. (1985). The narrative paradigm: An elaboration. *Communication Monographs*. 52(4), 347–367.
Fisher, W. R. (1989). Clarifying the narrative paradigm. *Communications Monographs*. 56(1), 55–58.
Flew, T. (2020). Globalization, neo-globalization and post-globalization: The challenge of populism and the return of the national. *Global Media and Communication*. 16(1), 19–39.
Flew, T., Iosifidis, P., & Steemers, J. (Eds). (2016). *Global media and national policies: The return of the state*. Palgrave Macmillan.
Fukuyama, F. (1992). *The End of History and the Last Man*. Simon & Schuster.
Frey, L., Botan, C., & Kreps, G. (2000) *Investigating communication: An introduction to research methods*. Allyn & Bacon.
Giddens, A. (1991). *Modernity and self-identity: Self and society in the late Modern Age*. Stanford University Press.
Gilboa, E. (2005a). Global television news and foreign policy: Debating the CNN effect. *International Studies Perspectives*. 6(3), 325–341.
Gilboa, E. (2005b). The CNN effect: The search for a communication theory of international relations. *Political communication*. 22(1), 27–44.
Guriev, S. & Treisman, D. (2019). Informational autocrats. *Journal of Economic Perspectives*. 33(4), 100–127.
Hagström, L. & Gustafsson, K. (2019). Narrative power: How storytelling shapes East Asian international politics. *Cambridge Review of International Affairs*. 32 (4), 387–406.
He, B. (2014). Deliberative culture and politics: The persistence of authoritarian deliberation in China. *Political Theory*. 42(1), 58–81.
He, B. & Warren, M. E. (2011). Authoritarian deliberation: The deliberative turn in Chinese political development. *Perspectives on Politics*. 9(2), 269–289.
Herman, E. S. & Chomsky, N. (2010). *Manufacturing consent: The political economy of the mass media*. Random House.
Hinck, R. S., Chinn, J., Kluver, R., & Norris, W. (2016). Interpreting and shaping geopolitics in Chinese media: The discourse of the "New Style of Great Power Relations." *Asian Journal of Communication*. 26(5), 427–445.
Hinck, R. S., Kluver, R., & Cooley, S. (2017). Russia re-envisions the world: Strategic narratives in Russian broadcast and news media during 2015. *Russian Journal of Communication*. 10(1), 21–37.
Hinck, R. S., Kluver, R., Norris, W., & Manly, J. (2018). Geopolitical dimensions of "The China Dream": Exploring strategic narratives of the Chinese Communist Party. *China Media Research*. 14(3), 99–110.
Hinck, R. S., Cooley, S., & Kluver, R. (2019). *Global media and strategic narratives of contested democracy: Chinese, Russian, and Arabic media narratives of the US presidential election*. Routledge.
Hinck, R. S. & Cooley, S. C. (2020). North Korean media penetration and influence in Chinese and Russian media: Strategic narratives during the 2017–2018 nuclear confrontation. *International Journal of Communication*. 14(22), 1331–1352.

Huysmans, J. (1998). Security! What do you mean? From concept to thick signifier. *European Journal of International Relations.* 4(2), 226–255.

IMF. (2019). *World Economic Outlook Database,* October 2019. www.imf.org/en/Publications/WEO/weo-database/2019/October.

Inglehart, R. (2020). *Modernization and postmodernization: Cultural, economic, and political change in 43 societies.* Princeton University Press.

Innes, A. L. & Steele, B. J. (2014). Memory, Trauma and Ontological Security. In E. Resende & D. Budryte (Eds), *Memory and Trauma in International Relations: Theories, Cases, and Debates,* 15–29. Routledge.

Kinnvall, C. (2004). Globalization and religious nationalism: Self, identity, and the search for ontological security. *Political Psychology.* 25(5), 741–767.

Kissinger, H. (2014). *World Order.* Penguin Books.

Kluver, R., Campbell, H. A., & Balfour, S. (2013). Language and the boundaries of research: Media monitoring technologies in international media research. *Journal of Broadcasting & Electronic Media.* 57(1), 4–19.

Krebs, R. R. (2015). How dominant narratives rise and fall: Military conflict, politics, and the Cold War consensus. *International Organization.* 69(4), 809–845.

Krolikowski, A. (2018). Shaking up and making up China: how the party-state compromises and creates ontological security for its subjects. *Journal of International Relations and Development.* 21(4), 909–933.

Krolikowski, A. (2008). State personhood in ontological security theories of international relations and Chinese nationalism: A sceptical view. *Chinese Journal of International Politics.* 2(1), 109–133.

Lagerkvist, J. (2010). *After the Internet, before democracy: Competing norms in Chinese media and society.* Peter Lang.

Lang, K. & Lang, G. E. (2004). Noam Chomsky and the manufacture of consent for American foreign policy. *Political Communication.* 21(1), 93–101.

Lasswell, H. D. (1941). The garrison state. *American Journal of Sociology.* 46, 455–468.

Lindsay, J. (2014). The most significant world events in 2014. *Council on Foreign Relations.* Blog Post, December 15, 2014. Available at www.cfr.org/blog/ten-most-significant-world-events-2014.

Lindsay, J. (2019). The most significant world events in 2014. *Council on Foreign Relations.* Blog Post, December 23, 2019. Available at www.cfr.org/blog/ten-most-significant-world-events-2019.

Lynch, M. (2011). After Egypt: The limits and promise of online challenges to the authoritarian Arab state. *Perspectives on politics.* 9(2), 301–310.

Mälksoo, M. (2018). Countering hybrid warfare as ontological security management: The emerging practices of the EU and NATO. *European Security.* 27(3), 374–392.

McCarthy-Jones, A. & Turner, M. (2011). Explaining radical policy change: The case of Venezuelan foreign policy. *Policy Studies,* 32(5). 549–567.

Michaelsen, M. (2017). Far away, so close: Transnational activism, digital surveillance and authoritarian control in Iran. *Surveillance & Society.* 15(3/4), 465–470.

Miskimmon, A., O'Loughlin, B., & Roselle, L. (2014). *Strategic narratives: Communication power and the new world order.* Routledge.

Miskimmon, A., O'Loughlin, B., & Roselle, L. (2017). *Forging the world: Strategic narratives and international relations.* University of Michigan Press.

Mitzen, J. (2006). Ontological security in world politics: State identity and the security dilemma. *European Journal of International Relations.* 12(3), 341–370.

Oates, S. (2007). The neo-Soviet model of the media. *Europe-Asia Studies*. 59(8), 1279–1297.
Oates, S., Walker, C., Deibler, D., & Anderson, J. (2020). *Sharing a playbook?: The convergence of Russian and U.S. narratives about Joe Biden*. American Political Science Association: 2020 APSA Annual Meeting: Democracy, Difference, and Destabilization.
Ottaway, M. (2013). *Democracy challenged: The rise of semi-authoritarianism*. Carnegie Endowment.
Price, M. E. (2002). *Media and sovereignty: The global information revolution and its challenge to state power*. MIT Press.
Rahim, B. (2015). Censorship and the Islamic Republic: Two modes of regulatory measures for media in Iran. *Middle East Journal*. 69(3), 358–378.
Repnikova, M. (2017). *Media politics in China: Improvising power under authoritarianism*. Cambridge University Press.
Robinson, P. (2001). Theorizing the influence of media on world politics: Models of media influence on foreign policy. *European Journal of Communication*. 16(4), 523–544.
Roselle, L., Miskimmon, A., & O'Loughlin, B. (2014). Strategic narrative: A new means to understand soft power. *Media, War & Conflict*. 7(1), 70–84.
Rozenas, A. & Stukal, D. (2019). How autocrats manipulate economic news: Evidence from Russia's state-controlled television. *The Journal of Politics*. 81(3), 982–996.
Samuel-Azran, T. (2009). Counterflows and counterpublics: The Al-Jazeera effect on western discourse. *Journal of International Communication*. 15(1), 56–73.
Schiller, D. (2008). The militarization of US communications. *Communication, Culture & Critique*. 1(1), 126–138.
Schumacher, T. (2015). Uncertainty at the EU's borders: Narratives of EU external relations in the revised European Neighbourhood Policy towards the southern borderlands. *European Security*. 24(3), 381–401.
Shehadey, B. D. (2013). Putting the "D" and "I" Back in DIME. *American Military University/Edge*. https://amuedge.com/putting-the-d-and-i-back-in-dime.
Silver, L., Devlin, K., & Huang, C. (2019). Attitudes toward China. *Pew*. December 5, 2019. www.pewresearch.org/global/2019/12/05/attitudes-toward-china-2019.
Simpson, C. (1994). *Science of coercion: Communication research and psychological warfare 1945–1960*. Oxford University Press.
Snow, N. (2002). *Propaganda, Inc*. (2nd ed.). Seven Stories Press.
Soleimanzadeh, S., Omidi, A., & Yazdani, E. (2018). A constructivist analysis of Iranophobia in the US foreign plicy in post-JCPOA era. *Strategic Research of Politics*. 7(24), 95–124.
Somers, M. R. & Gibson, G. D. (1994). Reclaiming the epistemological 'other': Narrative and the social construction of identity. In C. Calhoun (Ed.), *Social theory and the politics of identity*, 37–99). John Wiley & Sons.
SIPRI. (2019). *World military expenditure grows to $1.8 trillion in 2018*. April 29, 2019. www.sipri.org/media/press-release/2019/world-military-expenditure-grows-18-trillion-2018.
Steele, B. J. (2008). *Ontological security in international relations: Self-identity and the IR state*. Routledge.
Stockmann, D. & Luo, T. (2017). Which social media facilitate online public opinion in China? *Problems of Post-Communism*. 64(3–4),189–202.

Strauss, A. & Corbin, J. (1990). *Basics of qualitative research.* Sage Publications.

Subotić, J. (2016). Narrative, ontological security, and foreign policy change. *Foreign Policy Analysis.* 12(4), 610–627.

Taylor, P. M. (2013). *Munitions of the mind: A history of propaganda from the ancient world to the present era.* Manchester University Press.

Thussu, D. K. (2018). *International communication: Continuity and change.* Bloomsbury Publishing.

Tilly, C. (1994) The time of states. *Social Research.* 62(1): 269–295.

Tsygankov, A. P. (2017). The dark double: The American media perception of Russia as a neo-Soviet autocracy, 2008–2014. *Politics.* 37(1), 19–35.

White, S. & McAllister, I. (2014). Did Russia (nearly) have a Facebook revolution in 2011? Social media's challenge to authoritarianism. *Politics.* 34(1), 72–84.

Wight, C. (2004) State agency: Social action without human activity? *Review of International Studies.* 39(2): 269–280.

Woetzel, J., Madgavkar, A., Seong, J., Manyika, J., Sneader, K., Tonby, O., Cadena, A., Gupta, R., Leke, A., Kim, H., & Gupta, S. (2018). Outperformers: High-growth emerging economies and the companies that propel them. *McKinsey Global Institute.* September 11, 2018. www.mckinsey.com/featured-insights/innovation-and-growth/outperformers-high-growth-emerging-economies-and-the-companies-that-propel-them#.

Xiaoyu, P. (2012). Socialisation as a two-way process: Emerging powers and the diffusion of international norms. *The Chinese Journal of International Politics.* 5 (4), 341–367.

Xu, X. (2020). To Repress or to co-opt? Authoritarian control in the age of digital surveillance. *American Journal of Political Science.* 65(2), 309–325.

Yang, Y. E. & Liu, X. (2012). The 'China threat' through the lens of US print media: 1992–2006. *Journal of Contemporary China.* 21(76), 695–711.

3 Ontological Security Narratives in Chinese Media

Economic Anxieties and Cautious Optimism amid Evolving Identities

Introduction

China's rise has been the subject of much debate not only in academic and policy circles, but also the general public. According to Beckley (2011) the "rise of China" was the most read-about news story during the first decade of the twenty-first century. More recently, Harvard Historian Graham Allison's (2017) book on whether the US and China are destined for war was a national bestseller. Indeed, the past four decades have witnessed China's growth from a poor and internationally isolated nation to one of global prominence (Shambaugh, 2013). Today China tops the charts in many international categories of influence and power, including the second largest economy and annual military expenditure, leaving many wondering what the future holds (Bajpai, 2020; China Power Team, 2020).

A significant body of research has debated the implications of China's rise from the perspective power transition theory (Zhou, 2019; Graham, 2017; Mearsheimer, 2010, 2014; Lai, 2011; Beckley, 2011; Kirshner, 2008; Huiyun, 2009; Tammen & Kugler, 2006; Ross, 2006; Friedberg, 2005; Johnston, 2003) as well as studies theorizing China's impact on the global order more broadly (Pu, 2019; Acharya, 2018; Zhang, 2016; Smith, 2012; Breslin, 2013; Chin & Thakur, 2010; Foot & Walter, 2010; Jacques, 2009). Both bodies of literature are concerned with China's (dis)satisfaction with the current US-led order and whether it will exercise its growing power to change the rules of global interaction, potentially leading to conflict with the US.

From the perspective of ontological security (OS), power transitions are times of destabilization and uncertainty as established relations between states and patterns of hierarchy are revised or challenged (Chacko, 2014). During these periods of transition, previously cemented notions of identity, sense of place in the international community, and the routinized relationships and attachments with other actors and institutions become in flux. As Behravesh (2018) argues, revisionist powers could try to secure their identity by defining their relationships with others around dissatisfaction with the

DOI: 10.4324/9781003197478-3

global order, but in doing so cause greater feelings of ontological *in*security and exclusion from status quo powers.

Whether emerging powers are content, or can be persuaded to be, with the international system is of central importance (Ward, 2017; Xiaoyu, 2012), especially as it relates to established powers providing rising powers a sense of recognition and voice (Newman & Zala, 2018); or, in OS terms, agency. Although many assume China wants more status, Pu (2019) argues Chinese leaders project conflicting messages. Economically, Chinese leaders have both declared China's arrival as one of the world's major economic powers while insisting it is still a developing nation; likewise, Chinese officials project a vision towards a "great national rejuvenation" of its status as a great power while eschewing claims to global leadership, hegemony, or expansion. In essence, China remains a deeply conflicted power with a series of competing domestic and international identities (Shambaugh, 2011, 2013; Pu, 2017) with the nature and content of the future global order undoubtedly shaped by the roles China decides to play.

This chapter examines how Chinese media discourse narrates the future of global competition to its domestic populace by conveying the key challenges the nation faces and the solutions and instruments of power it should pursue. To make sense of these discourses, it argues for a lens perceiving the Chinese Communist Party (CCP) as functioning as an OS provider through which its national media discourse presents a vision of China's role in the global order driven by narratives legitimizing CCP policies and rule, as well as a vision for Chinese global leadership. Importantly, these narratives support Chinese official state discourse and promote its economic reform plans, reflective of its ongoing challenge in escaping the middle-income trap.

In sum, the narrative vision presented in Chinese media discourse regarding the future of global competition presents the global order as one needing multilateral cooperation and continued free trade. Within this order, China presents competition as one of economic contestation centered on free trade and innovation, rather than military conflict. The major antagonist is rising nationalism and isolationist policies in Europe and the US, portrayed as undermining global stability. As a result, this narrative defines and presents China as a global leader supporting international institutions such as the United Nations (UN) and the World Trade Organization (WTO). Taken together, China's narrative vision suggests that successful competition requires promotion of diplomatic ties, domestic technological innovation, and continued reforms, all of which support CCP policies and legitimacy. Importantly, Chinese media present the nation as optimistic in its ability to lead and shape the world within its current confines while also providing greater voice for developing nations.

Historical overview

Over the past two centuries, China has been a country in flux. The trauma experienced throughout the 1800s resulting in China's forced opening up at the hands of the British Empire during two Opium wars—in addition to the Tai-ping and Boxer rebellions and military defeats to Japan in 1895—shook the core of China's identity. As the Qing Empire waffled with its reforms, it ultimately proved unable to adapt to new Western currents of modernization, leading to the fall of the Chinese empire in 1906. Failed experiments with democracy led to warlordism, further weakening central authority. More trauma ensued, with China the victim of wartime atrocities at the hands of the Japanese empire, the legacy of which still impacts Sino-Japanese relations today (Hahm & Heo, 2019; Gustafsson, 2014; Moore, 2010; Yoshida, 2006). Out of this tumult, the CCP managed to wrest control from the democratic, albeit corrupt and authoritarian Kuomintang, with the communist revolution finally consolidating control of mainland China in 1949. However, under CCP authority, attempts at Chinese modernization and revival continued to transform and upend traditional Chinese culture and identities.

Krolikowski (2018) argues that since the founding of the People's Republic of China (PRC), CCP rule has sought to undermine Chinese citizens' OS through deliberate, top-down, and often coercive efforts in pursuit of revolutionizing Chinese society. Domestically during the 1950s, Krolikowski explains that CCP land reform policies and its agricultural collectivization campaign during the Great Leap Forward not only overturned the millennia of organized life centered around the extended-family unit to that of large collectives (Baum, 1964, Thaxton & Thaxton, 2008), but also erased local, traditional ways of life to install rigid structures conceived at the political center (Scott, 1999). Equally destabilizing, five years later, Mao's Cultural Revolution intentionally unfurled societal chaos by undermining sources of authority and knowledge in nearly every sphere of public life, including calling for the destruction of old customs, culture, habits, and ideas. The decade long experience of the Cultural Revolution traumatized Chinese both on the individual and societal level, impacting their shared recollections of historical experience (Heberer, 2009; Plankers & Hart, 2014; Plankers, 2011; Kleinman & Kleinman, 1994). Politically, the campaigns to root out party revisionists and capitalist roadsters led to the near total collapse of government authority at the hand of the Red Guards.

Throughout this period, China's international identity was also in flux. With the founding of the CCP in 1949, China's decision to initially align itself with the Soviet Union was not a foregone conclusion (Yufan & Zhihai, 1990). Ultimately, its decision to "lean" towards the USSR was cemented during the Korean War and first Taiwan Straits crisis, defining Chinese foreign policy as anti-imperialist and anti-capitalist. Thus, according to Johnston (2008), in the early 1950s, China's international rhetoric reflected the Five Principles of Peaceful Coexistence, developed with India, stressing norms of interstate relations that would minimize conflicts among independent, sovereign states. However, as domestic Chinese politics radicalized under Mao—with ideological conflict with the USSR and US sharpening—antagonistic discourse about world revolution and mobilization of anti-imperialist and anti-Soviet rhetoric rose into the 1960s. As conflict with the USSR began seriously threatening Chinese security, with China domestically in shambles as a result of the Cultural Revolution, Mao normalized relations with the US to form a strategic partnership in military and economic affairs.

After Mao's death in 1976, Chinese society again underwent profound changes both domestically and as internationally. In setting out to reform China's domestic economy, Deng Xiaoping fundamentally altered the economic relationship between the state and individual, this time reversing the basic social categories and attachments formed during the Maoist period to a hybrid socialist-market economy. By the 1980s over half of the rural farms had been decollectivized with state-owned enterprises (SOE) receiving less government support resulting in significant numbers of layoffs, ending the economic stability provided by the state through the iron rice bowl. This, in addition to the move away from state-assigned prices for goods to market-based prices led to not only rising prices but also corruption from party officials (Ma, 1989; Trinh, 2013; Nathan, 1990). Politically, Deng sought to stabilize Chinese politics by allowing for more open political discussion and by creating a consensus-led structure within the CCP leadership balancing conservative and moderate factions. However, as Chinese citizens embraced this incipient democratization, and grappled with their new economic challenges while witnessing the rampant corruption from government leaders, protests erupted resulting in the Tiananmen Square crackdown and retrenchment of CCP authority (Goldman, 1994; Zhao, 2004; Nathan, 2019).

Internationally at this time, changes in China's rhetoric included initially endorsing international institutions along a developmentalist perspective in the 1980s viewed as serving the economic development and security interests of the developing world (Johnston, 2008). However, after the Tiananmen crackdown, Chinese diplomatic discourse turned to more starkly absolutionist concepts of sovereignty combined with reactionary rhetoric designed to justify Chinese crackdown of political dissent and limit intrusive international commitments. To some extent this hyper sovereigntist discourse was diluted with themes of globalization and multilateralism as China increasingly sought to engage in global trade organizations deemed necessary for its economic development. By the 2000s China pursued new identity discourses describing it as a "responsible major power" albeit still a "developing country" willing to uphold some commitments to the status quo's international economic and security institutions (Scott, 2015; Zhang, 2010; Yi, 2005). As this brief historical review demonstrates, China's identity, routines, and attachments have been in significant flux for some time both domestically and internationally.

The Chinese Communist Party as ontological security provider

According to research on OS, individuals and social collectives require a sense of "security of being" or stable sense of self in order to manage the anxiety and unintelligibility of their world. According to Giddens (1991) OS is a prerequisite of agency and self-identity, which one develops through a sense of self through trust in routines and biographical narratives. Importantly, one's identity and trust system are tied to their interpersonal and organizational relationships in a particular time and space. According to Mitzen (2006) actors reinforce these trust systems by developing routines to minimizing uncertainty and impose cognitive order on their environment.

Of note, states are argued to be key providers of OS (Steele, 2008; Krolikowski, 2008, 2018; Chacko, 2014). According to Krolikowski (2018) states provide individuals with not only physical but also cognitive security and order by supplying them with the sense that the world around them is knowable despite the onslaught of unintelligible experiences. As Huysmans (1998) argues, the legitimacy of a state rests on its capacity to provide order for its citizens, making life intelligible. Thus, drawing from Huysmans, Krolikowski (2018) explains how state security policies can reinforce citizens' OS by ordering the state's social relations with others and introducing a level of certainty to abstract fears. However, if the state's "enemies and dangers multiply and cannot be coherently perceived or organized, this actor finds themselves in a state of crisis and loses trust in their capacity to manage these threats" (p. 915).

Paradoxically, as the history of China outlined above suggests, the CCP has created fundamentally destabilizing conditions both regarding individual Chinese citizens and the state's relation with major powers. As Ding (2006) explains, the CCP faced two crises of legitimacy, one in the aftermath of the Cultural Revolution and another following the Tiananmen Square protest; and yet, CCP rule continues demonstrating remarkable authoritarian resiliency (Pei, 2012; Hess, 2013). As Krolikowski (2018) argues, China's party-state has developed a unique mode of rule that both undermines its citizens' OS while also assuaging it through deeply embedded official state discourse anchoring their sense of biographical and ideological continuity. Thus, while CCP policies disrupted the conditions upon which Chinese citizens could maintain a stable sense of self by extirpating previous customs and social structures exacerbating the unintelligibility of their surroundings and aggravating their experience of existential anxiety, the CCP also supplied cultural and historical resources through official state discourse bolstering citizen's OS against the new threats arising from their shifting environment. In doing so, the state, through the CCP, ensures that "No entity but the party-state can both create this [ontological] need and address it in this way" (p. 927).

The current success of such efforts is evident by Chinese public opinion data showing government satisfaction increasing from 2003 to 2016 with Chinese citizens rating government officials as more capable and effective than ever before (Cunninghad, Saich, & Turiel, 2020). Xi's recent corruption campaign, while destabilizing the nation's political apparatus, has likewise garnered significant support. Whereas in 2011, only 35.5% of Chinese respondents approved of CCP corruption efforts in 2016, that number rose to 71.5%. As Cunninghad et al. (2020) conclude, polling data shows Chinese citizens are responsive to demonstrable changes in their material wellbeing—both positively and negatively, suggesting that future challenges arising from declining economic growth or a deteriorating natural environment can undermine such support if progress is not continued.

Narratives of continuity

According to Giddens (1991), individuals need a sense of biographical continuity to feel secure. As providers of OS, state agents fulfill this need by supplying citizens with compelling autobiographical stories about the nation (Steele, 2008; Chacko, 2014). Subotić (2016) adds that during crises and threats to state security, political elites selectively activate certain societal narratives preserving state OS to provide a sense of autobiographical continuity. In the case of China, Krolikowski (2018) identifies two narrative categories of continuity provided by the CCP. The first stresses China's civilizational continuity, including the situating of contemporary events within China's 5,000 years of civilizational history to its imperial past. These dialectical accounts, emphasizing historical ruptures, include: 1) contrasts between pre and post-revolutionary China, projecting a vision towards a progressively brighter future; and 2) China's Century of Humiliation, beginning with its traumatic initial experiences with the West whereby China was weak and victimized, thereby calling for a rejuvenation of its strength and restoration of its rightful place in the global order. The second category of continuity narratives is an ideological and normative one. Here, official state discourse produces a macro-narrative presenting the cumulative refinements and development of Marxist ideas as gradually built upon China's historical experience and ideologically consistent historiographies of the PRC. Krolikowski argues that official ideology sustains a relatively stable normative and ethical framework for organizing daily life with such normative structures repositioned and recomposed to maintain parameters of what counts as counter-normative, even if these normative structures evolve over time.

Thus, Chinese citizens draw upon these social and cultural narratives of continuity to maintain a sense of OS to which the Party has systematically propagated and embedded itself in throughout Chinese society (Krolikowski, 2018). In this case, the CCP utilizes multiple vehicles of transmission to spread its official state discourse to the masses and individuals. Some of these include patriotic education programs and social organizations while others extend to political work structures. Of importance to this study, however, is the role of Chinese media as a mode for connecting individuals to CCP state discourse, especially in relation to its perception of competition within the future global order.

Chinese media

Since the founding of the PRC, Chinese leaders have sought to control and define how their citizens understand their social realities in an effort to support and mobilize public backing of CCP policies. Censorship or access to information played a key role in the CCP's early propaganda policies with the general populace only made aware of positive developments while those in power were provided with a more comprehensive and somber depiction of affairs (Link & Qiang, 2013). Today, Chinese media employs a variety of influence tactics to maintain social cohesion and support for the CCP. These include state and self-censorship practices, positive framing techniques, information manipulation, and ideotainment (Chen & Xu, 2017; King et al., 2013; Stockmann, 2013); strategic managing of relationships with critical journalists (Repnikova, 2017; Lorentzen, 2014); authoritarian deliberation practices allowing for citizen feedback and promotion of state policy (Fishkin et al., 2010; He, 2014; He & Warren, 2011; Leib & He, 2006; Stockmann & Luo, 2017); and aspirational narratives such as the "China Dream" (Hinck et al., 2018; Sørensen, 2015).

Rhetorically, and on a more granular level, Schoenhals (1992) explains that Chinese leaders rely on key slogans and catchwords to legitimize policy action. Thus, Chinese political discourse takes the shape of formalized language characterized by slogans, clichés, jargon, and code words, constraining how political actors can advocate or defend policies. As Lu and Simons (2006) argue, Chinese leaders can be rhetorically inventive but only within the cultural and political traditions already in existence; those derived internally from its culture and history and the idea of the PRC as a nation state. This official state discourse not only travels through diverse media channels in China, including leaders' speeches, newspaper articles and editorials, televised news coverage, along with educational and reference materials, but also encompass a range of state sponsored entertainment products including books, films, and television programs for popular audiences. Together, these goods constitute "official culture" with their spoken and written elements constituting "official discourses" (Krolikowski, 2018).

China's domestic messaging is closely tied to its international communications. According to Edney (2012) Chinese officials have tried to elevate

China's cultural resources to augment its soft power abroad while emphasizing the promotion of a harmonious society at home. Efforts to do so focus on unifying domestic thought and coalescing popular feeling, with "national cohesion go[ing] hand in hand with international attractiveness" (pp. 912–913). Since 2003 the Chinese government has launched a series of Public Diplomacy and "going out" campaigns (Thussu et al., 2017; Hayden, 2012) to not only combat Western news organizations' dominance in international news reporting—including Chinese perceptions of foreign news agencies perpetuating a "China threat theory," but also bolster CCP legitimacy by advocating for an image of China as a "responsible nation," promoting a safer world through its "peaceful rise," and "national rejuvenation", and its role as a historic great power (Yang & Liu, 2012; Yi, 2005; Kerr, 2016; Wang, 2011; Hartig, 2016). As Lu and Simons (2006) explain, Chinese rhetorical requirements include China's role in the world economy and its geopolitical position among other nations with these rhetorical devices helping present China's national myth and create a narrative naming and affirming the identity of its people.

Nonetheless, Chinese officials walk a tight rope regarding its international rhetoric. Programs designed to reach foreign audiences leave the CCP susceptible to criticism at home in that spending millions of dollars abroad to bolster its image or promote Chinese language learning, like in the case of Confucius institutes, is contrasted with the hundreds of millions of Chinese lacking economic opportunities, tenuous health care, and social safety nets. Furthermore, although declaring Chinese return to strength could legitimize Party leadership at home, it can fuel fears by others regarding China's rise. Likewise, professing Chinese economic grandeur could undermine trade policy in that China strategically maintains its designation as a "developing" economy in WTO discussions to safeguard favorable trade regulations.

China and the future of global competition

While it is easy to assume China's rise has led to greater power, Chinese domestic politics remain in doubt. Under Xi Jinping, Chinese politics have returned to neo-authoritarianism with the throwing out of the political norms established by Deng. The constitutional amendment allowing Xi to more than two terms as president, in conjunction with his anti-corruption campaign purging the party of those aligned against him, has led many to deem Xi as the most powerful Chinese leader since Mao (Zhao, 2016; Phillips, 2017; Khan, 2018; Economy, 2018). Furthermore, Xi has attempted to retrench CCP authority within Chinese society, taking greater control of China's media and journalistic reporting as well as ideological messages intended to strengthen social cohesion and harness Chinese nationalism through narratives of the "China Dream" and China's "Great National Rejuvenation" (Jaros & Pan, 2018; Peidong & Lijun, 2018; Dimitrov, 2017; Callahan, 2015).

However, Xi's move to consolidate power can be understood, in part, by his belief in the profound challenges facing China. Indeed, while China has consistently grown economically over the past four decades, it now faces the crucial test of making the leap to a consumer driven economy capable of self-innovation to escape the middle-income trap (Woo et al., 2012; Lewin et al., 2016; Glawe & Wagner, 2020); thus, China has become dependent on the world economy. With CCP legitimacy tied to its ability to provide economic growth, China has doubled down on policies of opening up, forcing Chinese companies and SOEs to compete globally to stimulate innovation and pursue greater economic efficiency. As part of this plan, Xi has politically committed himself to growing China's international influence through its Belt and Road Initiative (BRI) by establishing trade routes with countries around the world (Ferdinand, 2016; Zhao, 2020).

Furthermore, China's two centenary goals marking the 100 year anniversaries of the founding of the CCP in 2021 and the PRC in 2049 represent clear benchmarks tied to Xi's China Dream, promising not only a modestly prosperous Chinese society, but also a return to national strength. This narrative not only calls forth Chinese identity in relation to its historical path, but also ties Chinese together in rectifying the trauma of its century of humiliation (Hinck et al., 2018). Thus, China's commitment to regaining its territorial claims in the South China Sea, as well as aspiring for control over Hong Kong and Taiwan represent flash points for jingoism and conflict.

In sum, the legitimacy of the CCP appears tied to its ability to successfully compete in the future global order in order to achieve its economic and military goals. With perceptions of declining US global influence, and challenges to the US-led liberal international order widely shared by academic and policy elites, in conjunction with fears of China's rise vis-à-vis the US, how China views the future global order and its ability to successfully compete within it holds significant implications both domestically for China, but also the world.

Thus, rather than focusing on physical security—like realist theories relating to great power politics and power transition, OS's focus on one's "security of being" points us to examine what goes into the stories we tell about ourselves and our relations to others, reflective of our environment. It also calls for an investigation of the cognitive and affective reasons states experience insecurity and their responses to such emotions (Kinnvall & Mitzen, 2017). In China's case, while the CCP's incorporation of its past narrative traumas could help to solidify Chinese identity, it could also lead to attachment of conflictual relations with its historical transgressors. Furthermore, although its routine relationships with the international order has served its past needs in providing a stable environment to develop its economy through export-led growth, whether this system continues to provide the space for China to grow is unclear. To determine how

Chinese media narrates to its citizen's what the future global order holds, and the implications of these narrative identities, relational attachments, and routine behavior, this chapter asks two questions:

RQ1. How do Chinese media narrate the future global order?
RQ2. How do Chinese media narrate the future of global competition?

Method

For a full description of the methodology, see Chapter 2. As a synopsis, researchers employed a mixed methodological design including qualitative narrative analysis aided by the text-mining program KH coder as well as a quantitative content analysis. The study analyzed 270 native language Chinese news articles across nine sources during December 2014–19. Data were collected using the Factiva platform, which aggregates and stores international news media. Researchers conducted a systematic random sampling at a 90% confidence interval of the articles collected by using a series of keywords (international/global influence, global order, international/global competition). For a full breakdown of sources and articles sampled, see Chapter 2.

The qualitative narrative analysis applied a grounded theory approach whereby researchers first read through the entire corpus of articles before identifying emerging patterns which were then used in the creation of larger thematic categories. Focus was placed on understanding the narrative structure of the news articles in relation to their depiction of the global order and competition within it. Narrative was broadly conceptualized using Burke's (1969) definition of narratives including act, agents, scenes, instruments, and purpose.

For the quantitative analysis, two coders analyzed the news articles using four general categories with subsequent subtopical categories. The first two broad categories were used to determine how China narrated the nature of global competition, including mentions of Chinese key vulnerabilities and necessary capabilities with subcategories related to the DIME instrument of power framework. Two further broad categories were included to capture Chinese media portrayals of the global order. The first included depictions of escalation management, deterrence, redlines, competitors, and alliances; the second included stated viewpoints related to China's depiction of the make-up of the future global order, China's role in the global order, and valence of US and Western Europe's role in the global order.

RQ1. How do Chinese media narrate the future global order?

As Figure 3.1 shows, the predominant themes surrounding Chinese media reporting on the global order are: Promote cooperation; China, development, global order, governance; Human community destiny; Defender, builder, contributor; New relations, mutual common; World war. These themes coalesce within the narratives Chinese media construct in defining the global order, including explicit depictions of China as upholding it both through China's past and current participation, and China's commitment to its continued existence with minor reforms ensuring all nations—specifically, developing nations—are able to benefit. However, despite China's willingness to support the global order, it notes that challenges remain from forces of isolationism and Cold War thinking.

Thus, concerns over the global order and its impact on China is extremely prominent in Chinese news (see Table 3.1). China views its role in the global order as overwhelmingly positive and frequently discussed (mentioned in n = 221; 82% of articles with a positive valance m = .62). Descriptions of the current order are also widely reported albeit in a more neutral manner (n = 203; 75% of articles with a slightly positive/neutral

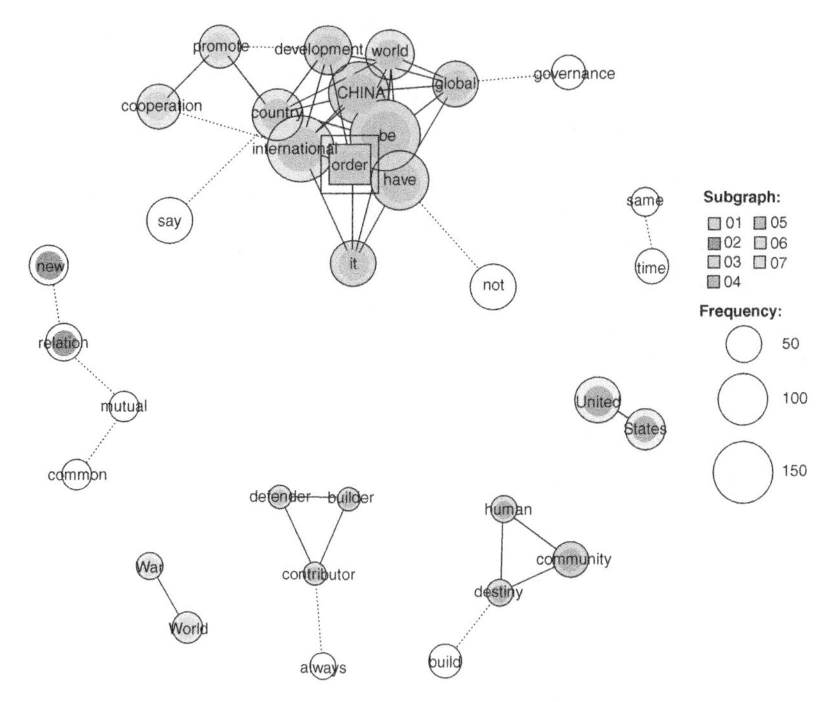

Figure 3.1 Co-occurrence Network of Chinese Media Reporting Referencing "Global Order"

Table 3.1 Chinese Media Views on the Global Order and the West

China's Role in Global Order	*Article Mentions*	*Valence (1=positive, -1=negative)*
Perspectives of Global Order	N = 221 (82%)	Mean = .62
Perspectives on the US	N = 203 (75%)	Mean = .10
Perspectives on Western Europe	N =108 (40%)	Mean = -.59

valence m = .1). However, the US and Western Europe are both perceived negatively, the US particularly so. As the narrative analysis following shows, the negative valence attached to the US and Western Europe stem primarily from concerns over rising nationalism and isolationism, with the US singled out for malapropos unitary action in possession of a Cold War mentality.

International order

Chinese media attach the identity of the current international order as represented by two institutions: the UN and WTO. The values embedded in both are key in regulating inter-state relations, providing the routinized framework by which nations cooperatively interact with each other. Chinese media emphasizes that, at its core, this framework is fundamentally multilateral with China explicitly stating its willingness to uphold and even defend the current system.

First, Chinese media impose cognitive order onto the international system through rhetorical identification of the UN and WTO as making up the substance of the international system. This is most clearly seen by reports stating that the international system is defined by the UN's Charter[1] with the UN characterized as ensuring not only basic respect for state sovereignty and cooperative relations—through its principles of equality, respect for sovereignty, and non-interference in nation's internal affairs, but also economically with countries needing to observe the multilateral, open economic trade system. As another article notes, it's difficult to distinguish who or what represents the "international" or "world" apart from the authority of the UN.[2] In other words, the UN is attributed as helping order international relations by playing the central role in providing stable expectations amid a turbulent world.[3] Similarly, Chinese media attribute the WTO as representative of the core of the multilateral trading system, described as providing a non-discriminatory, transparent, open and rule-based system which the Chinese are both committed to building and firmly supporting.[4] Importantly, Chinese media point out that all WTO members are supposed to be equal, and that the WTO is not a US institution, but a multilateral one.[5]

Second, Chinese media not only declare China's support for the current multilateral rules-based order, but also explains China's habitual participation within it. Regarding the UN, Chinese media frequently cite their country's position as firmly adhering to the international order while providing evidence of Chinese participation within it. This includes the 400 multilateral treaties China has joined and China's participation in all UN specialized agencies—in addition to approximately 90% of intergovernmental international organizations. From this, China is characterized as fully integrated into the contemporary global order.[6] Likewise, within the WTO, Chinese media express their nation's complete adherence to WTO rules. In support of their claim, reports cite positive comments from the WTO's Director General describing China's role as constructive and supportive in maintaining the multilateral trading system of which the

Director General is both highly appreciative and welcoming of China's growing role in the organization.[7]

Third, China attaches its identity not only as a regular contributor and faithful partner to the UN and WTO, but also as a defender and key source of its growth and prosperity. Articles repeatedly state how China will always be a staunch defender of both the current international trade system and the international order[8] through China's willingness to work with all countries to firmly safeguard the rules-based system by promoting development through cooperative relations.[9] In doing so, Chinese values of economic development are shown as aligned with international goals through China's firm support of the multilateral trading system—with the WTO described as being its core—with China's continuous promotion of the liberalization of the global economy and its key role in facilitating global trade and investment supporting the steady growth of the global economy.[10]

Finally, China's promissory rhetoric of upholding the international order is not just future oriented, but includes a sense of continuity of action through reports narrating how China has consistently had a salubrious effect on global trade. As one article explains, China has always been a stable source for global economic growth even during the 1997 Asian Financial crisis when the country underwent tremendous pressure from others to depreciate its currency. Chinese resistance to such efforts were reported as "correctly" enabling the country to weather such efforts with its "positive" crisis response injecting much needed confidence to the financial stability of the region, thereby showcasing both China's contribution to global financial security and its leadership ability. This story provides a moral lesson supportive of China's current role in the global economy as the article continues by noting China's economic clout today—as the world's second largest economy—having contributed to more than 30% to the world economic growth for decades; as a result, despite sluggish global economic growth with others questioning economic globalization, China's insistence on supporting an open global trading system will "undoubtedly" contribute and support global economic growth.[11]

Taken together, Chinese media construct a clearly defined international system where states engage in routine, multilateral cooperation in trade and diplomacy. Chinese media make this system "knowable" and "intelligible" for its citizenry by providing a clear and moral Chinese identity as committed to the international order's economic and diplomatic values over time. This narrative of global order thus provides Chinese citizens with a sense of OS creating a pathway to act *within* the international order, specifically through international trade, seen as benefiting all.

Threats to the global order

Despite Chinese media positively constructing the international order it reports this system as under attack. Two overarching plotlines portray the forces poised to unravel the international order: one focused on nationalism and isolationism and the other being unilateralism and a Cold War mentality. Both serve to define foreign threats to China's identity as attached to a multilateral, rules-based system promoting open trade. While these fears threaten Chinese OS, by providing a vision of an unstable future world order, it also allows serves as a motivational force for China to reaffirm its self-identities as a responsible, major power and leader of the developing world. As an article quoting China's foreign Minister Wang Yi explains, the current international system is being seriously undermined by the present rise of unilateralism and protectionism. According to Wang Yi, the solution is for the international community to unite under the banner of multilateralism to reaffirm the UN's central role in international affairs; with such efforts being the only way to provide stable expectations for nations amid a chaotic world.[12] This sentiment in reflected in other articles emphasizing the "unprecedented" and "severe" challenges to the multilateral trading system to which China is reported as responding to by standing against all forms of protectionism and unilateralism while reiterating its support for the WTO.[13]

In support of China's position, Chinese media portray globalization and multilateralism in progressive, historic forces. While these are the supposed, inevitable routines of state relations, Chinese media nonetheless note how the pattern of realist competition remains. Thus, reports explain that although the trend of economic globalization and cultural diversity, as well as multi-polarization and the democratization of international relations, is unstoppable, nonetheless, zero sum, Cold War mentalities are still present in the international relations.[14] Indeed reporters note how Cold War narratives negatively impact security cooperation in the Asia-Pacific[15] with media commentators reporting the smell of the new Cold War emerging.[16]

More specifically, the US is presented as the major source of this Cold War, isolationist mentality with Chinese media engaging in identity demarcation contrasting China's actions to the US. Whereas the examples above declare China's support for global trade and a multilateral rules-based order, Chinese media report how the US has, for some time now, withdrawn from various international organizations, including UNESCO, the UN Human Rights Council, and the Universal Postal Union.[17] Because of these actions, Chinese media report that the international community has developed its own "clear" vision of the US as a nation destroying the international contract through which nations cooperate in multilateral diplomacy by retreating from this group for individual US priorities.[18] Thus, whereas Chinese values are those of multilateralism, mutual respect, and win-win cooperation, the international community is deeply concerned about the US's practice of disagreeing with and abandoning multilateral institutions and treaties.[19]

Indeed, whereas China views itself as a stabilizing force for global growth, with Chinese culture emphasizing harmonious relations,[20] the US is juxtaposed as experiencing social division at home[21] leading to its decline and retreat from institutional institutions placing the global trading system in doubt. For instance, articles reference 2016 as a particularly deleterious year for the international community as black swan events such as Brexit and President Trump's election brought about significant drama and eccentricities across the international political spectrum.[22] The cause for these events is explained as coming from social division, both from within the US but also European countries more broadly, and resultant of the major contradictions present in the US-led global system; these contradictions are becoming ever more prominent, placing the global community at a new crossroads.[23] Other articles describe the problems the US faces as marking the decline of America's overall strength, thereby making it difficult for the US to lead the international order as well as limiting its ability to standalone in pursuit of its own self-interests. US withdrawal from global trade is reported as leaving no doubt that the global system formed after World War II is beginning to show a shocking crack.[24] Thus, the international order, which was previously dominated by the US and Western Europe is undergoing adjustment with the world in a period of transition as a new international order undergoes a process of struggle, collision, and gestation.[25]

In sum, the elements within Chinese media narratives portraying the global order provide stability and trust in the international system, but also reflect growing anxieties about its future. Importantly, these stories portending conflict also serve an OS function in ensuring that the Chinese people commit to its leaders' vision of China, especially as China's projected international identity is argued to provide stability for the international order.

China's role

The uncertainty over the future global order appears not to have resulted in a lack of Chinese agency, but actually augments it with Chinese media projecting confidence in China's identity as a global leader in possession of the resources to lead this period of transition. Specifically, Chinese media present a coherent Chinese identity by linking it to CCP leaders' statements and policy doctrine defining China's role in a transitioning world order. For instance, Chinese media covering Xi Jinping's speech at the UN in January 2017 describe how the nation is in the position to help build a stable global order. In his speech, Xi explains how China, as a fast-growing, emerging power naturally occupies an important position in discussions of global governance and development, and thus, under these circumstances, the government's doctrinal concept of building a human destiny will play an increasingly important role in leading the transformation of the world and the international order.[26] Likewise, coverage of the CCP's 19th National Congress report how not only is Chinese global leadership and guidance needed, but that the international community itself is looking forward to hearing China's voice and seeing China's plan; as a result, China cannot be absent in global affairs as it has always played the role of a defender of the international order and has always been a builder of world peace and contributor to global development.[27] These statements demonstrate how China's identity and role in the international order are connected in Chinese media to CCP policies in portraying an image of Chinese prestige and global benevolence.

While China's identity is attached to the current international system, Chinese media also present China's identity as a reformer. These two narrative strands are not contradictory, but reinforce a consistent Chinese identity in that these reforms are argued as necessary for maintaining the current system of international relations. Thus, China's willingness to safeguard the authority of the multilateral trading system comes from its desire to cooperatively build an open world economy by promoting economic globalization to be more open and inclusive.[28] This need for a more inclusive system comes from reports calling developing countries' lack of voice as the main problem in today's global governance practices; Chinese media note that while developing nations account for 70% of the world's total population their representation and influence in international institutions fail to match their proportion of global population.[29] As a result, developing countries are reported as hoping for China to take steps in promoting a more just and reasonable global governance system to which China is reported as answering this call by being an advocate and promoter of this new international order and using its role as a permanent member of the UN Security Council to actively participate in reforming the global governance mechanisms.[30]

China's identity as a leader of developing nations is most prominent in its association with the BRICS nations. These nations, like China, explain their desire to reform, rather than remake the international system. As one article explains, China is willing to work together with BRICS to adhere to international fairness and justice and jointly safeguard multilateralism and the global trading system with the WTO as its core, and in doing so, oppose unilateralism and protectionism to promote the development of the international order in a more just and rational direction.[31] Likewise, Chinese media reports BRICS support for the UN, with the association reaffirming their shared commitment to world peace and stability as defined by the UN's central role in promoting a fair, just, equitable, democratic, and ultimately more representative global order.[32] These positions are argued as not only representing BRICS nations, but also the common aspirations of developing countries who desire to strengthen unity and cooperative efforts to safeguard common interests and boost confidence of all parties in building an open world economy.[33] Taken together, through Chinese leadership, and in partnership with developing nations, the forces threatening the global order can thus be resisted and reformed.

Partnerships, competitors, and conflict management

Reflective of Chinese media's depiction of the international order, the threats undermining it, and China's vision for its role, the frequencies of references to potential competitors (n = 51; 19%) and allies (n = 68; 25%) are roughly balanced, albeit leaning towards more alliances. As the qualitative narrative accounts illustrate, China's competitors are primarily the US and Japan, with European nations at times brought into the fold against China. However, through China's relationships with the Shanghai Cooperation Organization (SCO) and BRICS organizations, in addition to its BRI, China enjoys the possibility of numerous alliances or partnerships with developing nations and other countries willing to support China in reforming the international system and supporting multilateralism and free trade.

Table 3.2 provides further validation of China's narrative and interests in maintaining a peaceful, stable world order whereby countries resolve their differences mostly through multilateral institutions but also through bilateral consultations. Here Chinese media emphasize how disputes or differences in opinion among WTO members should be resolved through negotiation[34] while lending credibility to the WTO as a neutral party that balances the interests of all parties.[35] Even security issues like denuclearization of the Korean peninsula and disputes in the South China Sea are explained as needing to be resolved through dialogue and consultation[36] with persistence and friendly consultations between directly affected parties allowing for the peaceful resolution of disputes.[37] This cooperative and conflict avoidant narrative affirms China's national and international level narratives describing global order, specifically China's belief, preference, and commitment towards a rules based system. In contrast, China stands opposed to the anarchical forces, such as unilateral action and great power politicking. As China embodies these conflict avoidant values, its media present few if any mentions of specific redlines to action or explicit messages of deterrence. Indeed, as the next section describing Chinese views of its vulnerabilities and capacities compete in the global suggest, China sees global competition far less in militaristic terms and instead through an economic and diplomatic lens.

Table 3.2 Chinese Media Reporting of Conflict Dynamics

	Article Mentions
Mentioned Competitors	N = 51 (19%)
Mentioned Alliances	N = 68 (25%)
Legitimate Deterrence	N = 3 (1%)
Conflict/Escalation Management	N = 40 (15%)
Redlines to Action	N = 5 (2%)

RQ2. How do Chinese media narrate the future of global competition?

Reflective of China's depiction of the global order, Chinese media define China's ability to compete in the global order primarily around issues of economics and diplomacy. Both categories are the highest mentioned when discussing Chinese vulnerabilities and capabilities, followed by informational, with military least frequently occurring (See Table 3.3). Importantly, Chinese media discuss its capabilities to compete far more frequently than its vulnerabilities, suggesting China's relative optimism in its ability to compete in the future global order.

Vulnerabilities

Chinese media report the nation's competitive vulnerabilities as stemming primarily from its economic (n = 54; 20%) and diplomatic position (n = 45; 17%). Elements of both reflect its vision of the global order, namely the importance of multilateralism avoiding Cold War like conflict with economic development particularly crucial for China. China's military and informational vulnerabilities are referenced less frequently (n = 23; 9% and n = 26; 10% respectfully). Regarding informational elements, concerns primarily revolve around cultural harmony domestically and foreign narratives described as incorrectly perpetuating China as a threat intended to marshal states to contain China. Military concerns are few and regionally focused with concerns over Japanese militarism in particular.

Economic vulnerabilities

China's economic vulnerabilities are anchored within its concerns about domestic economic growth. This concern revolves primarily around the middle-income trap and whether China can innovate. Articles explain how China is a relatively poor country measured by per capita GDP. Thus, although the country has enjoyed considerable success modernizing, Chinese media warns it now faces the middle income trap and makes sure to

Table 3.3 Chinese Vulnerabilities and Capabilities in News Media

	Articles Mentioning Key Vulnerabilities	*Articles Mentioning Necessary Capabilities*
Diplomatic	N = 45 (17%)	N = 120 (44%)
Informational	N = 26 (10%)	N = 53 (20%)
Military	N = 23 (9%)	N = 27 (10%)
Economic	N = 54 (20%)	N = 147 (54%)

define the phenomenon for Chinese audiences as the final threshold that developing countries face in their transition to becoming a developed nation.[38] Articles further detail the challenges of this transition explaining how developing nations, after entering the middle income stage, face special difficulties in overcoming this last stage of economic development as low-income nations lose their competitive advantage in the form of low labor costs while still lacking the innovative and technological advantages enjoyed by high-income countries; this places countries like China at a disadvantage in global competition.[39] As a result, China's chief concern then, is described as a lack of innovative capacity poised to weaken its development momentum and lead to an increase in income inequality.[40] Importantly, Chinese media warn that if these problems are not handled well, China might not only fail to escape and grow out of the middle-income trap, but also stagnate for a long period of time.[41]

The worry regarding innovation arises in a variety of issues, including China's space program, education system, and more broadly in areas such as its original contributions to basic research, development of core algorithms and the manufacturing of key equipment, high-end chips, and major products and systems. In all these areas, China is reported as experiencing shortcomings and problems with Chinese advancements in these areas still relatively small.[42] China also faces problems with talent acquisition and skill development, both of which are described as far from satisfactory, especially as China has yet to develop industrial chains in possession of international influence.[43]

To break free of the middle-income trap, Chinese media emphasize the importance of global trade in adding development and innovation. Chinese media explain how historically, under CCP leadership, China's past 40 years of reform and opening up brought more and more development opportunities.[44] Reaffirming this habit, other articles note how development is the basis and key to solving all problems in our country with focus on economic growth being the key to rejuvenating the country.[45] Therefore, only through global trade and cooperation can China obtain global innovation and research and development (R&D) capabilities enabling China to transform from a manufacturing driven economy to a real market economy based on innovation.[46]

Diplomatic vulnerabilities

Chinese media report its diplomatic vulnerabilities as stemming from other nations' unilateralism and Cold War thinking and fears over China's rise in global influence. First, Chinese media suggests China is vulnerable to US actions, with China's diplomatic position vis-à-vis the US explained as a choice of two roads: one of which is to choose peaceful coexistence and peaceful competition thereby maintaining the existing global governance system while making appropriate adjustments; the second is to continue the old routine of dealing with the rise of other big powers through various means to suppress and contain them reflective of US attempts to maintain its long-term status as the global hegemon.[47] US actions are often criticized as embodying the latter with it unfairly characterizing Chinese actions, pursing a Chinese-Russiam threat theory, and attempting to contain China economically.[48] Further examples of this comes from reports portraying the Trump administration's trade war with China as forcing Europe into jointly suppressing China through economic and trade policies[49] with others explaining how the West in general is worried over new Chinese international institutions such as the AIIB, viewing such as posing a threat to current international standards for foreign aid.[50]

Finally, China's diplomatic influence in the Pacific is reported as particularly tenuous. Chinese media see Japan as wooing countries concerned with China's rise and working with such nations to enact a containment policy targeting China through a variety of tools, including: financial assistance to the Philippines; providing patrol ships to Malaysia; building shared values with Myanmar; and Japan strengthening economic cooperation with Kazakhstan.[51] Other articles warn how Japan and the US utilize diplomatic security conferences—like those dedicated to discussing the influence of Chinese soft power, strategic threats arising from China's network technology, and concerns over China's BRI and its disputes in the South China Sea—to sway global diplomatic competition against China's interests.[52]

Informational vulnerabilities

Chinese informational vulnerabilities are rarely mentioned, but when they are they center on the importance of Chinese culture and concerns over cyber security and public opinion related to China's image in the world. While Chinese culture is reported as an important force for the survival and development of the nation,[53] in relation to the future of global competition, emphasis is on its implications in the international realm. Therefore, while domestically Chinese media occasionally define elements of Chinese culture as harmonious or supporting the harmony of the state,[54] more prominent are discussions regarding the need to spread Chinese culture into the international cultural market[55] with Chinese cultural products and services becoming digital and networked.[56] As a result, Chinese media note how network culture has become a key global industry as the growth in Internet use and mobile technology holds the potential for China's culture industry to go abroad and further enhance the country's international influence. While this represent a new growth opportunity for China, the country is reported as having a long way to go before its culture industries can become globally competitive, with China needing better understanding of the global market to solve problems related to its cultural product positioning.[57]

In the cybersecurity realm, Chinese media report that global and national cyber security issues have erupted with insufficient security of the Internet; this reportedly occurs because, basic global rules are missing, leading to a disordered cyberspace that is becoming more and more serious.[58] Other concerns arise from China's public image, reported as vulnerable from primarily Japanese and Western countries' attempts to suppress and contain China in international public opinion, specifically through the propagation of a China threat theory, contributing to Chinese isolation.[59] Likewise, Chinese media note the vulnerability BRICS nations face from Western media dominance controlling who has the right to speak internationally, thereby resulting in a bias against developing countries such as the BRICS; in response, Chinese media call for BRICS to strengthen cooperation and develop a voice different from the Western media to show the true side of each country.[60]

Military vulnerabilities

Like informational vulnerabilities, Chinese media rarely mention military vulnerabilities when discussing the competition in the future global order. Concerns related to security are discussed in more diplomatic terms arising from great power competition and attempts at isolating and containing China. Nonetheless, Chinese media do present worries stemming from US and Japanese actions in the Asia Pacific where the US is viewed as undoubtedly focusing on the Asia-Pacific which leads to the militarization of the South China Sea. Importantly, the US is always viewed as the initiator of conflict through its daily patrols and reconnaissance activities. Such actions are described as strategically intended to pressure China through military action and arising from the US's hegemonic mentality.[61] Thus, while the US is reported as rushing military personnel to the South China Sea, thereby ratcheting tensions in the region, the US also is characterized as using its voice and power to hype the international community against China.[62] Additional Chinese concerns arise from worries over Japanese revisions to its pacifist constitution and actions stemming from WWII. Here Chinese media state that China must remain vigilant by not sitting back and watching the resurrection of Japanese militarism; Chinese audiences are exhorted to never forget or underestimate the ambitious and treachery of Japanese militarism, specifically Japan's heinous crimes not just against China, but against humanity itself, as well as the world.[63]

In sum, few articles place China's security in doubt. Nonetheless, while they note that China presently faces no security threats of large-scale maritime military incursions into China, Chinese media still warns that traditional security threats still exist, mainly from the strategic containment of marine military powers and disputes over island sovereignty and maritime rights; such complex dynamics still present a security crisis with the long-term, versatile characteristics of China's marine safety being their primary concern.[64]

Capabilities

To succeed in the current and future global order, Chinese media narratives overwhelmingly focus on promoting diplomatic partnerships with both developing and developed nations which allows for China to continue to economically modernize. Diplomatic and Economic capabilities are again far more frequently cited (n = 120; 44% and n = 147; 54% respectfully) than Informational and Military capabilities (n = 53; 20% and n = 27; 10% respectively). Diplomatic partnerships, both multilaterally and bilaterally, go nearly hand in hand in aiding Chinese companies' growth and innovation in addition to penetration of foreign markets.

Diplomatic capabilities

The largest areas of diplomatic success reported in Chinese media are those surrounding the BRI. As one article noted, China's BRI international cooperation summit had participants from 29 foreign heads of state including1,500 representatives from more than 130 countries and 70 international organizations, thus demonstrating how the BRI has entered a new stage of comprehensive promotion.[65] A number of Asian, South American, and African countries are reported as signing bilateral partnerships with China to boost trade relations. Guinean Prime Minister Kabine Komara is quoted as stating how great an opportunity China's BRI has been for the African continent in that over the past five years writ large as it has brought more investment and technological development to a continent forgotten by others.[66] Likewise, the BRI is reported as recognized and supported by an ever increasing number of countries because of the substantial investment and economic growth opportunities it provides, especially for BRICS nations; most notably with Russia reported as a particularly ardent supporter of the it, thereby demonstrating full extent to which China and Russia have built a community of interests.[67]

Beyond the BRI, China reports its diplomatic capabilities as increasing within the UN, even supplanting that of the US. One article concludes that China's influence is becoming increasingly widespread, owing to its proposed idea of a community of human destiny having been included in UN documents with the reportedly smooth operation of the Asian Infrastructure Investment Bank (AIIB) demonstrating how this concept has moved from concept to action.[68] With its new economic partnerships, such as the AIIB and BRI, Chinese media note that international publics believe that China can quickly occupy the vacuum left by the US's retreat from international institutions, specifically in the post-Trans Pacific Partnership world.[69]

Economic capabilities

With China's capacity for building diplomatic partnerships supporting global trade, Chinese media report that the nation will succeed in economic competition by bolstering its ability to innovate. For instance, the continuous development of the BRI is explained as leading to more domestic funds and production capacity to enter the international market thereby helping Chinese industries and consulting services to go out and compete. This competition is described as furthering China's attempts at defining engineering construction standards as well as supporting Chinese internationalization strategies and basic research projects, thereby aiding Chinese companies' competiveness through serving more foreign companies and developing China's soft power brand within its engineering consulting services.[70] As other articles note, although innovation and development is the general trend of international competition, through China's striving to innovate the nation can keep up with the world and rapidly move towards becoming a global research leader; the Chinese government is viewed as leading this process by its placing of great emphasis on the importance of research as driving innovation and economic growth.[71] Chinese optimism in such endeavors is also evident in reports explaining that over the next few years China could become one of the countries that contributes the most to global R&D[72] with CCP policies hailed as successfully resulting in China's manifold economic advantages in the areas of technological and economic innovation, educational and financial reforms, branding, and increased quality standards and productivity; all the while with the CCP calling for continued support for opening up policies and further domestic reform.

Informational capabilities

China's informational capabilities derive from its successes in its ability to innovate in the telecommunications and AI industries as well as some ability to promote Chinese culture and product brands. Chinese media connect its technological innovation capabilities as part of its China Dream Digitalization program with China attaching great importance to the digital economy and cyberspace as new territories for global competition.[73] China's innovation in this area is reported as worthy of pride[74] with China becoming a global leader in the 5G field[75] as well as in cyber security in which China is described as having stood out while now facing an historic opportunity to be at the forefront of a new round of change.[76]

Likewise, in the area of culture, Chinese media report how China's going out campaigns in international business have helped build a Chinese investment brand as select multinational companies and key projects have achieved a level of international influence and competitiveness establishing a positive international image.[77] Taken together, China shows itself as somewhat capable in building technological innovation to ensure its information environment with its international brands helping promote a positive Chinese image to the world.

Military capabilities

Military capabilities, although rarely mentioned, emphasize China's successful military modernization and strategic military partnerships with Russia and SCO member nations. For instance, articles note how in the next five years China is expected to achieve concrete results and significant breakthroughs in its military preparedness, owing to military reforms to its leadership and command systems allowing China to further enhance its strength and national status.[78] In addition to military modernization, strategic partnerships with the SCO and Russia are hailed as demonstrating Chinese diplomatic and strategic policy success with active cooperation between China and Russia over the past ten years resulting in strengthened military ties bound by common goals such as competition with the US for regional and global influence.[79] Through such cooperation, including that with BRICS and the SCO, Russia and China are reportedly able to hedge against the isolation of Western countries.[80]

In sum, China's vulnerabilities and capabilities largely reflect its narratives of the current and future global order. Here, the focus is not on realist calculations measuring the size or influence of one's military resources, but instead accounts of Chinese diplomatic and economic relations allowing it to develop its economy into one capable of self-innovation.

Discussion

Taken together, Chinese media narrate the future global order as one that is, and should be, moving towards greater multilateralism and continued free trade. For China, competition within this order is described primarily as economic, but also diplomatic, with China in particular needing to build global trade relations to ensure Chinese economic growth and domestic innovation while preventing diplomatic isolation. From the perspective of OS, this narrative worldview of the global order stems from Chinese leaders' anxieties over China's economic growth. Evidence of the fidelity of this narrative can be seen today with Chinese Premier Li Keqiang in November 2019 stating that, in contemplating the direction of China's 14th Five Year Plan, China's external environment could become more complicated with increasing uncertainties and challenges requiring more measures to promote reform and opening up in order to inject vitality into its market growth and foster industrial competitiveness through innovation (State Council, 2019).

The uncertainty and challenges promoting economic growth is not new for Chinese audiences. As Krolikowski (2018) argues, since its inception the CCP has repeatedly and drastically remade Chinese society, fostering new links between individuals and the economy. And yet, the difficulty in overcoming the middle-income trap and the manifold environmental and social challenges facing China today place CCP legitimacy at risk. Thus, the CCP's role as both an OS provider and destabilizer become important tools in not only maintaining order, but more importantly, continuing to push Chinese society towards greater opening and reform, despite domestic reluctance or even backlash potentially challenging CCP legitimacy.

As Giddens (1991) and Kinnvall (2004) argued, the forces of globalization significantly challenge traditional social relations pushing social collectives to seek out and reaffirm their collective identities. In China's case, CCP influence within its media and control over Chinese political thought supply the discursive resources for the Chinese people to collectively understand their world (Krolikowski, 2018), and in the context of the future global order, China's role in the international system. Here we see Chinese media imposing cognitive order on how states are to behave more broadly by characterizing the routines and values of inter-state cooperation governed and embedded in multilateral institutions. These behaviors are then reinforced with Chinese leaders' repeated sloganeering of "win-win cooperation," "mutual respect, benefit, and equality," support for "sovereignty and non-interference," among others, which provide continuity of Chinese political thought, as they reflect China's Five Principles of Peaceful Coexistence first introduced in the 1950s.

Furthermore, these depictions of appropriate state behavior enable Chinese citizens to envision how CCP policies of continued economic reform and opening up will function in the global order, thereby aiding or sustaining China's domestic agency related to CCP policies with a vision of what China can become within a larger global order. Here narratives of China's autobiographical continuity selectively highlight China's identity as a nation that has always participated in this global trading and governance structure, including its historical past as a great power prior to its century of humiliation pointing towards China's great national rejuvenation if it continues to partake in international trade and global governance. This developmental mindset coincides with its narrative claims to leadership and attachment to the global order by defining itself as a developing country, albeit a moderately prosperous one, representing and advocating for other developing nations to garner greater voice and benefit in the international order.

Nonetheless, while this vision of the global order provides stability and predictability for Chinese audiences in understanding how nations are supposed to act, Chinese media also create instability by portraying the order as unraveling. The forces of protectionism, isolationism, unilateralism, and Cold War thinking are ever present, especially with reported US and Japanese desires to contain China. However, these antagonistic forces, and actors, provide resources for Chinese identity formation, and thus realization of even greater agency by contrasting China's self to these others. In this case, China's role in the global order becomes more important, with Chinese leadership necessary and wanted by other nations as China writes itself as the protagonist championing the current, "correct" global order espousing open trade, multilateralism, global governance, and peaceful coexistence. This diplomatic value advocacy reflects Steele's (2008) argument of states providing compelling stories to their populace along moral values, further solidifying Chinese sense of purpose and harmonious leadership.

Trajectory/self-reflection

To some extent these narratives provide a directional force towards China's national rejuvenation, but reflect less of what Eberle (2019) argues to be a fantasy narrative moving towards an object of desire. Whereas Eberle describes fantasy narratives as sensemaking devices to help subjects grapple with their sense of ontological incompleteness by creating a black and white scenario where the subject obtains or fails to obtain its desired object, China's identity narratives suggest it is to some extent whole enough, perhaps achieving a sense of "security of becoming" (Kinnvall et al., 2018). This acceptance of a "fragile nature" of self could be a function of Krolikowski's (2018) account of the push and pull of the CCP's suppling of OS and could even contribute to China's ability to adapt and change its identity narratives as needed when considering the future global order. The higher frequency of Chinese capabilities to compete in the global order compared to vulnerabilities as well as its identity narratives demonstrate China as having already made substantial economic progress, enjoying significant diplomatic influence and prestige, and playing an active leadership role in global governance, and yet still suggests more can be done. Thus, China's narrative trajectory points to a nation that is progressing, step-by-step to further global prominence.

Whereas Mitzen (2006) argues that states can become attached to conflict leading identities or routines, Chinese media discourse reports a significant level of reflection and adaptability. For instance, while the US is often characterized in negative terms, Chinese media also note the importance and possibility of building stronger US-China ties. Furthermore, Chinese media both affirm the global governance institutions while also portraying them as needing revision and similarly provide both stable and unstable depictions of the global order. In doing so, Chinese leaders are afforded room to maneuver and adapt depending upon which narrative elements of are emphasized, reflecting Subotić's (2016) argument of narratives' flexible nature. Indeed, as Pu (2019) explained, Chinese messaging regarding its own identity are often contradictory, with the self-identity narratives present in this study supporting those identified by Pu with China being both a developing nation but also one with significant economic clout; a supporter and reformer of global governance; an influential leader but also a follower of multilateral negotiations; and one capable and incapable of economic innovation.

Perhaps this adaptability, or capacity not to fall into rigid attachments is a function of China's present optimism in its current position or its belief in analyzing larger historical trends. In other words, although China faces challenges, its belief in its ability to compete in the global order allows for greater flexibility for change. Indeed, despite the instability resulting from globalization, and in contrast to isolationist currents in the US and Europe, China appears remarkably confident, optimistic, and highly attached to the international system. As Krolikowski (2008) explains, actors with healthy basic trust systems have the capacity for rational deliberation and the ability to learn and adapt to changing circumstances. In contrast, those with low basic trust are likely to fail to engage in self-monitoring and updating of autobiographical narratives. In China's case, it appears to trust the international rules-based order while also believing in China's ability to learn from the past. Articles report how China should study the lessons from the US and the UK's great power pasts by maintaining an innovative method of strategic thinking to understand the flow of international trends while avoiding getting lost in the ever-changing international chaos.[81] Chinese media even report some humility, noting that while they are confident in China's eventual arrival to prominence on the global stage, they nonetheless recognize its influence is still limited.[82]

In sum, China's narrative trajectories and reported attachments to current international institutions suggests that, at least in the short and medium term. it will continue to work within and support this system as part of the future global order. However, it is important to note that the logic driving China's narrative views point to a resolution around the PRC's centenary in 2049. By that point China is expected to have developed a moderately prosperous society with its national strength rejuvenated. Thus, assuming by then that China has escaped its middle income trap and developed an economy capable of self-innovation, the extent to which China will still need the current global order's international institutions could become less clear.

Notes

1 Reference News (December 4, 2018). Factiva.
2 *Global Times* (May 10, 2016). Factiva.
3 China.Net (September 2018). Factiva.
4 China News Service (November 7, 2018). Factiva.
5 *People's Daily* (November 23, 2018). Factiva.
6 China.Net (December 23, 2018). Factiva.
7 *People's Daily* (November 23, 2018). Factiva.
8 Xinhua (April 5, 2018). Factiva.
9 Cankao Xiaoxi (November 17, 2018). Factiva.

10 Ibid.
11 China.Net (December 23, 2018). Factiva.
12 Ibid.
13 China News Service (November 7, 2018). Factiva.
14 Xinhua (October 14, 2015). Factiva.
15 China News Service (June 4, 2014). Factiva.
16 *People's Daily* (May 6, 2016). Factiva.
17 163 (November 22, 2018). Factiva.
18 Ibid.
19 Ibid.
20 *People's Daily* (September 26, 2018). Factiva.
21 China.Net. (November 24, 2016). Factiva.
22 Ibid.
23 Ibid.
24 *Global Times* (November 28, 2016). Factiva.
25 China.Net (November 24, 2016). Factiva.
26 China.Net (January 20, 2017). Factiva.
27 China.Net (November 30, 2017). Factiva.
28 China News Service (April 9, 2018). Factiva.
29 Xinhua (October 14, 2015). Factiva.
30 China.Net (November 30, 2017). Factiva.
31 China News Service (July 13, 2018). Factiva.
32 Xinhua (November 30, 2018). Factiva.
33 Ibid.
34 163 (November 22, 2018). Factiva.
35 163 (December 30, 2018). Factiva.
36 Xinhua (June 14, 2018). Factiva.
37 China News Service (April 28, 2016). Factiva.
38 *Global Times* (November 28, 2016). Factiva.
39 *People's Daily* (September 18, 2017). Factiva.
40 Ibid.
41 Ibid.
42 *People's Daily* (July 22, 2017). Factiva.
43 Ibid.
44 Xinhua (April 5, 2018). Factiva.
45 *People's Daily* (July 14, 2017). Factiva.
46 Ibid.
47 *Global Times* (February 7, 2018). Factiva.
48 Cankao Xiaoxi (January 23, 2019). Factiva.
49 China.Net (April 3, 2018). Factiva.
50 *Global Times* (December 8, 2014). Factiva.
51 China.Net (January 12, 2017). Factiva.
52 *Global Times* (February 23, 2019). Factiva.
53 *People's Daily* (December 4, 2017). Factiva.
54 Ibid.
55 Xinhua (December 6, 2016). Factiva.
56 *People's Daily.* (December 25, 2017). Factiva.
57 Xinhua (December 6, 2016). Factiva.
58 *Global Times* (October 18, 2017). Factiva.
59 *People's Daily* (June 10, 2015). Factiva.
60 Xinhua (July 19, 2018). Factiva.
61 *People's Daily.* (April 16, 2016). Factiva.
62 *Global Times* (March 18, 2016). Factiva.
63 *People's Daily* (July 2, 2014). Factiva.

64 China News Service (June 23, 2015). Factiva.
65 China News Service. (October 30, 2017). Factiva.
66 Xinhua (September 28, 2018). Factiva.
67 *People's Daily* (August 28, 2017). Factiva.
68 China.Net (February 22, 2018). Factiva.
69 *Global Times* (November 28, 2016). Factiva.
70 *People's Daily* (August 4, 2018). Factiva.
71 Xinhua (May 28, 2016). Factiva.
72 Ibid.
73 *Global Times* (August 27, 2018). Factiva.
74 *People's Daily* (August 23, 2017). Factiva.
75 Ibid.
76 *Global Times* (October 27, 2018). Factiva.
77 China News Service (June 21, 2018). Factiva.
78 Xinhua (November 29, 2015). Factiva.
79 163 (December 28, 2018). Factiva.
80 China.Net (January 20, 2017). Factiva.
81 *Global Times* (November 28, 2016). Factiva.
82 *Global Times* (May 29, 2015). Factiva.

References

Acharya, A. (2018). *Constructing global order: Agency and change in world politics.* Cambridge University Press.

Allison, G. (2017). *Destined for war: Can America and China escape Thucydides's trap?.* Houghton Mifflin Harcourt.

Baum, R. D. (1964). "Red and expert": The politico-ideological foundations of China's Great Leap Forward. *Asian Survey.* 4(9), 1048–1057.

Beckley, M. (2011). China's century? Why America's edge will endure. *International Security.* 36(3), 41–78.

Behravesh, M. (2018). State revisionism and ontological (in)security in international politics: The complicated case of Iran and its nuclear behavior. *Journal of International Relations and Development.* 21(4), 836–857.

Bajpai, P. (2020). The 5 largest economics in the world and their growth in 2020. *NASDAQ.* January 22, 2020. www.nasdaq.com/articles/the-5-largest-economies-in-the-world-and-their-growth-in-2020-2020-01-22.

Breslin, S. (2013). China and the global order: Signaling threat or friendship? *International Affairs.* 89(3), 615–634.

Burke, K. (1969). *A Grammar of Motives.* University of California Press.

Callahan, W. A. (2015). Identity and security in China: The negative soft power of the China Dream. *Politics.* 35(3–4),216–229.

Chacko, P. (2014). A new "special relationship"?: Power transitions, ontological security, and India–US relations. *International Studies Perspectives.* 15(3), 329–346.

Chen, J. & Xu, Y. (2017). Information manipulation and reform in authoritarian regimes. *Political Science Research and Methods.* 5(1), 163–178.

Chin, G. & Thakur, R. (2010). Will China change the rules of global order? *The Washington Quarterly.* 33(4), 119–138.

China Power Team. (2020). What Does China Really Spend on its Military? *CSIS.* September 15, 2020. https://chinapower.csis.org/military-spending/.

Cunninghad, E., Saich, T., & Turiel, J. (2020). Understanding CCP resilience: Surveying Chinese public opinion through Time. *Harvard Kennedy School.* Available at https://ash.harvard.edu/files/ash/files/final_policy_brief_7.6.2020.pdf.

Ding, X. L. (2006). *The decline of communism in China: Legitimacy crisis, 1977–1989.* Cambridge University Press.

Dimitrov, M. K. (2017). The political logic of media control in China. *Problems of Post-Communism.* 64(3–4), 121–127.

Eberle, J. (2019). Narrative, desire, ontological security, transgression: Fantasy as a factor in international politics. *Journal of International Relations and Development.* 22(1), 243–268.

Economy, E. C. (2018). China's new revolution: The reign of Xi Jinping. *Foreign Affairs.* (97), 60–74.

Edney, K. (2012). Soft power and the Chinese propaganda system. *Journal of Contemporary China.* 21(78), 899–914.

Ferdinand, P. (2016). Westward ho—the China dream and 'one belt, one road': Chinese foreign policy under Xi Jinping. *International Affairs.* 92(4), 941–957.

Fishkin, J. S., He, B., Luskin, R. C., & Siu, A. (2010). Deliberative democracy in an unlikely place: Deliberative polling in China. *British Journal of Political Science.* 40(2), 435–448.

Foot, R. & Walter, A. (2010). *China, the United States, and global order.* Cambridge University Press.

Friedberg, A. (2005). The future of U.S.-China relations: Is conflict inevitable? *International Security.* 30(2), 7–45.

Giddens, A. (1991). *Modernity and self-identity: Self and society in the late Modern Age.* Stanford University Press.

Glawe, L. & Wagner, H. (2020). China in the middle-income trap? *China Economic Review.* vol. 60, April 2020.

Goldman, M. (1994). *Sowing the seeds of democracy in China: Political reform in the Deng Xiaoping era.* Harvard University Press.

Gustafsson, K. (2014). Memory politics and ontological security in Sino-Japanese relations. *Asian Studies Review.* 38(1), 71–86.

Hahm, S. D. & Heo, U. (2019). History and territorial disputes, domestic politics, and international relations: An analysis of the relationship among South Korea, China, and Japan. *Korea Observer.* 50(1), 53–80.

Hartig, F. (2016). How China understands public diplomacy: The importance of national image for national interests. *International Studies Review.* 18(4), 655–680.

Hayden, C. (2012). *The rhetoric of soft power: Public diplomacy in global contexts.* Lexington Books.

He, B. & Warren, M. E. (2011). Authoritarian deliberation: The deliberative turn in Chinese political development. *Perspectives on Politics.* 9(2), 269–289.

He, B. (2014). Deliberative culture and politics: The persistence of authoritarian deliberation in China. *Political Theory.* 42(1), 58–81.

Heberer, T. (2009). The "great proletarian cultural revolution": China's modern trauma. *Journal of Modern Chinese History.* 3(2), 165–181.

Hess, S. (2013). From the Arab Spring to the Chinese Winter: The institutional sources of authoritarian vulnerability and resilience in Egypt, Tunisia, and China. *International Political Science Review.* 34(3), 254–272.

Hinck, R., Manly, J., Kluver, R., & Norris, W. (2018). Geopolitical dimensions of "The China Dream": Exploring strategic narratives of the Chinese Communist Party. *China Media Research*. 14(3).

Huiyun, F. (2009). Is China a revisionist power? *Chinese Journal of International Politics*. 2(3), 313–334.

Huysmans, J. (1998). Security! What do you mean? From concept to thick signifier. *European Journal of International Relations*. 4(2), 226–255.

Jacques, M. (2009). *When China rules the world: The end of the western world and the birth of a new global order*. Penguin.

Jaros, K. & Pan, J. (2018). China's newsmakers: Official media coverage and political shifts in the Xi Jinping era. *The China Quarterly*. 233, 111–136.

Johnston, A. I. (2003). Is China a status quo power? *International Security*. 27(4), 5–56.

Johnston, A. I. (2008). *Social states: China in international institutions, 1980–2000*. Princeton University Press.

Kerr, D. (Ed.). (2016). *China's many dreams: Comparative perspectives on China's search for national rejuvenation*. Springer.

Khan, S. W. (2018). *Haunted by chaos: China's grand strategy from Mao Zedong to Xi Jinping*. Harvard University Press.

King, G., Pan, J., & Roberts, M. E. (2013). How censorship in China allows government criticism but silences collective expression. *American Political Science Review*. 107(2), 326–343.

Kinnvall, C. (2004). Globalization and religious nationalism: Self, identity, and the search for ontological security. *Political Psychology*. 25(5), 741–767.

Kinnvall, C. & Mitzen, J. (2017). An introduction to the special issue: Ontological securities in world politics. *Cooperation and Conflict*. 52(1), 3–11.

Kinnvall, C., Manners, I., & Mitzen, J. (2018). Introduction to 2018 special issue of European Security: "Ontological (in)security in the European Union." *European Security*. 27(3), 249–265.

Kirshner, J. (2008). The consequences of China's economic rise for Sino-US relations: Rivalry, political conflict, and (not) war. In R. S.Ross & Z. Feng (Eds.), *China's Ascent: Power, Security, and the Future of International Politics*, 238–259. Cornell University Press.

Kleinman, A. & Kleinman, J. (1994). How bodies remember: Social memory and bodily experience of criticism, resistance, and delegitimation following China's Cultural Revolution. *New Literary History*. 25(3), 707–723.

Krolikowski, A. (2008). State personhood in ontological security theories of international relations and Chinese nationalism: A sceptical view. *Chinese Journal of International Politics*. 2(1), 109–133.

Krolikowski, A. (2018). Shaking up and making up China: How the party-state compromises and creates ontological security for its subjects. *Journal of International Relations and Development*. 21(4), 909–933.

Lai, D. (2011). *The United States and China in power transition*. Strategic Studies Institute, US Army War College. Available at https://publications.armywarcollege.edu/pubs/2166.pdf.

Leib, E. & He, B. (Eds.). (2006). *The search for deliberative democracy in China*. Springer.

Lewin, A. Y., Kenney, M., & Murmann, J. P. (Eds.). (2016). *China's innovation challenge: Overcoming the middle-income trap*. Cambridge University Press.

Link, P. & Qiang, X. (2013). From grass-mud equestrians to rights-conscious citizens: Language and thought on the Chinese internet. In P. Link, R. P. Madsen, & P. G. Pickowicz (Eds), *Restless China*, 83–106. Rowman & Littlefield Publishers.

Lorentzen, P. (2014). China's strategic censorship. *American Journal of Political Science*. 58(2), 402–414.

Lu, D. (2016). China's "Two Centenary Goals": Progress and challenge. *East Asian Policy*. 8(2), 79–93.

Lu, X. & Simons, H. W. (2006). Transitional rhetoric of Chinese communist party leaders in the post-Mao reform period: Dilemmas and strategies. *Quarterly Journal of Speech*. 92(3), 262–286.

Mearsheimer, J. J. (2010). The gathering storm: China's challenge to US power in Asia. *The Chinese Journal of International Politics*. 3(4), 381–396.

Mearsheimer, J. J. (2014). Can China rise peacefully? *The National Interest*. 25(1), 1–40.

Ma, S. K. (1989). Reform corruption: A discussion on China's current development. *Pacific Affairs*. 62(1), 40–52.

Mitzen, J. (2006). Ontological security in world politics: State identity and the security dilemma. *European Journal of International Relations*. 12(3), 341–370.

Moore, G. J. (2010). History, nationalism and face in Sino-Japanese relations. *Journal of Chinese Political Science*. 15(3), 283–306.

Nathan, A. J. (1990). *China's crisis: Dilemmas of reform and prospects for democracy*. Columbia University Press.

Nathan, A. J. (2019). The new Tiananmen papers: Inside the secret meeting that changed China. *Foreign Affairs*. 98(4), 80–91.

Newman, E. & Zala, B. (2018). Rising powers and order contestation: Disaggregating the normative from the representational. *Third World Quarterly*. 39 (5), 871–888.

Peidong, Y. & Lijun, T. (2018). "Positive energy": Hegemonic intervention and online media discourse in China's Xi Jinping era. *China: An International Journal*. 16(1), 1–22.

Pei, M. (2012). Is CCP rule fragile or resilient? *Journal of Democracy*. 23(1), 27–41.

Phillips, T. (2017). Xi Jinping becomes most powerful leader since Mao with China's change to constitution. *The Guardian*. October 24, 2017. Available at www.theguardian.com/world/2017/oct/24/xi-jinping-mao-thought-on-socialism-china-constitution.

Plankers, T. (2011). Psychic impact and outcome of the Chinese Cultural Revolution (1966–1976). *International Journal of Applied Psychoanalytic Studies*. 8(3), 227–238.

Plankers, T. & Hart, J. (2014). *Landscapes of the Chinese soul: The enduring presence of the Cultural Revolution*. Karnac Books.

Pu, X. (2017). Controversial identity of a rising China. *The Chinese Journal of International Politics*. 10(2), 131–149.

Pu, X. (2019). *Rebranding China: Contested status signaling in the changing global order*. Stanford University Press.

Repnikova, M. (2017). *Media politics in China: Improvising power under authoritarianism*. Cambridge University Press.

Ross, R. S. (2006). Balance of power politics and the rise of China: Accommodation and balancing in East Asia. *Security Studies*, 15(3), 355–395.

Schoenhals, M. (1992). *Doing things with words in Chinese politics: Five Studies.* University of California Press.

Scott, D. (2015). China's public diplomacy rhetoric, 1990–2012: Pragmatic image-crafting. *Diplomacy & Statecraft.* 26(2), 249–265.

Scott, J. C. (1999). *Seeing like a state: How certain schemes to improve the human condition have failed.* Yale University Press.

Shambaugh, D. L. (2013). *China goes global: The partial power.* Oxford University Press.

Shambaugh, D. L. (2011). Coping with a conflicted China. *The Washington Quarterly.* 34(1), 7–27.

Smith, M. A. (2012). *Power in the changing global order: the US, Russia and China.* Polity.

Sørensen, C. T. (2015). The significance of Xi Jinping's "Chinese Dream" for Chinese foreign policy: From "Tao Guang Yang Hui" to "Fen Fa You Wei". *Journal of China and International Relations.* 3(1), 53–73.

State Council, The People's Republic of China. (2019). *China mulls over 14th Five-year plan.* November 26, 2019. http://english.www.gov.cn/premier/news/201911/26/content_WS5ddd1626c6d0bcf8c4c17d87.html.

Steele, B. J. (2008). *Ontological security in international relations: Self-identity and the IR state.* Routledge.

Stockmann, D. (2013). *Media commercialization and authoritarian rule in China.* Cambridge University Press.

Stockmann, D. & Luo, T. (2017). Which social media facilitate online public opinion in China? *Problems of Post-Communism.* 64(3–4), 189–202.

Subotić, J. (2016). Narrative, ontological security, and foreign policy change. *Foreign Policy Analysis.* 12(4), 610–627.

Tammen, R. L. & Kugler, J. (2006). Power transition and China-US conflicts. *Chinese Journal of International Politics.* 1(1), 35–55.

Thaxton Jr, R. A. & Thaxton, R. (2008). *Catastrophe and contention in rural China: Mao's Great Leap Forward famine and the origins of righteous resistance in Da Fo village.* Cambridge University Press.

Thussu, D. K., De Burgh, H., & Shi, A. (Eds.). (2017). *China's media go global.* Routledge.

Trinh, D. D. (2013). Corruption driven reform: China's economic reforms in the Post-Mao Period. *Inquiries Journal.* 5(4).

Wang, J. (Ed.). (2011). *Soft power in China: Public diplomacy through communication.* Springer.

Ward, S. (2017). *Status and the challenge of rising powers.* Cambridge University Press.

Woo, W. T., Lu, M., & Sachs, J. D. (Eds). (2012). *A new economic growth engine for China: Escaping the middle-income trap by not doing more of the same.* World Scientific.

World Bank. (n.d.). China Overview. www.worldbank.org/en/country/china/overview.

Xiaoyu, P. (2012). Socialisation as a two-way process: Emerging powers and the diffusion of international norms. *The Chinese Journal of International Politics.* 5(4), 341–367.

Yang, Y. E. & Liu, X. (2012). The 'China Threat' through the lens of US print media: 1992–2006. *Journal of Contemporary China.* 21(76), 695–711.

Yi, X. (2005). Chinese foreign policy in transition: Understanding China's "peaceful development". *The Journal of East Asian Affairs.* 19(1), 74–112.
Yoshida, T. (2006). *The making of the "Rape of Nanking": History and memory in Japan, China, and the United States.* Oxford University Press.
Yufan, H. & Zhihai, Z. (1990). China's decision to enter the Korean War: History revisited. *The China Quarterly.* 121, 94–115.
Zhang, B. (2010). Chinese foreign policy in transition: Trends and implications. *Journal of Current Chinese Affairs.* 39(2), 39–68.
Zhang, Y. (2016). China and liberal hierarchies in global international society: Power and negotiation for normative change. *International Affairs.* 92(4), 795–816.
Zhao, D. (2004). *The power of Tiananmen: State-society relations and the 1989 Beijing student movement.* University of Chicago Press.
Zhao, S. (2016). Xi Jinping's Maoist Revival. *Journal of Democracy.* 27(3), 83–97.
Zhao, S. (2020). China's Belt-Road Initiative as the signature of President Xi Jinping diplomacy: Easier said than done. *Journal of Contemporary China.* 29 (123), 319–335.
Zhou, J. (2019). Power transition and paradigm shift in diplomacy: Why China and the US march towards strategic competition? *The Chinese Journal of International Politics.* 12(1), 1–34.

4 Ontological Security Narratives in Russian Media

The Besieged Fortress Capable of Spectacular Foreign Campaigns

Introduction

Regardless of its relative power, Russia today maintains a perception of itself as an influential actor in world politics. Indeed, the nation has long been regarded as a great power, from its Czarist roots through to its great power status during the Cold War, and many argue that it still deserves to be considered as such today (Heller, 2019; Lo, 2015). Others, however, label Russia as a declining power beset by internal weaknesses (Krickovic, 2017) with limited material capabilities to project power; marking it as a status-overachiever enjoying more recognition than it deserves (Freire & Heller, 2018). In this sense, Russia's search for recognition and affirmation of its identity appears to drive much its international behavior even when this ideational view of itself falls short of its material capabilities (Freire & Heller, 2018; Kanet, 2019).

Because of this, understanding Russia's role in the global order requires examination of its constructed national identity. As students of social identity theory posit, a state's status aspirations are often linked to its historical identity rather than to its relative capabilities (Larson, 2019). This is especially true for Russia as the nation found itself confronted with a crisis of identity following the collapse of the Soviet Union. As a result, Russia underwent a period of complex and difficult economic and political reconstruction, forcing it to re-create or re-discover a sense of self (Roselle, 2017). Although integrating itself into the Western economic order was a viable option at the time, ultimately attempts to do so failed (Mankoff, 2012) with Russia coming to define itself in opposition to the West (Hansen, 2016; Szostek, 2017).

Thus, today Russia appears discontented with its position in the global arena with Russian elites clearly dissatisfied by their perception of the international community's insufficient recognition of Russia's international position and status (Forsberg, Heller, & Wolf, 2014; Heller, 2019). These perceptions further drive Russian antagonism towards the West (Mis-kimmon & O'Loughlin, 2017; Snetkov, 2012). As Krickovic (2017) states, evident by Russia's annexation of Crimea, support for separatists in

DOI: 10.4324/9781003197478-4

Eastern Ukraine, military intervention in Syria, and hacking of the 2016 US presidential elections, "Russia, a declining power, has emerged as the most assertive challenger to the US-led global order" (p. 299).

The importance of Russia's identity as driving its international behavior suggests a focus not on its search for physical security but what scholars define as one's need for ontological security (OS), or the securing of the subjective sense of who one is (Mitzen, 2006). While all social collectives require a stable sense of self in order to actualize a sense of agency (Giddens, 1991; Kinnvall et al., 2018), this becomes particularly important during times of disruption when one's relationships and understandings of the world are destabilized. This leads to new, or reformulated, narratives providing autobiographical continuity (Subotić, 2016) with nostalgia, reaffirmation of the homeland, and historical narratives all serving as key narrative resources to draw upon (Cash & Kinnvall, 2017; Agius, 2017; Combes, 2017); serving to buttress domestic political legitimacy (Krolikowski, 2008, 2018; Huysmans, 1998). In Russia's case, as it holds onto notions of past grandeur yet continues to experience a faltering economy, domestic political unrest, and a shifting global order, reinforcing a stable sense of self becomes increasingly important for the nation's future.

To shed light on the implications of Russia's identity, this chapter examines Russian media discourse reporting on the future global order and the nature of global competition through the lens of OS. Specifically, it argues that Russia's OS-seeking is fueled by its desire for recognition as an agentic great power. In doing so, Russian media presents narratives of autobiographical continuity, including visions of a Russian World and identity demarcation separating itself from the West, designed to bolster its OS in confronting the manifold challenges it faces in the world and at home, as well as its disillusionment from its Cold War fall. In turn, these narrative worldviews influence how Russian media present the current and future global order and competition within it. While others have noted similar narrative elements as important to Russian identity (Biersack & O'Lear, 2014; Szostek, 2018; Hinck et al., 2017), we argue that the cornerstone of these narratives, from the perspective of OS, is Russia's need for recognition, both at home and abroad. Thus, demonstrations of Russian strength, autonomy, and prestige, through various attempts at recognition seeking, helps assist Russian populations in formulating a sense of much desired agency within the contemporary global order, harkening back to its historical status as a great power, and, explaining in part, Russia's continued truculent foreign policy. In this sense, even reports showcasing Western nations characterizing Russia as a destabilizing agent in the world order, stress not only Russia's ability to obstruct Western dominance within the international system, but also depict a Russia as courted, even needed by the West to solve our global problems, thereby resonating with Russian recognition narratives affirming its sense of OS.

Russian ontological security: A tale of two Russias

Rather than focusing on physical safety, OS refers to one's "security of being" (Kinnvall & Mitzen, 2017) or the securing of the subjective sense of who one is (Mitzen, 2006). According to Giddens (1991) the need for OS arises from individuals' continuous confrontation with ineradicable anxiety drawn from their environment. Individuals, then, must manage this anxiety in order to achieve a sense of agency by developing a continuous sense of self. Like individuals, states, and social collectives more generally, require OS (Mitzen, 2006; Zarakol, 2010). Thus, state governments function as key OS suppliers for their citizenry by telling convincing stories about itself through autobiographical narratives. In doing so, these narratives provide cognitive order and security, making the world appear intelligible. These narratives not only define the state's identity, but also establish its routine behaviors and relations with other actors on the global stage (Mitzen, 2006).

Importantly, however, while these identities are durable, they are not permanent and can change over time through various socialization processes (Hansen, 2016; Browning & Joenniemi, 2017), especially by elites through media during times of crisis (Subotić, 2016). For Russia, this changing of identity has proven tumultuous with long running debates over whether it is a Western or Eurasian nation, impacting its views of the global order today (Mankoff, 2012). Indeed, Russia's sense of self appears driven by its ability to define its identity in opposition to others, specifically the West (Hansen, 2016; Szostek, 2017; Medinskiy, 2010). In this case, previous research suggests Russian OS reflects practices of "closed identities" intended to preserve the stability of the self (Kazharski, 2020) or the "securitization of identities" by symbolically rigidifying, bordering, and closing down its identity (Rumelili, 2015; Browning & Joenniemi, 2017, p. 39). While such ontological coping mechanisms undoubtedly furnish Russia with a sense of OS, as Mitzen (2006) notes, these rigid attachments to past identity and routine relations can lead nations towards unwanted, continued conflict. Therefore, to appreciate Russia's ontological worldview, its search for OS, and the implications of Russia's identity regarding the future global order, one must first understand the crucible in which these identities emerged, beginning with the collapse of the Soviet Union in 1991.

Post-Soviet debate: Rejecting the West and introduction of the Russian World

After the fall of Soviet Union, Russia felt an unprecedented collective identity void, even a crisis of identity (Russo & Stoddard, 2018), acknowledged by President Boris Yeltsin himself (Breslauer & Dale, 1997). As it searched for a new post-Cold War identity, two options emerged: on one side, were "Westerners" who saw Russia as a European and a Western country; on the other side, were the "fundamentalist nationalists" who defined Russia through its distinctiveness from the West, stressing Russia's Eurasian roots and reaffirming its great power status (Light, 2003, p. 44). Initially, the advocates of the former won out, with Russia liberalizing its economy and working with the US on a number of foreign policy issues.

Indeed, the immediate years after of the Soviet Union's fall brought previously unthinkable levels of cooperation between the US and Russia (Mankoff, 2012), including reversal of Saddam Hussein's occupation of Kuwait, facilitation of German reunification, dismantling of Soviet occupation of Eastern Europe, and securement of the USSR's nuclear arsenal. Reflective of this cooperation, hope emerged that a more enduring US-Russian partnership was possible with George H. W. Bush's inclusion of Russia in his vision of a "new world order" and Gorbachev's dreams of a "common security community stretching from Vancouver to Vladivostok" (p. 89). During this time, and as the identity of the Russian state was being redefined, Russian leaders openly expressed a desire to imitate the West by embracing liberal democracy, free-market economics, and share ideas of Western states (Hansen, 2016).

However, the aspired partnership between Russia and the West quickly unraveled (Mankoff, 2012). The liberal reform agendas of 1990s led to the breakdown of social support systems and near-anarchic conditions throughout the country. This ruin resulted in Russia's belief that the West had failed to lend its support when Russia needed it most (Hansen, 2016), leading to bitter feelings compounded by residual mistrust inherited from the Cold War era (Mankoff, 2012). While some attribute this failure by contending that Russia was unready to be a part of the liberal democratic community in late 1990s (Jackson, 2004), others place blame on the West, arguing they were reluctant to recognize the former Soviet state as a part of the new world and systematically misinterpreting Russia's position by holding on to an image of Russia as a Soviet rather than contemporary state (Krashenninikova, 2007). Ultimately, Russian elites and publics sided with the latter and developed the "unreasonable rejection" notion where the West was assigned blame for causing the deterioration of relationships (Hansen, 2016, p. 363). Thus, coming to recognize the Russian self as fundamentally unlike the West (Steele, 2008) "the Russian state was trapped in a struggle between domestic survival and international acceptance" (Akchurina & Della Sala, 2018, p. 1644). The ensuing domestic tumult and desire for recognition led Russia to look inwards, reviewing its past identities to guide its future actions, and resulted in Putin's rise and articulation of a narrative identity defining the "Russian World."

Putin's rise: The Russian worldview and conflicting relations with the West

During Putin's rise to power in the late 1990s he began institutionalizing the idea of the Russian World as the ontological foundation of the young

Russian state. According to Herspring (2009), Putin had two major goals when he first took office: first, recreating the Russian state by consolidating Russian society and strengthening government control, including addressing Russia's economic inefficiencies, need for results-based social policies, and support for science, education, culture, and health care. The second was gaining back international respect and influence in foreign policy. In support of both, Putin presented the notion of a "Russian World" understood as a community of ethnic Russians, or simply Russian speakers, bound by shared culture and extending past the physical boarders of Russia (Kazharski, 2020). Thus, within this narrative, Putin expressed the idea of borders as a relational concept defined by shared history and ancestry with an abstract, imagined spiritual bond and understanding of Russian political leadership (Akchurina & Della Sala, 2018).

From the perspective of OS, Putin's articulation of the Russian world reflected the role state governments play as key suppliers of OS (Steele, 2008; Krowlikowski, 2008, 2018). As Huysmans (1998) argues, the legitimacy of a state rests on its capacity to provide order for citizens with Krolikowski (2018) adding that states create or reinforce citizens' OS by ordering social relations and introducing a level of certainty to abstract fears. In drawing upon Russia's past at a time of social unraveling, Putin preserved a sense of autobiographical continuity, a necessary feature in maintaining OS (Kazharski, 2020), especially during times of great ruptures or crisis (Subotić, 2016). More specifically, as Kazharski (2020) explains, the historic nature of the Russian World, with its origins in the 11th century, held already established imaginings within the minds of the Russian people, and provided strategic purchase by allowing Russian leaders to articulate a holistic unity across its ideological, societal, and spatial cleavages.

At first, US interests appeared misaligned with Putin's Russian World narrative. The late 1990s saw a deterioration of US–Russian relations, from events such as US support for North Atlantic Treaty Organization (NATO) expansion to US interest in stopping the bloodshed in Yugoslavia with both viewed as encroaching on Russia's sphere of interest. However, the September 11, 2001 terrorist attacks provided an opportunity not only for renewed US-Russian partnership (Mankoff 2012), but also an avenue for Russia's return to the international stage as an equal and active participant cooperating with other great powers against international terrorism (Snetkov, 2012). Here, US and Russian perceptions of the threat of global terrorism finally aligned, with Russia having identified terrorism, specifically Islamic terrorism, as its most immediate security challenge long before the September 11 attacks, owing to its war in Chechnya and wave of terrorist bombings in Russian cities. Thus, Putin significantly contributed to the US campaign in Afghanistan, while noting that US military presence in Central Asia needed to be temporary.

However, this cooperation was short lived. According to Mankoff (2012), Russia's cooperative goals with the US in Afghanistan included the elimination of Afghanistan as a source for radical Islam, enhancement of Russia's role as a global power and ally in Afghanistan, and greater freedom in Chechnya. But, the US misread Russia's calculus with the Bush administration viewing Putin's support in Afghanistan as a "strategic, even civilizational, choice to ally with the West" (p. 106). In this case, when another round of NATO expansion in the early 2000s brought in the former-Soviet Baltic states into the historically anti-Soviet alliance, NATO's frontiers reached less than 100 kilometers from St. Petersburg challenging Russia's narrative vision of a Russian World while also posing a security threat. This in combination with the US's second Iraq war renewed Russian criticism and fear of unilateral projection of US power.

Further challenges emerged with the 2004 Rose Revolution in Georgia and 2005 Orange Revolution in Ukraine, pitting the US and Russia on opposite sides within the political and ideological struggles taking place within the former Soviet Union with Russia opposing both out of fear that they could serve as a template for regime change within Russia itself (Mankoff, 2012). Within the Kremlin, these revolutions represented "the most dangerous steps yet in a US-led campaign to surround, contain, and weaken Russia" (p. 110) with US support of former Soviet states applying for NATO membership in conjunction with liberalizing trends in Kyrgyzstan and Ukraine leading Russia to see the situation as "spiraling increasingly out of control" (p. 112). Consequently, US-Russian relations hit a nadir with Putin reversing much of the liberalization efforts taking place within Russia in addition to intimidation of its neighbors culminating, at that time, with Russian troops marching into Georgia in 2008 to reinforce Russian influence. As relations between Putin's Russia and the West once again deteriorated, along with Russia's economy, anti-Western narratives re-emerged. As McFaul and Stoner-Weiss (2008) argue, Russia's weakening economy and unsettling foreign landscape required a new justification for Putin's leadership, resulting in a narrative of Russia besieged by the hypocritical and morally decadent West while promising economic growth in exchange for diminishing rights.

New narratives of conflict: Re-set and breakdown in US–Russian cooperation

Fearing a "permanent doom" for US-Russian relations, the elections of President Barack Obama and Dimitri Medvedev allowed for a re-set of relations (Mankoff, 2012; Gerber, 2015). Focusing on areas where agreement appeared easier, like arms control and deepening economic ties, the two nations made some progress in re-establishing cooperative habits. At the April 2009 G20 summit the two expressed a shared commitment to a new arms control agreement, collaboration in curbing Iranian and North

Korea's nuclear programs, and next steps on Russian entry to the WTO. These actions were made tangible in Obama and Medvedev's July 2009 bilateral meeting where the US and Russia committed to a number of agreements, including a new Bilateral Presidential Commission and use of Russian airspace to move forces and equipment into Afghanistan. Indeed, cooperation in Afghanistan resumed with the Obama administration providing additional olive branches by backing away from missile defense plans in Eastern Europe and relations with Georgia and Ukraine by prioritizing relations with Russia (Mankoff, 2012).

Nonetheless, the ideational divide between the two nations continued with a new rupture in relations ossifying Russia's antagonistic identity towards the West. Most notably, Hillary Clinton's support for Russian protestors during Vladimir Putin's election campaign to return to Russia's presidency had lasting effects on Putin's view towards the US. According to Crowley and Ioffe (2016), protests in Russia about voter fraud during Putin's 2012 election were blamed by the Kremlin as incited by the West and encouraged personally by Hillary Clinton. Consequently, Putin saw Western officials as attempting to undermine his own position as leader of the Russian Federation, resulting in increasingly anti-Western rhetoric and populist policies (Zygar, 2016). Thus, the attempt at reconciliation with the US, symbolized by Medvedev's presidency, was viewed as a failure in Russia with Putin's return to the Russian Presidency ushering in a new wave of Russian nationalistic identity poised in contrast to the West.

In support of Putin's new anti-Western posturing, in 2014, political observers noted a powerful wave of nationalism often referred to as the "Russian spring," which held the foundational ideas of Russian World at its heart (Kazharski, 2020). Levada reported public opinion data showing Russian's ranking of the US as the country most hostile towards Russia as rising from 78 in 2018 from a low of 26 in 2010. As Skalamera (2018) notes, Russian authorities pursued an active policy of narrative building in 2013–16, including Russia's shifting identity distancing itself from Europe to support economic ties with China. In support of these actions, Russian foreign policy and narratives reflecting its own power, prestige, and cultural heritage were used to strengthen Russian identity vis-à-vis the West (Szostek, 2017), including Russian media discourse perpetuating narratives of Russia as a great power (Miskimmon & O'Loughlin, 2017).

Therefore, when Ukraine turned towards a Westernized, pro-democratic regime in 2014, Russia interpreted this as a rejection of the Soviet legacy and a threat to Putin's Russian World narrative identity (Akchurina & Della Sala, 2018). As President Putin stressed during his 2014 speech to the Federal Council and the State Duma, Ukraine—the Crimean peninsula in particular—held a "'strategic importance for Russia' because it is 'where our [Russian] people live' and because it is the place where the Grand Prince Vladimir was baptized in the tenth century, subsequently uniting the Eastern Slavic tribes and lands around Christianity"

(Akchurina & Della Sala, 2018, p. 1645). In response to the pro-democratic demonstrations, Russia mobilized to support its political allies in Ukraine and annexed Crimea despite international condemnation and costly Western sanctions, enhancing Russian prestige and its identity as a global power (Freire & Heller, 2018).

Like Russia's response in Ukraine, Freire and Heller (2018) argue that Russia's Syria policy reflected an exercise of power politics designed to improve Russia's international status driven by Russian identity concerns. Specifically, they argue that Russia's self-image as a central player in international diplomacy became in doubt with the Arab Spring and rise of the Islamic State. Thus, Russian identity and opportunistic cost-calculations drove Russia's active military involvement in Syria as a means to reverse its partial international isolation following its actions in Ukraine and increasing Russian influence in the Middle East, despite incurring a number of costs likely to weigh on Russia in the long term.

To mitigate the blow back from international sanctions and subsequent domestic fallout from a weakening economy, Russian media continued to project new narratives of economic resiliency and spiritual solidarity reinforcing Russian identity. As Cooley and Stokes (2018) argue, during the economic sanctions of 2014–15, Russian broadcast and online media scapegoated the US and its Western allies by reporting them as insidiously attempting to weaken Russia. Despite these attempts, Russian narratives of economic resiliency presented its economy as strong enough to weather the crisis by emphasizing Russian solidarity. Likewise, Damm & Cooley (2017) argue that Putin introduced narratives of Russian spiritual identity in his 2015 Russian National Security Strategy in response to a weakening economy again by stressing common bonds, but this time through the Russian Orthodox Church as an attempt to enhance Russian legitimacy. Indeed, public opinion regarding Church trust had risen consistently over the past two decades (Levada, 2018) with the Russian Orthodox Church deployed as a symbol and unifier of Slavic people (Damm & Cooley, 2017) further supporting narratives of the Russian world as a distinct Russian civilization (Kazharski, 2020) and highlighting the influence of media in support of Russian OS constructions.

Russian state–media relations

As noted above, Russian media serves as a key instrument for political control and defining of the Russian state identity. Following the collapse of the USSR, Russian media reforms unfolded amidst significant political and economic transformations. Media outlets began struggling financially as state subsidies disappeared (Roselle, 2017) leading to their pursuit of Western-based media models (Lehtisaari & Miazhevich, 2019). While journalists traversed this new emerging media landscape, looking forward to the development of the media as a fourth estate capable of serving as a watchdog for democratic development (Roselle, 2017), politicians and business leaders quickly found the value in controlling the national narrative. As Gehlbach (2010) notes, Putin came of political age during this time, witnessing Russian politicians and oligarchs wielding television as a weapon in the struggle for power and money with the 1991 coup against Gorbachev failing, owing in large part to the plotters' inability to control the airwaves and oligarchs challenging government policies which awarded shares to rival tycoons.

The importance of Russian media solidified in the mid-1990s with Russian political and business communities viewing the media as the crucial factor contributing to Yeltsin's victory in the 1996 presidential campaign (Belin, 2002; Gehlbach, 2010). As Belin (2002) argues, Yeltsin's victory proved that media could shape Russia's political landscape by significantly impacting public opinion with political actors proving capable of mobilizing journalists to support a political agenda making control over the media sector the "passport to power and influence in Yeltsin's Russia" (p. 144).

Thus, in pursuit of solidifying Russian identity and reasserting state control, Putin acquired or reasserted state ownership of key parts of the media sector. Although the Russian state does not control all facets of Russian media, its control over the media's commanding heights appears sufficient (Gehlbach, 2010). As Herspring (2009) explains, although Putin did not initially take the press back to its level of censorship during the Soviet Union, Putin felt that the government had the right to set the parameters for debate by deciding what could or could not be published. Indeed, as President Putin experienced during the Yeltsin years, personal connections or ownership of the media allowed for significant political influence. What emerged, then, is a unique media-political clientelism with powerful patrons—including politicians, governors, oligarchs, and financial tycoons—offering financial and political support for media outlets in exchange for deference and other forms of political service (Lowrey & Erzikova, 2010; Roudakova, 2008). Consequently, since the 2000s there has been a decrease in commercial capital while an increase in state and mixed capital flowing into the Russian media industry (Vartanova, 2016) resulting in the instrumentation of media outlets "whereby outlets' owners and sponsors use the media under their control to advance their particularistic interests" (Roudakova, 2008, p. 43); rather than engaging in neutral and objective reporting, many news media outlets engage in advocacy reporting providing positive publicity for the patrons or negative publicity for one's opponents.

Reflective of these structural and political developments in the Russian media system are the Russian people's ostensible support of this system. According to Oates (2006), the Russian people themselves reject the idea of objectivity or balance in mass media reporting and consume media through the lens of political players deployed in the service of their financial and political patrons. Thus, they view and understand media content as "an arrangement of information through strong political filters" (Oates, 2007, p. 1285) with many Russian journalists (even the post-Soviet generation of journalists) interpreting their role not as contributors or supporters of civil society (Pasti, 2005; Voltmer, 2000), but more akin to political agents.

Today Russia's media actively promotes Russian interests both at home and abroad. At home, Russian state media has invested in strategic publicity campaigns to enhance Putin's charismatic leadership (Hill & Gaddy, 2015). Abroad, according to Paul and Matthews (2016), Russian media engages in deliberate propaganda techniques utilizes high numbers of communication channels, such as the Internet, social media, journalism, and other media outlets to disseminate partial truths or outright fictions for the purpose of entertaining, confusing, and overwhelming its audiences. Indeed, the Russian state appears surprisingly adept at evolving with the times with Russian backed trolls succeeding in influencing the 2016 US election in support of Donald Trump at the cost to Hillary Clinton (Jamieson, 2020). Thus, the importance of Russian media, both in supporting Putin's narrative vision and Russian OS, remains crucial to Russia's future ambitions, especially in defining the Russian world view and the nation's ability to influence and compete in the future of global competition.

Russia and the future of global competition

Despite Russia's investment in defining a new civilizational identity, in today's global order Russia still struggles materially. As Friere and Heller (2018) note, Russia's status-seeking strategies and desire to overturn the current international order is at odds with typical status-overachiever nations, posing an interesting paradox for scholars of international relations. In this case, although Russia appears relatively successful in promoting its hard-power-based status seeking, these actions have not solved the country's problems more broadly with the Russian state falling upon narratives supporting its OS to make up for its shortfalls and maintain support for Putin's continued political rule.

Indeed, economically, Russia faces significant challenges with Russian experts themselves recognizing that their country is not an economic great power (Clunan, 2018). Fueled by the global financial crisis of 2008 and post-Ukraine economic sanctions, Russia's economy entered into a deep recession, making economic difficulties "one of the most important challenges facing Russia today" (Aleksashenko, 2012, p. 33). The Russian economy not only lacks labor resources and technological skills (Aleksashenko, 2012), but also, because of its tight control and nationalization of key economic sectors, suffers from the suppression of innovation and diversification.

To address these challenges, and reflective of Russia's ideational pursuits, Russian policy has moved towards a "sovereign globalization" strategy (Clunan, 2018, p. 54), resting on limited economic interdependence between

Russia and the outside world. Whether this strategy can solve Russia's economic problems is uncertain. As Clunan (2018) states, despite this policy leading to some success in 2016, "Russian foreign policy elites are now markedly more sober and somber about the future of the international order and Russia's place in it" (p. 45).

Importantly, Russia places significant blame for its economic woes on the West. Russian media not only attributes the US-liberal order as creating the conditions for a struggling global economy, but also as intentionally implementing policies designed to marginalized Russia's growth (Cooley & Stokes, 2018). This, in combination with Russian political discourse more generally offended by Western countries' reluctance to treat Russia in line with its perceived great power status (Miskimmon & O'Loughlin, 2017; Snetkov, 2012), drives antagonism towards the West and provides Russia with a clearly defined identity and sense of self in opposition to the US-led global order (Hansen, 2016).

Whether this narrative can continue to hold sway among Russia's populace remains uncertain, especially if Russia is unable to compete globally. As Mitzen (2006) explains states can become attached to certain identities and routinized relationships, even when it appears irrational to do so, resulting in continued conflict. In Russia's case, the directionality of its identities will influence whether its investment in Eastern economic cooperation produces dividends; or, if not, could portend further diplomatic machoism and military flexing to satiate its ontological identity constructions despite facing an eroding economic base to support its great power identity. To determine how Russian media narrates to its citizens what the future global order holds, and the implications of these narrative identities this chapter asks two questions:

RQ1. How do Russian media narrate the future global order?
RQ2. How do Russian media narrate the future of global competition?

Method

For a full description of the methodology, see Chapter 2. As a synopsis, researchers employed a mixed methodological design including qualitative narrative analysis aided by the text-mining program KH coder, as well as a quantitative content analysis. A total of 166 Russian news articles were examined across 20 native Russian news media sources. Data was collected using the Factiva platform, which aggregates and stores international news media. Researchers conducted a systematic random sampling at a 90% confidence interval on the articles collected by using a series of keywords (international/global influence, global order, international/global competition). For a full breakdown of sources and articles sampled, see Chapter 2.

The qualitative narrative analysis applied a grounded theory approach whereby researchers first read through the entire corpus of articles before identifying emerging patterns which were then used in the creation of larger thematic categories related to global competition and the prospective futures of the global order from the perspective provided by Russian news media. As with all the chapters in this manuscript, narrative was broadly conceptualized using Burke's (1969) definition of narratives including act, agents, scenes, instruments, and purpose, with the qualitative analysis taking a grounded approach. Researchers also employed a quantitative analysis with coders analyzing news articles using four general categories with subsequent subtopic categories related to global competition, alliances, and security. The first two categories examined how Russian media presented global competition, specifically assessing vulnerabilities and capabilities related to the DIME framework of diplomatic, informational, military, and economic sources of system power. The next two categories examined Russian media presentation of the global order. These categories included reports of conflict management and escalation, deterrence, redlines, competitors, and alliances; as well as stated viewpoints related to the composition of the global order, Russia's role in the global order, along with presentations of US and WE's role in the global order.

RQ1. How do Russian media narrate the future global order?

Figure 4.1. visually presents Russian media discourse regarding the future global order as associated with the following themes: new international order;

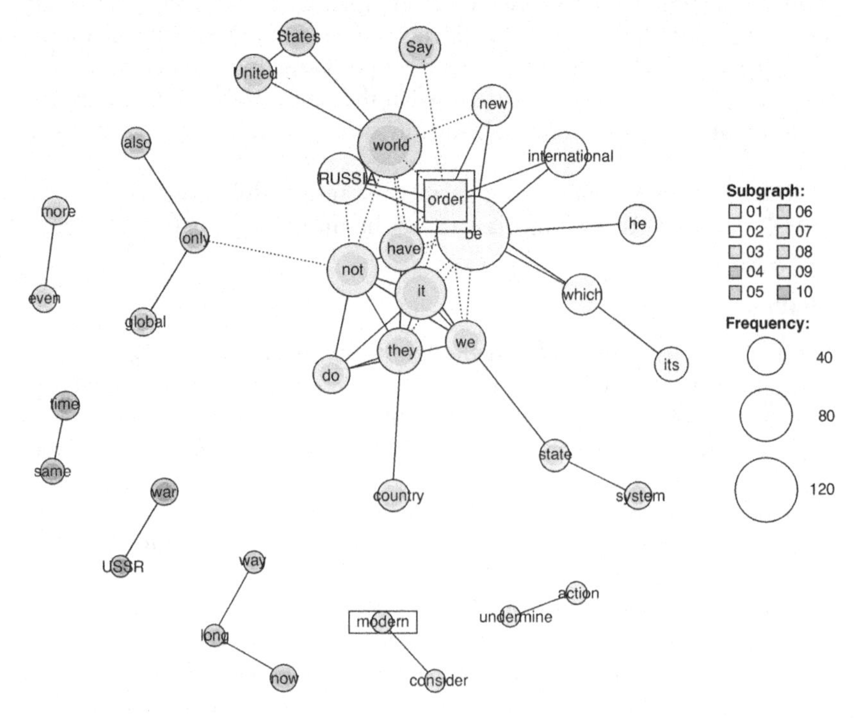

Figure 4.1 Co-occurrence Network of Russian Media Reporting Referencing "Global Order"

USSR, war; state system, they/we; United States, world; consider modern; undermine action; long way now. According to the qualitative analysis, these portrayed themes represent a narrative of Russia clinging to its previous identity of a strong USSR reminiscent of its prestige during the Cold War bolstered by narrative of "othering" via frequent mentions of "us" verse "them" themes in relation to the US and the West, as well as narrative constructions of a new world order.

Quantitatively, the manifestation of Russian World identity in discussion of the global order is represented by Table 4.1 with Russian media negatively portraying the larger global order (m = -.32), the US (m = -.51), and Western Europe (m = -.21) in contrast to the positive influence assigned to Russia's role in the global order (m = .35). Evident by the qualitative data, Russian media makes sweeping accusation on the failings of the current international order's leadership. Specifically, Russian media consistently others Western global leadership to distinguish itself and its sphere of influence. This narrative worldview allows for a justification for Russia to pivot towards conversations partnering with China in support of carving out a Russian World niche in a newly emerging global order.

Global order

Russian media portray the global order as defined by the actions of three key players, the US, China, and Russia. As such, the interactions among these great powers dictate the terms of the current and future order, with the growing contradictions between these major world powers increasing its instability leading Russian media to portend the current global world order as on the verge of collapse. Thus, Russian media focus on narratives emphasizing the changing process, or need for change of the international system, with Russia seen as leading the move towards a multipolar order out of criticism of US and Western nations' current dominant positions. As *RBC* reports, today's global order rests on the principles of multipolarity resulting from the growth of developing countries' economies[1] with an article from *RIA Novosit* more explicitly expressing the need for change in global leadership now that the US has lost its position in the international system.[2]

The decline of the current global order manifests itself in narratives characterizing its problems and outdated nature in contrast to the world's

Table 4.1 Russian Media Views on the Global Order and the West

	Article Mentions	*Valence (1=positive, -1=negative)*
Perspectives of Global Order	N = 94 (57%)	Mean = -.32
Russia's Role in Global Order	N = 55 (33%)	Mean = .35
Perspectives on the US	N = 98 (59%)	Mean = -.51
Perspectives on Western Europe	N = 72 (43%)	Mean = -.21

new centers of power. Russian media report that the current state of global affairs are the worst they have been since 1945, with *Vedomosti* quipping how the world's evolving political architecture is not a new world order, but stem from disorder from the old system. In contrast to the failings of the current order as stemming from the past, Russian media envisions a new order that will be built around two centers: (1) a large Eurasian center around the Chinese Belt and Road Initiative (BRI), which Russia will join as an independent actor; and (2) a center that will be formed around the US.[3] Regardless of the centers of power, Russian media report that the rivalry of such power centers will increase with political and economic processes becoming more unstable against the backdrop of increasingly complicated international relations.[4]

Reflective of this increasing antagonism between power centers is Russian reporting on the state of the global order as occurring in the context of one country impugning another as the actor causing global instability. For instance, European countries (UK, Ukraine, Poland, Estonia, etc.) and the US are reported as blaming Russia for destabilizing the global order with UK Member of Parliament, Jeremy Hunt, quoted as stating how Russians support anything that shatters the current system with Moscow intentionally trying to destabilize the world order.[5] Likewise, the US is reported as blaming Russia as actively undermining the international order from the inside through attempts to unravel the underlying economic and security structures in Europe and the Middle East, as well as NATO partnerships.[6] Other examples include quotes by the Polish Defense Minister labeling Russia as the only country in Europe today that, through its military actions, undermines European relations and the global order[7] with Ukrainian President Petro Poroshenko contending that Russia not only rejects the current global system, but also tries to build an alternative reality based on alternative values such as tyranny and intolerance instead of democracy and respect.[8] Although Russian media's ample reporting on foreign leaders' criticism of the Russian state could arguably undermine Russia's image, it nonetheless grants Russia significant agency in world affairs by demonstrating Russia's ability to influence global politics even if that influence falls to Russia playing spoiler.

Russian media does not shy from blaming other international actors for the disruption of world order. Regarding US behavior, *Rossiyskaya Gazeta* quotes Medvedev as explaining how US sanctions destroy both the political and economic order.[9] Ironically, the US is viewed as the primary actor attempting to dismantle the post-World War II international order it built, with its actions standing in contrast to the international community, which is portrayed as counterbalancing US unilateralism. Furthermore, Russian media characterizes US interests as self-serving, reporting how the US only established the foundations of the current global order because it was politically and economically expedient for them at the time, and so now, as the current system no longer serves US interests, it is the US taking actions that shake the system's foundations. As one article claims, the US became a hostage to the system they themselves created in the 1990s, and now the US is the primary actor interested in destabilizing it.[10]

Because of US self-interest, Russian media claims that not only has the US lost its leadership in the global order but also that there is a need to change its leadership rather than allowing the US to reshape the system to suit its own needs. Evidence of this include reports that Western Europe is unsatisfied with US actions in the global arena with an European riot breaking out on the American ship, which is good news for Russia.[11] US foreign policy is discussed as unilateral and destructive, like in the case of its US actions in Syria which typify its attempts to preserve a unipolar world order while leading to destructive ends. As an article from *RIA Novosti* explains, US missile attacks on the Syrian air base of Shairat creates a dangerous precedent that undermines the modern world order if such acts are passed with impunity and without condemnation from the global community; without which might cause the international order to collapse with chaos spreading throughout the world.[12]

Russian media also accuse the US of distrusting Russian and Chinese intentions claiming that the two nations are trying to undermine international norms and institutions while working together to change the global order in their favor. Unsurprisingly, Russian media reports that Moscow strongly disagrees with this claim and notes the opposite as true, expressing how both Russia and China stand firmly in defense of peace and remain committed to the fair values of the post-war order.[13] Again, US criticism of Russia, this time through its partnership with China, portrays Russia as an agentic threat by emphasizing its partnership with the preeminent emerging power thereby bolstering a sense of Russian influence.

Russia's role within global order

When reporting upon the global order, Russia's role is both prominent, with a third of articles explicitly covering Russia's role, and also positive (m = .35; see Table 4.1). In general, Russia is viewed as not only a key actor in international relations, but also gaining strength and influence. Russian media reports how Russia has proved itself in areas where it has been historically strong, like power politics, military strategy, and diplomacy[14] with other articles noting the impossibility of creating a new global order without Russian participation.[15] Indeed, articles explain how Russia is on the rise and increasing its international influence[16] with *Nezavisimaya Gazeta* reporting Russia as aspiring to become not only a major player in the international economic arena but also in becoming a global economic leader.[17]

Russian media narrates the nation's foreign policy actions in Syria as a vivid example of how Russian conceptualizes itself as an international power. In this case, its Syrian policy presents a story of success where, using relatively few military forces and means, Russian is reported to have reversed the course of a long-term conflict in its favor; Russia is further characterized as playing a balancing role in the international arena, capable of smoothing out contradictions of interests surgically by being a scale-tipper of sorts in a new multipolar world where equality and parity will dominate. As *Vedomosti* reports, while Russia's actions in Syria cost the nation dearly, they paid far less than the whole price demonstrating that the world is no longer one characterized by unipolarity.[18]

Despite the positive outlook on Russia's role within global order, Russian media depicts the nation as an unlikely actor to occupy the first place in any new system of international power. Thus, although Russia is seen as a key actor and a proponent in the construction of a new global order,[19] this rebuilding requires partnerships with another great power, China. In this case, Russia is reported as playing a key role in building a Greater Eurasian partnership (proposed by Russia and supported by China) which strategically aligns Russia with the Chinese BRI. Not only does Russian media positively report upon the BRI, viewing it as a new model of global order, but also borrows from Chinese rhetoric by describing Russia's support of the initiative as promoting the spirit and principles of peace and cooperation, openness and tolerance, and the sharing of positive experiences and benefits for all.[20]

In sum, Russian media showcases a global order defined by the aspirations and conflict among great powers carving spheres of influence, of which it is one. Emphasis is placed on the criticizing of US leadership as self-serving and even undermining the current global order. Despite this, Russia is viewed as growing in international influence and partnering with other great powers, like China, in rebuilding a new, more multipolar world order. This overarching narrative plotline is further evident in Russian media reporting regarding its allies, competitors, and approach to managing conflict in the international order.

Partnerships, competitors, and conflict management

Aligning with its presentation of the global order as in a state of decline and requiring new leadership, Russian media describes the state's key allies or partners as those capable of helping Russia form a new sphere of influence outside of Western control, most notably China and former Soviet states. Thus, the US and Western Europe are viewed as Russia's main competitors, with the global order in which they support depicted as the source of global conflict.

Partnerships

China most notably appears as a strategic ally in Russian media coverage regarding the global order. China represents a key ally for Russia, with

Table 4.2 Russian Media Reporting of Conflict Dynamics

	Article Mentions
Mentioned Competitors	N = 31 (19%)
Mentioned Alliances	N = 41 (25%)
Legitimate Deterrence	N = 21 (13%)
Conflict/Escalation Management	N = 23 (14%)
Redlines to Action	N = 5 (3%)

Itar-TASS explicitly stating how, the development of a strategic partnership with China marks an unconditional priority of Russia's foreign policy strategy.[21] Much of this coverage is in the context of Russia's pursuit of a great Eurasian partnership with China's BRI allowing for Russia's joining as a strategic partner and thereby providing economic possibilities for Kamlykia, Stavropol Territory, and Dagestan. Russian media also reports Russian desires to strengthen relations with China on initiatives in Central Asia and the South Caucasus. Beyond economic opportunities to Russia's partnering with China, Russian media also highlights the strategic benefits of doing so as well. In this case, Russian media portray a narrative of Russia and China working together against the US with *Rosbalt* reporting how doing so allows Moscow and Beijing to strongly press against the US[22] while other articles reporting that relations between China, Russia, and the US represents a multifaceted triangle with Russia and China's relationship being the most positive and stable.[23]

In addition to China, Russian media also presents FSU countries as allies. Reports repeatedly stress Russia's shared cultural roots, historical ties, and common religion with former Soviet states. Specifically, the Shanghai Cooperation Organization is portrayed as symbolizing Russia's strategic economic, political and security alliances with Kazakhstan, Kyrgyzstan, Tajikistan, and Uzbekistan. Importantly, Russian media narrate FSU countries as falling under Russia's sphere of regional influence and urges both the US and China to agree not to intervene in regional conflicts.[24] In this case, the Ukrainian crisis is presented as an attempt to show the borders of Russian influence with Russia ultimately striving towards creating a powerful Russian World branded under Eurasian terminology through its moving towards the creation of a large Eurasian space of peace and cooperation.[25]

Competitors

Unsurprisingly, the US spearheads the list of Russia's main competitors. *Vedomosti's* reporting of Vladimir Putin's Valdai-Sochi speech makes the message clear by calling the US world order as both bad and as the source of almost all ills.[26] Other articles note how diametrically opposed Russia and the US are, regarding their understanding of their security interests.[27] Indeed, throughout Russian media reporting, the US is presented as an enemy of a stable global order evident by its reckless and frivolous behavior,[28] including its role as a harsh criticizer of Russia and China, service as an anti-Russian propaganda force, and characterization as an overall aggressive player regularly breaking strategic rules. Other themes include portrayals of US selfishness as an enforcer of its own hegemony and behavior as an isolationist and nationalist actor, marking it as a country unable to solve a single international conflict by itself, and, through its attempts to do so, only worsening everything.[29] Likewise, the US is vividly described as using petrodollars not just as a weapon, but as the basis for world domination with it able to bomb, kidnap, and torture anyone they want with impunity as long as the US maintains its control over international finance.[30]

Although the US is criticized for destabilizing the global order, another theme in Russian coverage is that of the US losing its global power and hegemony. For instance, an article from *RBC Daily* uses the metaphor of the US as an aging celebrity in search of former glory and spotlight in that the US, desperately fights for a place on stage, including courting new figures like China.[31] As such, Russian media explains its perception of America's aggressive and irrational behavior by attributing its behavior to losses within the global marketplace to rising powers like China as well as diminishing US influence through the gradual losing of Western Europe as a long-standing ally.[32]

Despite these critiques, some articles still report the need for US-Russian cooperation, or at least management of conflict. Indeed, the US, at times, is argued as serving as an ally to Russian interests, specifically in the fight against global terrorism and Sunni radicals with Itar-TASS quoting Pentagon Chief Ashton Carter as stating how the US must keep the door open for cooperation with Moscow and does not want to see Russia as its enemy.[33] Additional areas of cooperation include operations in cyberspace, dialogue between the two countries' militaries in order to prevent miscalculations or unwanted incidents, and the conflict in Ukraine, and a political settlement in Syria.[34] In these areas, as *Vedomosti* reports, although it is unrealistic to expect the elimination of the fundamental contradictions between Russia and America, it is reasonable to expect a relationship where both parties are able to take a sober and serious approach to risk management.[35]

Similar to the US, Western Europe is presented in a negative light. Europe is reported as an anti-Russian propaganda force accusing Russia of trying to destabilize world order, as agents responsible for the collapse of USSR (and the associated Russian prestige as a superpower), involved in unjust economic sanctions towards Russia and as champions of democratic totalitarianism. As an article from RIA Novosit explains, Western Europe claims civilizational leadership in the world while subordinating the rest to their ideas about how to live and what domestic and foreign policy issues others should pursue.[36] Although media narratives on Western Europe are predominantly negative, Russian media still portray the Russian state as urging for more cooperation with Europe, especially with regards to balancing US actions, and positing that Western Europe needs to take into account Russia's point of view and realize its needs for positive relations with Moscow.[37]

Conflict management

Regarding conflict management, and reflective of its referenced competitors, Russian media narratives include conversations on escalating tensions between Russia and the US and the West. Articles report how today US-Russian relations are as bad as they were since the end of World War II; *Vedomosti* reports that after a roller-coaster of mutual illusions and disappointments over the past 25 years a new model of relations is now preferable.[38] In this case, Russian media expresses how dialogue between the West and the Russian military are needed to avoid mishaps and miscommunication leading to unwanted conflict.

In addition to conflict with the West, Russian media draws upon the Ukrainian crisis as an example of managing disputes within Russia's sphere of influence and the need for Russia to remain steadfast in preserving its regional influence. Russia's response to events in Ukraine are portrayed as an attempt by Russia to show the world the extent of Russian influence, and where it sees the borders of that influence. Although the conflict is viewed as exacerbating tensions within the world order, the conflict is characterized as necessary; thus, despite Russia having paid a high price of for its Ukrainian gambit[39] the conflict is narrated as a quarrel of fraternal people and a fight that Russia has historically fought, not once, twice, or even a third time.[40] Furthermore, while Russia is actively engaged in Ukraine, Russia's involvement is not one of an antagonist, with *Argumenty I Fakti* stating that under no circumstances can Russia become an aggressor country, despite many in the world convinced of the opposite.[41]

RQ2. How do Russian media narrate the future of global competition?

Russian media narrate its potential to compete in the future global order mostly through discussions of necessary capabilities, rather than mentions of its vulnerabilities, averaging 20% and 9.75% respectfully. These findings point to Russia's purported optimism in its ability to compete on a world stage. More specifically, results suggest Russia's primary concerns fall within the economic and diplomatic spheres with both vulnerabilities and capabilities most frequently discussed through issues of economics (n = 27; 16% and n = 36; 22% respectfully) and diplomacy (11% and 25%

respectfully) while informational and military issues presented less often (see Table 4.3). Importantly, Russian military vulnerabilities are rarely mentioned, suggesting some sense of Russian military self-assurance.

Vulnerabilities

Russia's chief competitive vulnerabilities stem from its economy, viewed as hindering its status as a great power (n = 27; 16%). The second most frequently cited area of disadvantage is diplomatic (n = 19; 11%) whereby Russia is placed in a defensive position vis-à-vis the West. Similar in frequency to diplomatic concerns are Russia's informational vulnerabilities (n = 15; 9%) stemming from Russia's IT infrastructure, but also growing concerns of Western soft power and cultural encroachment. Military vulnerabilities are rarely discussed (n = 5; 3%) and focus on new challenges related to Russia's navy.

Economic vulnerabilities

Russian media presents Russia as a nation gradually losing its economic advantages. Examples of this narrative are abundant, including reports stating how the Russian economy represents only 2–3% of global GDP[42] and thus unable to become an equal part of the global economy.[43] Importantly, these developments are viewed as part of a larger trend with Russia's lack of global economic clout falling within a long-term negative trend[44] as Russia experiences economic stagnation without a strategy for growth.[45] Causes of Russia's inability to grow its economy are attributed to a variety of factors from a lack of resources for new investment projects and modern technologies to weaknesses in human resource management and economic diversification in industry, and dependency on oil exports. An article from *Rossiyskaya Gazeta* summarizes the situation with Russia's economy remaining largely ineffective and lagging behind other leading nations, owing to labor productivity.[46] Importantly, these economic vulnerabilities are viewed as undermining Russia's position and aspirations as a great power, with *Nezavisimaya Gazeta* reporting that Russia's economic relations with China can never reach a level worthy of great powers as it remains several times smaller than that of US-Chinese trade.[47]

Table 4.3 Russian Vulnerabilities and Capabilities in News Media

	Articles Mentioning Key Vulnerabilities	*Articles Mentioning Necessary Capabilities*
Diplomatic	N = 19 (11%)	N = 42 (25%)
Informational	N = 15 (9%)	N = 24 (15%)
Military	N = 5 (3%)	N = 30 (18%)
Economic	N = 27 (16%)	N = 36 (22%)

Additional reasons for Russia's economic vulnerabilities come from economic sanctions imposed by the West. Here Russian media engage in narrative "othering" portraying the West as an outsider trying to contain Russia. As *Nezavisimaya Gazeta* reports, the US leads the West in endeavoring to economically and politically isolate Russia from the world in every way, including the use of the crisis situation in Ukraine.[48] These actions implicate Russia's vision of the Russian World, leading Russian media to call for greater Russian economic solidarity and closer ties in that if Russia is shown unable to create its own macro-economic region, then Russia itself will be torn apart.[49]

Diplomatic vulnerabilities

Russian media's depiction of its diplomatic landscape is reminiscent of its Soviet past with its current diplomatic resources seen as more limited. Numerous references to Russia's Soviet legacy with the USSR occur, with the term occupying a prominent placement in Russia's media discussions regarding global competition and order (See Figure 4.1). Specifically, the USSR is romanticized in that it provided order and stability but its collapse led to the destruction of equilibrium in the world order.[50] This nostalgia for the past is placed into conversation with the future, with Russian media noting how the same forces that broke the USSR are now breaking the US and the whole world.[51]

Beyond discussions of the USSR, Russian media characterizes the country's diplomatic efforts largely in a defensive posture against the US while Russia attempts to provide an alternative voice in global affairs. Articles express how the West fails to consider Russian perspectives and legitimate interests, with Itar-TASS quoting Gorbachev as explaining how Western nations' reluctance to take into account Russia's point of view ignores the nation's legitimate security interests.[52] Thus, operating as an outsider nation, articles note Russia's need to make the whole world reckon with its opinion[53] and defend the nation's interests by confronting the lies and an outright aggression of Western nations.[54] In other words, Russian media discuss Russia's voice within the diplomatic arena as often challenged by the West, undermining not only interpretations of basic facts about global affairs, but also the facts themselves.[55] Such actions, arising from the West's diplomatic partnerships and accusations of inappropriate Russian behavior on the world stage, thereby diminish Russia's diplomatic influence.

Informational vulnerabilities

Russia is presented as a weak player within the informational and communication environment which undermines is geopolitical position. Like its depiction of the Russian economy, Russian media reports how its IT technologies are under 1% of world market[56] and that in the digital space, Russia is only able to minimally participate in the competition of "civilizational" technological platforms, which in turn poses a strategic deficit for Russia moving into the future.[57] Russian media claim that its lack of communication power undermines its soft power capabilities and thus defenses against Western influence while also leading to increased misunderstanding and diverging cultural values. Specifically, Russian media views the US and UK's soft power capabilities as a vulnerability, with RIA Novosti reporting that British soft power gets "installed" in Russian citizens when they use British technologies.[58] Likewise, concerns of Western soft power play into Russian leaders' fears regarding the negative effects of foreign cultural penetration into Russian lives, with further worries regarding the implications of direct contact of the Western world with their own; as *Vedomosti* reports, US and Russian societies share little in culture or common values, thereby developing in opposite directions.[59]

Military vulnerabilities

Russian media rarely report upon Russian military vulnerabilities, but out of the few articles that do, emphasis is placed on Russia's navy. As RIA Novosti reports Russia's navy faces challenges from foreign states' territorial claims, the aspirations of a number of countries to limit Russia's access to ocean resources, and concerns over international terrorism, piracy, and poaching—as well as illicit transportation of weapons, drugs and radioactive materials.[60] Other articles warn that the development of new-generations of weapons systems will require a shift towards the field of science, technology and education[61] which the Russian military is unable to match. Some concerns even include long term worries over Russia's ostensible ally, China, with an article from Rosbalt discussing the implications of closing of the Manas airbase in Kyrgyzstan with China posing as a certain danger to Russia by reducing Russia to a junior partner in Central Asia and other regions of the world.[62] Nonetheless, the fact that few articles report on Russian vulnerabilities when discussing the future of global competition suggests Russia is relatively self-assured with its military position.

Capabilities

Russian media reporting on the nation's necessary capabilities come from a variety of areas, most frequently through discussion of diplomatic partnerships (n = 42; 25%) with China and de-escalation of relations with the US. Closely followed is its needed capabilities to secure its economic growth (n = 36; 22%) amid Western sanctions. Its military capabilities are also prominent (n = 30; 18%), focusing on its navy and how innovation in the military sphere can contribute to its economic growth. Finally, its informational capabilities (n = 24; 15%) primarily revolve around cultural protection of Russian society.

Diplomatic capabilities

Russian news media does not underestimate the importance of diplomatic relationships, as this category constitutes the most frequently mentioned necessary capability for the future. As one article explains, countries can settle their differences by working together in a harmonious manner that both maintains the global order while mitigating chances of peace slipping into conflict between great powers.[63] Indeed, Russian leaders are often quoted on the importance of dialogue in establishing future diplomatic relationships, with articles citing Medvedev as stating how Russia believes cooperation is better than refusing to cooperate, communication better than not communicating, and negotiation preferable to conflict.[64] Most often, necessary diplomatic capabilities are discussed in the context of Russian-US relations; for example, one article quotes Gorbachev as explaining the need for Russia and the US to talk to each other, calling it an axiom forgotten in vain.[65] Other examples include quotes from Putin as stating how Russia is ready for constructive dialogue with the US, albeit only on an equal basis.[66]

Diplomatic relationships with China are also of importance as Russia considers China not only as a powerful global player, but also a key economical ally. As such, several articles report on various diplomatic meetings between China and Russia, especially discussing opportunities provided by the BRI like its development of a Eurasian transit corridor described as certainly having a positive effect on the economic situation in the Kalmykia, Dagestan, Astrakhan, Volgograd, Rostov, and Stavropol Krai regions.[67] As an article from *Trud* explains, today is the best period in the history of Sino-Russian relations with the two nations enjoying a high-level of mutual trust and perfect cooperation across multiple platforms of engagement.[68] Such trust and positive relations stem from their ability to find common ground as they enjoy similar interests in many aspects of their relationship allowing for the two nations to closely coordinate their positions and cooperate across many international venues, including defending the world order.[69] Other articles note how Russia and China firmly support each other on important issues relating to their mutual key interests with both countries pledging to do everything to support their efforts to provide stability in the world.[70]

Economic capabilities

Russian media frequently report upon the state's potential economic capabilities, primarily by identifying areas Russia can strengthen to ensure its ability to compete. These areas include stimulating its domestic economy, building human capital, and advancing technological innovation largely for the purpose of reducing Russia's economic dependency on the West. For instance, Russian media report on aggressive plans to reform and invest in the Russian economy, including changes in the tax system and a focus on defense industry equipment to boost its exports.[71] Likewise, a more robust science and technology sector is discussed as part of a larger economic revitalization program[72] including the need for internal IT development.[73] These programs are explained as helping support Russian economic development by reducing dependency on US currency, accumulation of gold in international reserves, and the creation of ruble settlement zones through the organization of custom unions that will increase economic efficiency and establish closer political and cultural ties between member countries.[74]

In addition to financial and technological development, Russian media place an emphasis on reducing dependency on imported foods and the need to support small, and medium-sized local businesses. Part of the concern for these sectors arise from US and Western sanctions on Russia's economy, but Russian media cite government officials as noting how these sanctions could have a positive impact by reducing Russia's dependency on imported goods and even suggest policies to reduce the efficacy of sanctions through the formation of international consortia designed to circumvent trade rules.[75] Ultimately, Russian discussions of its economic capabilities are tied to its international prestige, as an article from *Argumenty I Fakti* states, no matter how unpopular the steps, Russians must find the economic resources to maintain its leading position in the world.[76]

Finally, conversations on necessary economic capabilities are often entangled with discussions regarding investments in human resources. An article form *Rossiyskaya Gazeta* explains, in today's 21st-century economy human capital is the key factor for all nations, but especially Russia, in competing economically through the development of innovative technologies.[77] As other articles note, Russia must unleash its full potential to stimulate, initiate, develop, and increase human capital in order to lay its own path to success[78] as today's global competition is not just a competition over technological development or innovative solutions, but a competition for individuals.[79]

Military capabilities

Although Russian media presents competitiveness in science and technology as more important than competitiveness in traditional military developments, Russian media note the opportunities for Russian military technology as a means to enhance its economic competitiveness and fund further military development. For instance, Russian media explains the commercialization of space as a way to boost the Russian economy through partnerships with foreign companies leading to greater foreign investment into the Russian economy. Competition in space is viewed as a key sector in that the moon is both the object of future exploration of Earth's civilization as well as a potential source for twenty-first century geopolitical competition over lunar resources.[80]

Most prominent, however, is Russian media's emphasis on development of its navy. Russian media portrays the navy as the dominant force that will provide Russia with a competitive position in a multipolar political landscape with maritime leadership viewed as essential in the implementation and protection of Russia's national interests. As RIA Novosit puts it, only a strong fleet can provide Russia with a leading position within the multipolar world of the twenty-first century.[81] Likewise, RT reports the importance of strengthening the position of the Russian Federation among the leading maritime powers in order to protect its national interests and secure its oceanic borders.[82]

The importance of Russia's navy is further highlighted in discussions about Russian development in the Artic, which, like its discussions regarding its space program, tie together Russian military development to potential economic development. Russian media stresses the economic and political importance of the region, portraying Russia as the ultimate leader in the Arctic and its Northern Sea Route. For instance, Russian media brags that no other country has similar power capabilities and infrastructure to rival it within the Arctic region, boasting that Russia possess the world's largest icebreaking fleet.[83] Even with this advantage, Russian media report how Russia is further increasing its Artic infrastructure through development and deployment of more air bases, ports, armaments, troops, data collection, resources for search and rescue, commercial hubs, and even floating nuclear power plants.[84] In sum, Russian media portray the Northern Sea Route as essential for freight traffic and trade routes between continents and a key area to boost its ability to compete in the future global landscape.

Informational Capabilities

Although informational capabilities are the least frequently described, Russian media still maintains their importance in safeguarding Russian culture and political cohesion. Here reporting focuses on the intensifying nature of competition in the information space with calls for Russia to invest in its culture industries to maintain a sense of unity and common identity. Articles note how global competition in the ideological and informational sphere is becoming increasingly aggressive[85] with others analogizing the competitive nature of today's informational battles as akin to those during the Cold War albeit with the Internet representing a more powerful weapon with its ability to scatter information instantly over millions of people.[86] In the context of this new age of informational warfare, RIA Novosit reports that the Russia government should develop both foreign and domestic defense policies that include psychological and informational abilities as the fall of the USSR only occurred once it suffered psychological defeat within its own society.[87]

To prevent such a collapse from reoccurring, Russian media report upon the need for significant investment in Russian cultural programs. These cultural initiatives are characterized as vital for Russia's competitiveness in the future global order, emphasizes the importance and relevance of developing a state cultural policy, to ensure the strengthening of the civil, national and cultural identity of the Russian people. At the heart of this culture program, is the notion that the self-actualization of its citizens, through cultural education, represents a key element to global competition.[88]

Other issues connected to Russia's cultural programs are its informational initiatives. As an article from *Vedomosti* reporting on Russia's Strategy for the Development of the Information Society in the Russian Federation for 2017–2030 explains, Russia should become a more capable player within the informational environment and set an ambitious goal to increase the role of Russia in the global humanitarian and cultural space.[89] Here, Russia is presented as an informational and cultural hub, and as a center of the Russian World, from where all direction to its areas of influence will flow. However, in addition to developing its cultural resources, and as part of its strategy for developing an information society, Russian media debates challenges regarding Russia's ability to balance open and closed information systems; while these initiatives are necessary for innovation, they are also recognized as posing security concerns as Russia wants to build a digital economy like the rest of the world while also fencing itself off from the world for security purposes.[90]

Discussion

This chapter set out to determine how Russian news media narrate, and thus define to its citizens, Russia's outlook on the future global order and the nation's ability to successfully compete within it through the lens of Russian OS. In sum, Russia's conception of the global order appears agent-centric, focused on the competition and action among great powers, of which Russia is one. As such, growing antagonism among the US, China, and Russia, contribute to a narrative by which the current global order is unraveling, owing primarily to US self-interest. As a result, Russian media envisions an emerging multipolar future order whereby Russia maintains an important place, albeit one shifting towards the East, rather than engaging with the West. The general outline of this narrative thereby places Russia in conflict with, or at the very least outside of, the Western-led global order and those aligned with the West.

From media coverage reporting on the future of global order, Russia's OS-seeking appears driven by its need for recognition amongst the backdrop of narratives portraying the world as driven by great power politics and its visions of the Russian World. Specifically, these narrative visions provide key sources of OS by cognitively ordering Russia's external and internal environments as the nation anxiously considers its economic and cultural ability to compete in the global order. As the data demonstrates, the major concerns expressed by Russian media relating to global competition revolve around economic and diplomatic issues, as well as concerns over Russian cultural identity. Here the depression of the Russian economy and lack of investment place Russia at significant competitive disadvantages in the US-aligned global order pushing the nation to optimistically pursue an Eurasian economic partnership and planned investments in sweeping educational and cultural programs to ensure domestic cohesion, technological innovation, and economic growth.

Thus, to compensate for its domestic challenges and diplomatic isolation from Western nations, the findings suggest that Russia relies upon OS building by emphasizing its Cold War attachments and anti-West routines to maintain a sense of autobiographical continuity amidst a changing world order. As previous OS research notes, the destabilizing forces of economic globalization has led to reaffirmation of past identities (Kinnvall, 2004) and securing of a sense of place (Cash & Kinnvall, 2017) with states returning to past identities when faced with perceptions of insecurity (Mitzen, 2006). In Russia's case, Roselle (2017) notes how its great power narrative identity in particular helps the state secure domestic political support and enhance its power (Roselle, 2017) with others noting the importance of defining Russian identity in opposition to the West to bolster its sense of self (Szostek, 2017; Hansen, 2016; Medinskiy, 2010). These two narrative elements and their importance to Russia's OS are perhaps best exemplified by an article published in *Vedomosti*, stating how the legitimacy of the Russian government is largely based on the idea of the country as a besieged fortress and on building the image of Russia as a great power capable of conducting spectacular foreign campaigns.[91] Here the West represents the besieging force with Russian grandeur and power, in other words—agency, embodied by the image of it being the great fortress. This metaphor resonates well with Wertsch's (2008) identification of the expulsion-of-foreign-enemies narrative schematic template allowing for the construction of national collective memory; as well as OS literature more broadly pointing to processes of "othering" in pursuit of constituting a distinct "self" (Rumelili, 2015, p. 54), Russia's recognition of its Russian self as distinct from its Western "self" more specifically (Steele, 2008), and the legitimizing role of OS more broadly (Huysmans, 1998; Kroliwkoski, 2008, 2018).

In support of these findings, we argue that central to Russian media's portrayal of the current and future global order is affirmation of Russian agency in world affairs as evidence of its international influence. Thus, Russian media's portrayal of the global order as an arrangement of three key players (Russia, US, and China) stresses great powers as the major actors in global affairs. Russia, being one of those powers, is shown as possessing considerable agency in the current global order evident by US and Western leaders' criticism of its ability to play spoiler in today's global order and projections of the future global order where Russian media emphasizes the nation's strong relationship with China—the preeminent rising power, suggesting Russia's continued agency in the future. Further feeding into Russian narratives regarding the importance of great powers within the global order are portrayals of its military strength. Here Russian media depicts the nation's military prowess, including its navy, newest missile technology, and space program and emphasizes future areas of dominance such as the Arctic regions and the Northern Sea Route. All this implicitly suggests that only a great power, like Russia, can boast such strong military forces, with articles making this more explicit by characterizing Russia as the main guarantor of security in the new world order,[92] thereby providing autobiographical continuity from its Soviet past to the present, and projected into the future.

Narrative trajectory/self reflection

As Browning and Joenniemi (2017) note, the general presupposition of most OS research is that actors prefer stability and certitude over change, as change is viewed as having a disturbing, anxiety-inducing effect leading to ontological *in*security. In Russia's case, while its narratives regarding its place in the current and future global order appear somewhat optimistic, focusing on projecting Russian influence and agency on the world stage; nonetheless, its doubling down on past anti-Western routine relationships, attachment to its military prestige harkening to days of Soviet strength, and reassertion of its sense of place through narratives of the Russian World, suggests the country is fixated by its previously held identities. As Mitzen (2006) explains, when confronted with moments of deep ontological insecurity, states can become consumed by crisis thereby falling back on previous routines to regain a limited sense of agency, even if past behaviors lead to continued conflict. This appears the case for Russia, in that the tumult it experienced in the 1990s combined with the failure to integrate into the US-led liberal order led the Russian state to return to its anti-Western worldview. Continued fears of Western encroachment into FSU territory combined with economic malaise due first to the collapse of oil prices and second from Western economic sanctions all solidify Russia's outsider identity, leading to identity securitization and closure (Rumelili, 2015; Kazharski, 2020).

The consequences of such rigid identity attachment include Russia being driven into flexing its military might and expression of general opposition to the West as a means to make tangible its identity as it as little economic or cultural success to fall back upon. In doing so, the inertial effects of its OS-seeking behavior makes substantive cooperation with the West unlikely. Indeed, even if relations temporarily warm, the deep-rooted nature of distrust, ossified by Russia's identity defined by its othering of the West makes any lasting partnership unlikely, unless Russia can develop new, more constructive means to define its sense of self.

Nonetheless, Russia's narrative ties to the East, specifically relations with China offer more flexibility. As part of its Russian World narrative, the salience and protection of a distinctive Russian identity through investments and cultivation of Russian civilizational grandeur might offer alternative means to strengthen Russian OS and reduce its geopolitical anxieties. As one article explains, competition is won not by who is smarter, stronger or richer, but by who becomes the dream for everyone else.[93] Thus, Russia's push to create an Eurasian economic union, if successful, might contribute to a sense of Russian OS by highlighting the common civilizational bonds that strengthen regional integration efforts in Eurasia (Russo & Stoddard, 2018). Furthermore, cooperative relations and deepening economic integration with China could not only produce economic growth within Russia but also provide a valuable ally on Russia's border, providing Russia with trust systems necessary for reflecting upon and evolving its sense of identity.

However, contradictions and challenges remain. As Russo and Stoddard (2018) note, the Russian view of Eurasianism does not imply equal status among Eurasian states. Rather, Russia is thought to remain the primary force within a Eurasian civilizational context. Not only does this place pressure on Russia to provide leadership among Eurasian nations, a challenge if Russia is unable to provide the soft power resources making such leadership attractive to its Eurasian partners, but China's rise relative to Russia could lead to eventual competition over who is Eurasia's pre-eminent power. Furthermore, as Russian media notes, the dangers of external, weaponized information undermining Russian cultural identity remains a significant concern. From discussions on the openness of the internet to even more mundane concerns regarding how to best deal with and Russify rap music, Russia's cultural challenges remain one of the most significant forms of competition Russia will face in the future global order.

Notes

1 RBC Daily (April 14, 2015). Factiva.
2 RIA Novosit (May 11, 2018). Factiva.
3 Itar-TASS (October 17, 2017). Factiva.
4 RIA Novosti (July 20, 2017). Factiva.
5 Itar-TASS (September 29, 2018). Factiva.
6 Ria Novosit (January 19, 2018). Factiva.
7 Rosbalt (July 12, 2016). Factiva.
8 Rosbalt (April 19, 2017). Factiva.
9 *Rossiyskaya Gazeta* (October 19, 2018). Factiva.
10 RIA Novosti (August 8, 2017). Factiva.

11 RIA Novosti (May 11, 2018). Factiva.
12 RIA Novosti (April 18, 2017). Factiva.
13 *Trud* (September 5, 2017). Factiva.
14 *Kommersant* (January 10, 2018). Factiva.
15 RiA Novosit (November 22, 2015). Factiva.
16 RBK (May 27, 2016). Factiva.
17 *Nezavisimaya Gazeta* (February 2, 2016). Factiva.
18 *Vedomosti* (August 26, 2014). Factiva.
19 *Rossiyskaya Gazeta* (September 8, 2017). Factiva.
20 *Rossiyskaya Gazeta* (July 27, 2018). Factiva.
21 Itar-TASS (July 3, 2014). Factiva.
22 Rosbalt (July 17, 2014). Factiva.
23 Itar-TASS (January 25, 2016). Factiva.
24 Izvestiya (February 14, 2017). Factiva.
25 Itar-TASS (October 17, 2017). Factiva.
26 *Vedomosti* (October 29, 2014). Factiva.
27 *Vedomosti* (March 15, 2017). Factiva.
28 Itar-TASS (October 17, 2017). Factiva.
29 *Argumenty I Fakti* (November 9, 2016). Factiva.
30 *Komsomolskaya Pravda* (May 15, 2014). Factiva.
31 RBC Daily (April 14, 2015). Factiva.
32 RIA Novosti (May 11, 2018); RIA Novosti (August 28, 2018). Factiva.
33 Itar-TASS (December 3, 2016). Factiva.
34 *Vedomosti* (March 15, 2017). Factiva.
35 *Vedomosti* (March 15, 2017). Factiva.
36 RIA Novosit (April 11, 2016). Factiva.
37 Itar-TASS (October 15, 2014). Factiva.
38 Ibid.
39 RBK (May 27, 2016). Factiva.
40 *Argumenty I Fakti* (March 5, 2014). Factiva.
41 Ibid.
42 *Moskovskiy Komsomolez* (June 13, 2018). Factiva.
43 Vesti.ru (November 20, 2014). Factiva.
44 *Vedomosti* (May 28, 2015). Factiva.
45 *Vedomosti* (December 8, 2017). Factiva.
46 *Rossiyskaya Gazeta* (September 24, 2015). Factiva.
47 *Nezavisimaya Gazeta* (July 3, 2015). Factiva.
48 Ibid.
49 *Nezavisimaya Gazeta* (September 21, 2016). Factiva.
50 *Moskovskiy Komsomolez* (December 8, 2016). Factiva.
51 Ibid.
52 Itar-TASS (October 15, 2014). Factiva.
53 Rosbalt (February 12, 2019). Factiva.
54 RIA Novosti (February 9, 2018). Factiva.
55 RBK (May 27, 2016). Factiva.
56 *Moskovskiy Komsomolez* (June 13, 2018). Factiva.
57 *Kommersant* (1/10/18). Factiva.
58 RIA Novosti (3/23/18). Factiva.
59 *Vedomosti* (3/15/17). Factiva.
60 RIA Novosti (7/20/17). Factiva.
61 Itar-Tass (2/26/19). Factiva.
62 Rosbalt (7/17/14). Factiva.
63 Itar-TASS (January 25, 2016). Factiva.
64 *Rossiyskaya Gazeta* (October 19, 2018). Factiva.

65 Itar-TASS (October 15, 2014). Factiva.
66 *Nezavisimaya Gazeta* (July 2, 2014). Factiva.
67 *Nezavisimaya Gazeta* (November 24, 2016). Factiva.
68 *Trud* (September 5, 2017). Factiva.
69 Ibid.
70 Itar-TASS (July 3, 2014). Factiva.
71 Itar-TASS (December 1, 2016). Factiva.
72 *Moskovskij Komsolets* (June 13, 2018). Factiva.
73 Itar-TASS (December 1, 2016). Factiva.
74 *Nezavisimaya Gazeta* (September 21, 2016). Factiva.
75 *Nezavisimaya Gazeta* (February 2, 2016). Factiva.
76 *Argumenty I Fakti* (March 5, 2014). Factiva.
77 *Rossiyskaya Gazeta* (May 14, 2015). Factiva.
78 Vesti.ru (November 20, 2014). Factiva.
79 *Rossiyskaya Gazeta* (May 14, 2015). Factiva.
80 *Izvestiya* (May 8, 2014). Factiva.
81 RIA Novosit (July 20, 2017). Factiva.
82 Itar-TASS (August 12, 2015). Factiva.
83 RT (April 23, 2019). Factiva.
84 Ibid.
85 Itar-TASS (March 31, 2014). Factiva.
86 *Argumenty I Fakti* (March 5, 2014). Factiva.
87 RIA Novosit (April 11, 2016). Factiva.
88 Itar-TASS (March 31, 2014). Factiva.
89 *Vedomosti* (May 12, 2017). Factiva.
90 Ibid.
91 *Vedomosti* (March 15, 2017). Factiva.
92 Itar-TASS (October 17, 2017). Factiva.
93 *Moskovskiy Komsomolez* (October 27, 2014). Factiva.

References

Agius, C. (2017). Drawing the discourses of ontological security: Immigration and identity in the Danish and Swedish cartoon crises. *Cooperation and Conflict*. 52 (1), 109–125.

Akchurina, V. & Della Sala, V. (2018). Russia, Europe and the ontological security dilemma: Narrating the emerging Eurasian space. *Europe-Asia Studies*. 70(10), 1638–1655.

Aleksashenko, S. (2012). Russia's economic agenda to 2020. *International Affairs*. 88(1), 31–48.

Belin, L. (2002). The Russian media in the 1990s. *The Journal of Communist Studies and Transition Politics*. 18(1), 139–160.

Biersack, J. & O'Lear, S. (2014). The geopolitics of Russia's annexation of Crimea: Narratives, identity, silences, and energy. *Eurasian Geography and Economics*. 55 (3), 247–269.

Breslauer, G. W. & Dale, C. (1997). Boris Yel'tsin and the invention of a Russian nation-state. *Post-Soviet Affairs*. 13(4), 303–332.

Browning, C. S. & Joenniemi, P. (2017). Ontological security, self-articulation and the securitization of identity. *Cooperation and Conflict*. 52(1), 31–47.

Burke, K. (1969). *A Grammar of Motives*. University of California Press.

Cash, J. & Kinnvall, C. (2017). Postcolonial bordering and ontological insecurities. *Postcolonial Studies*. 20(3), 267–274.

Chacko, P. (2014). A new "special relationship"?: Power transitions, ontological security, and India–US relations. *International Studies Perspectives*. 15(3), 329–346.

Clunan, A. L. (2018). Russia and the liberal world order. *Ethics & International Affairs*. 32(1), 45–59.

Combes, M. D. (2017). Encountering the stranger: Ontological security and the Boston Marathon bombing. *Cooperation and Conflict*. 52(1), 126–143.

Cooley, S. C. & Stokes, E. C. (2018). Manufacturing resilience: An analysis of broadcast and Web-based news presentations of the 2014–2015 Russian economic downturn. *Global Media and Communication*. 14(1), 123–139.

Crowley, M. & Ioffe, J. (2016). Why Putin hates Hillary. *Politico*. July 25, 2016. www.politico.com/story/2016/07/clinton-putin-226153.

Damm, E. B. & Cooley, S. (2017). Resurrection of the Russian Orthodox Church: Narrative of analysis of the Russian national myth. *Social Science Quarterly*. 98 (3), 942–957.

Forsberg, T., Heller, R., & Wolf, R. (2014). Status and emotions in Russian foreign policy. *Communist and Post-Communist Studies*. 47(3–4),261–268.

Freire, M. R. & Heller, R. (2018). Russia's power politics in Ukraine and Syria: Status-seeking between identity, opportunity and costs. *Europe-Asia Studies*. 70 (8), 1185–1212.

Gehlbach, S. (2010). Reflections on Putin and the media. *Post-Soviet Affairs*. 26(1), 77–87.

Gerber, T. P. (2015). Foreign policy and the United States in Russian public opinion. *Problems of Post-Communism*. 62(2), 98–111.

Giddens, A. (1991). *Modernity and self-identity: Self and society in the late Modern Age*. Stanford University Press.

Hansen, F. S. (2016). Russia's relations with the West: Ontological security through conflict. *Contemporary Politics*. 22(3), 359–375.

Heller, R. (2019). From community politics to the politicisation of community: The role of identity in Eurasian economic integration. *East European Politics*. 35(2), 122–142.

Herspring, D. (2009). *Civil-military relations in the United States and Russia: An alternative approach. Armed Forces & Society*. 35(4), 667–687.

Hill, F. & Gaddy, C. G. (2015). *Mr. Putin: Operative in the Kremlin*. Brookings Institution Press.

Hinck, R. S., Kluver, R., & Cooley, S. (2017). Russia re-envisions the world: Strategic narratives in Russian broadcast and news media during 2015. *Russian Journal of Communication*. 10(1), 21–37.

Huysmans, J. (1998). Security! What do you mean? From concept to thick signifier. *European Journal of International Relations*. 4(2), 226–255.

Jackson, W. D. (2004). Russia and the council of Europe: The perils of premature admission. *Problems of Post-Communism*. 51(5), 23–33.

Jamieson, K. H. (2020). *Cyberwar: How Russian hackers and trolls helped elect a president*. Oxford University Press.

Kanet, R. E. (2019). Russian strategic culture, domestic politics and Cold War 2.0. *European Politics and Society*. 20(2), 190–206.

Kazharski, A. (2020). Civilizations as ontological security?: Stories of the Russian trauma. *Problems of Post-Communism: Russia and Europe*. 67(1), 24–36.

Kinnvall, C., & Mitzen, J. (2017). An introduction to the special issue: Ontological securities in world politics. *Cooperation and Conflict*. 52(1), 3–11.

Kinnvall, C., Manners, I., & Mitzen, J. (2018). Introduction to 2018 special issue of European security: "Ontological (in)security in the European Union." *European Security*. 27(3), 249–265.

Kinnvall, C. (2004). Globalization and religious nationalism: Self, identity, and the search for ontological security. *Political Psychology*. 25(5), 741–767.

Krashenninikova, V. (2007). *Amerika-Rossiya: Kholodnaya voina kultur*. Evropa.

Krickovic, A. (2017). *The symbiotic China-Russia partnership: Cautious riser and desperate challenger. The Chinese Journal of International Politics*. 10(3), 299–329.

Krolikowski, A. (2008). State personhood in ontological security theories of international relations and Chinese nationalism: A skeptical view. *Chinese Journal of International Politics*. 2(1), 109–133.

Krolikowski, A. (2018). Shaking up and making up China: How the party-state compromises and creates ontological security for its subjects. *Journal of International Relations and Development*. 21(4), 909–933.

Larson, D. W. (2019). Status competition among Russia, India, and China in clubs: A source of stalemate or innovation in global governance. *Contemporary Politics*. 25(5), 549–566.

Lehtisaari, K. & Miazhevich, G. (2019). Introduction: the Russian media system at a crossroads. *Russian Journal of Communication*. 11(1), 1–5.

Levada Analytical Center. (2019). *Russian public opinion*. www.levada.ru/cp/wp-content/uploads/2019/07/2018-Eng.pdf.

Light, M. (2003). In search of an identity: Russian foreign policy and the end of ideology. *Journal of Communist Studies and Transition Politics*. 19(3), 42–59.

Lo, B. (2015). *Russia and the New World Disorder*. Brookings Institution Press/Chatham House.

Lowrey, W. & Erzikova, E. (2010). Institutional legitimacy and Russian news: Case studies of four regional newspapers. *Political Communication*. 27(3), 275–288.

Mankoff, J. (2012). *Russian foreign policy: The return of great power politics* (2nd Ed,). Rowman & Littlefield Publishers.

McFaul, M. & Stoner-Weiss, K. (2008). The myth of the authoritarian model: How Putin's crackdown holds Russia back. *Foreign Affairs*. 87(1), 68–84.

Medinskiy, V. (2010). *Ob 'osobom puti' i zagadocnoi russkoi dushe*. Olma.

Miskimmon, A. & O'Loughlin, B. (2017). Russia's narratives of global order: Great power legacies in a polycentric world. *Politics and Governance*. 5(3), 111–120.

Mitzen, J. (2006). Ontological security in world politics: State identity and the security dilemma. *European Journal of International Relations*. 12(3), 341–370.

Oates, S. (2006). *Television, democracy and elections in Russia*. Routledge.

Oates, S. (2007). The neo-Soviet model of the media. *Europe-Asia Studies: Symposium on the Post-Soviet Media*. 59(8), 1279–1297.

Pasti, S. (2005). Two generations of contemporary Russian journalists. *European Journal of Communication*. 20(1), 89–115.

Paul, C. & Matthews, M. (2016). *The Russian "firehose of falsehood" propaganda model*. Rand Corporation.

Roselle, L. (2017). Strategic narratives and great power identity. In A. Miskimmon, B. O'Loughlin, & L. Roselle (Eds.), *Forging the world: Strategic narratives and international relations*, 56–84. University of Michigan Press.

Roudakova, N. (2008). Media-political clientelism: Lessons from anthropology. *Media, Culture & Society.* 30(1), 41–59.

Rumelili, B. (2015). Identity and desecuritisation: The pitfalls of conflating ontological and physical security. *Journal of International Relations and Development.* 18(1), 52–74.

Russo, A. & Stoddard, E. (2018). Why do authoritarian leaders do regionalism? Ontological security and Eurasian regional cooperation. *The International Spectator.* 53(3), 20–37.

Skalamera, M. (2018). Understanding Russia's energy turn to China: Domestic narratives and national identity priorities. *Post-Soviet Affairs.* 34(1), 55–77.

Snetkov, A. (2012). When the internal and external collide: A saocial constructivist reading of Russia's security policy. *Europe-Asia Studies.* 64(3), 521–542.

Steele, B. J. (2008). *Ontological security in international relations: Self-identity and the IR state.* Routledge.

Subotić, J. (2016). Narrative, ontological security, and foreign policy change. *Foreign Policy Analysis.* 12(4), 610–627.

Szostek, J. (2017). Defence and promotion of desired state identity in Russia's strategic narrative. *Geopolitics.* 22(3), 571–593.

Szostek, J. (2018). News media repertoires and strategic narrative reception: A paradox of dis/belief in authoritarian Russia. *New Media and Society.* 20(1), 68–87.

Vartanova, E. (2011). The Russian media model in the context of post-Soviet dynamics. In D. Hallin & P. Mancini (Eds), *Comparing media systems beyond the Western world*, 119–142. Cambridge: Cambridge University Press.

Vartanova, E. (2016). Media ownership and concentration in Russia. In E. Noam (Ed.), *Who owns the world's media? Media concentration and ownership around the world*, 276–310. Oxford University Press.

Voltmer, K. (2000). Constructing political reality in Russia: Izvestiya - Between old and new journalistic practices. *European Journal of Communication.* 15(4), 469–500.

Wertsch, J. V. (2008). The narrative organization of collective memory. *Ethos.* 36 (1), 120–135.

Zarakol, A. (2010). Ontological (in)security and state denial of historical crimes: Turkey and Japan. *International Relations.* 24(1), 3–23.

Zygar, M. (2016). The Russian reset that never was. *Foreign Policy.* December 6, 2016. https://foreignpolicy.com/2016/12/09/the-russian-reset-that-never-was-putin-obama-medvedev-libya-mikhail-zygar-all-the-kremlin-men/.

5 Ontological Security Narratives in Venezuelan Media

Imperial Sharks and Identity Attachments amidst a Collapsing Domestic Order

Introduction

Over the past two decades Venezuela has positioned itself as a regional leader in Latin America aligned against US interests and neoliberal policies. Led by its populist president, Hugo Chávez, from 1999 until 2013, the country underwent profound political and social transformations (Hawkins, 2010); with Chavismo becoming Venezuela's guiding political ideology and grand strategy (Mijares, 2017) characterized by Manichean juxtaposing of socialism, participatory democracy, and Latin Americanism against neoliberalism, bourgeois-liberal democracy, and US imperialism (de la Torre, 2017). Thus, departing from previous Venezuelan administrations, Chávez reoriented Venezuela's foreign policy by placing the US as its main adversary with Venezuela actively trying to counter and frustrate US goals (Corrales, 2011) while also promoting policies of regional political integration in Latin America and the Caribbean to keep US influence and interventionism at bay (Angosto-Ferrández, 2013). While Venezuela largely succeeded in these endeavors, with Angosto-Ferrández (2013) concluding that Venezuela "is an increasingly influential agent in the international arena, a leader in regional integration projects, and a referent for transcontinental movements advocating a multipolar world" (p. 3); Romero and Mijares (2016) argue that Venezuela's continuation of this foreign policy positioning is unsustainable, owing to low oil prices, and key allies, like Brazil and Russia, facing their own socioeconomic problems.

Indeed, despite Venezuela boasting the world's largest known oil reserves, today the country faces widespread unemployment, crumbling infrastructure, corruption, and a humanitarian crisis, among a host of other problems. As Tarver (2018) argues, the age of Chavismo ended with Chávez's death in 2013 with Venezuela entering a new age of socialist collapse. Likewise, even though Venezuela's current, albeit disputed, president Nicolás Maduro was Chávez's handpicked successor, Smilde (2015) concludes that Maduro's widespread disapproval, lack of charisma, inability to govern, and Venezuela's crumbling economic and social system

DOI: 10.4324/9781003197478-5

suggests that, under Maduro, Chavismo "does not seem a sustainable form of governance or even a viable electoral contender" (p. 54). Over the past few years, Venezuela's domestic situation has only worsened. In 2018 inflation hit 80,000 percent, marking the collapse of the Venezuelan economy. This led to widespread violence and a worsening humanitarian crisis with 80% of households unable to access enough food in addition to the severe lack of public healthcare (Pérez, 2019; Specia, 2019; Krygier & Faiola, 2018).

And yet, despite these ominous conditions for his people, Maduro continues to refuse international aid and blames US sanctions for Venezuela's hardships (Kiger, 2019; Krygier & Faiola, 2018). From the perspective of OS, while nations require a sense of biographical continuity, with Venezuela appearing to prioritize its sense of self through its attachment to its Chavismo identity, these attachments can trap nations into unhealthy conflict and routine behaviors. As Mitzen (2006) explains, although "routines that perpetuate physical insecurity can provide ontological security (OS), states can become attached to physically dangerous relationships and be unable, or unwilling, to learn their way out" (p. 354). In the case of Venezuela, as its domestic situation deteriorates, leading to declining support for Maduro's continuation of Chavismo policies and pursuit of abrasive and isolationist policies in the region (Romero & Mijares, 2016), the government's ability to provide OS for its citizens is in jeopardy. As Krolikowski (2018) argues, if a state's "enemies and dangers multiply and cannot be coherently perceived or organized, this actor finds themselves in a state of crisis and loses trust in their capacity to manage these threats" (p. 915).

How then Venezuela manages its identity as a regional leader and challenger to US influence in Latin America while battling its domestic crises has significant impact on the international order and Venezuela's much needed ability to participate and compete within the global economy. Thus, this chapter examines how Venezuelan media report upon the future of global competition and Venezuela's tenuous position in the current and future world order. Specifically, it argues that Venezuela's postcolonial identity and attachment to Marxist-Leninist ideology provides some narrative continuity and cognitive order in describing the routine relationships constituting the global order to its citizens, reflective in part of its Chavismo identity. Nonetheless this narrative characterization fails to provide a sense of security for self, arising from Venezuela's failed material realities, both domestically and internationally, marking it as a target for foreign military invasion and informational/cultural encroachment. As a result, globally, Venezuelan media depicts the country at the hands of imperial nations, both past but also present and emerging ones, like the US and China; domestically, its media portray a Venezuela in crisis with humanitarian and political concerns regarding the state's ability to provide for its citizens suggesting the basic trust systems promised in

Chávez-Maduro's vision for a socialist state is unraveling. The consequences of Venezuela's self-reported weakened state are seen in its inability to influence its international environment and general decline in diplomatic and economic capabilities from years past. In sum, Venezuelan media narratives construct the global order as broken and corrupt with Venezuela domestically incapacitated to act or exert influence to safeguard the nation in the present, let alone the future.

Historical overview

Venezuela was, in recent history, a stable democracy flush with funds from its natural supply of oil, marking it as one of the fastest growing economies in Latin America. After the discovery of oil in the early 1920s, its political system began shifting from a dictatorship towards more democratic rule, with democracy taking root in the late 1950s. During this time a representative presidential model and power sharing between three dominant political parties was put into place, though democratic rule continued to be guided by an economic elite (McCarthy-Jones & Turner, 2011). As a result, Venezuela's political stability relied on stable economic growth premised on healthy oil prices in the international market, with Mijares (2017) concluding that Venezuela reflects Karl's (1997) archetypal petro-state.

However, owing to its reliance on oil revenue, and following the oil shocks of 1970s and 1980s, Venezuela's economy began to collapse with social mobility falling, eventually leading to political and economic crises in the 1990s. As a result, Venezuela was forced to seek an IMF bailout with subsequent imposition of austerity measures allowing for Hugo Chávez's rise (McCarthy-Jones & Turner, 2011). Although Chávez led a failed coup intended to oust President Carlos Pérez in 1992, for which Chávez was jailed; two years later he was pardoned. Following his release, he formed a political party known as the Fifth Republican Movement (Kiger, 2019). Aided by the economic impact of collapsing oil prices from the 1997 Asian financial crisis (Mijares, 2017), Chávez successfully led his populist movement and was elected president in 1998 whereby he began a massive socialist overhauling and transformation of Venezuelan politics through his Bolivarian Revolution and Chavismo ideology (Hawkins, 2010; Kiger, 2019).

Early in his presidency, Chávez implemented new domestic politics aimed at the total transformation of Venezuelan society, solidifying a new national ideology known as Chavismo (Mijares, 2017; Hawkins, 2010). According to Krygier and Faiola (2018) his vision was premised on empowering the poor working class through welfare programs and leftist labor laws with Hawkins (2003) characterizing the Chavismo populist movement as reliant on constructing charismatic linkages between voters and politicians by pitting the people versus the elite. Thus, under the guise of promoting more participatory models of democracy and pursuing nationalist redistributive economic policies, Chávez was able to convene a constitutional assembly to remake Venezuela's existing institutions (de la Torre, 2017). This resulted in the writing of a new constitution, the disbandment of the previous Congress and Supreme Court, and the holding of mega elections to elect a new unicameral parliament with Chávez as president (McCarthy-Jones & Turner, 2011).

According to Mijares (2017) Venezuela's new Chavismo ideology not only became Venezuela's guiding political ideology but also its grand strategy dictating the country's domestic and international policy goals born against the backdrop of the emerging unipolar order from the fall of the Soviet Union. Specifically, Chávez's foreign policy was fueled by an ideological component with Chávez viewing his mission to liberate Venezuela and Latin America from US imperialism (Levisky & Roberts, 2011), thereby shifting Venezuela's foreign policy from previous presidents by placing the US as the country's main adversary (Correles, 2011). In support of this vision, Chávez aimed to reshape international geopolitics towards multicentrism and pluripolarity (Angosto-Ferrández, 2013). According to de la Torre (2017) evidence of this vision was clear in Venezuela's 2001–2007 Economic Development plan, which presented Venezuela's policy promoting participative democracy worldwide as well as a multipolar world order as a corrective to US hegemony. In support of these aims, Venezuela sponsored policies designed to build regional political integration in Latin America and the Caribbean (Angosto-Ferrández, 2013), largely fueled by Venezuela's oil industry. Thus, Chávez promoted profligate spending both at home and abroad to win over key allies with offers of investments, aid, and subsidies to other nations with few conditions. This policy won Venezuela international allies: mainly those who refused to criticize the Chávez government, those willing to accept his financial support, and those with anti-American and populist politics; marking this strategy as Chávez's "centerpiece" of Venezuelan foreign policy (Corrales, 2009, p. 100).

Ontological security and Venezuela

Introduced to International Relations scholarship around 2004, ontological security (OS) is a 60-year-old concept that draws from psychoanalysis, sociology, and political psychology (Kinnvall et al., 2018; Mitzen, 2017). Above all, OS examines the relationship between identity, security, and agency. For individuals, OS refers to a "person's fundamental sense of safety in the world and includes a basic trust of other people" (Giddens, 1991, p. 38). As Vieira (2016) notes, like individuals, state actors also have a need for stable and consistent identities. This stability is achieved through routines embedded in biographical narratives created by entities such as the government, media, and public intellectuals. Thus, OS is formed and maintained via a state's relationship with others, including recognition from other international actors, constituting the actor's basic trust system through the regularizing of social life making the actor's environment and sense of self knowable, thereby providing the capacity to act (Mitzen, 2006).

Importantly, states are argued to be key providers of OS for their citizenry (Steele, 2008; Krolikowski, 2008, 2018; Chacko, 2014) with Huysmans (1998) and Krolikowski (2018) arguing state legitimacy is predicated on the government's ability to provide cognitive security and order by making abstract fears knowable and manageable. In relation to Venezuela, OS studies on populism provide a particularly useful lens to understand the rise and appeal of Chávez and his Chavismo ideology. As Steele and Homolar (2019) argue, the rise of populism around the globe has been driven by both a loss of confidence in mainstream politics and political candidates and perceptions of an increasingly "runaway world" beyond our control (p. 214). In this sense, the economic malaise, political corruption, and anti-elitism endured by Venezuela in the 1990s created the ontologically *in*secure conditions for a populist uprising led by Chávez.

More specifically, Steele and Homolar (2019) posit three primary connections between populism and OS: first, both OS and populism attempt to manage anxiety through routine—this often comes in the form of resistance to expertise, where ignorance and rejection of facts becomes a key coping mechanism. Second, both also focus on a relationship between narratives and memory. Specifically, narratives of the past offer continuity and become "an entry point for a populist politics that utilizes promises to regenerate and reinforce past notions of belonging and inclusion" especially when states or agents have experienced trauma or anxiety (p. 216). Finally, the rise of "radical disruptions" that have come with late modernity call into question our notions of "self" and "others" fostering high anxiety and loss of confidence in biographical continuity. These critical situations "both enable and are created and performed by the populist politics" (p. 216), owing to their high unpredictability.

The Chavismo ideology and larger Bolivarian movement promoted by Chávez fit nicely within Steele and Homolar's (2019) framework in that Chávez's radical democratic socialism and nationalization of key industries undermined both economic and technical elites pitting them against the "people" while setting up new institutions designed to routinize this form of participatory democracy and large scale populist elections. Furthermore, Chávez was able to legitimize his movement by initially making good on his promise to deliver a new 21st-century democratic socialism by increasing direct subsidies for the poor and new social programs providing health care, educational services, and food funded by Venezuela's windfall oil profits (de la Torre, 2017).

Importantly, Chávez was also able to draw upon past narratives and national memory. Specifically, Chávez's construction of a larger Bolivarian movement drew upon narratives of past trauma drawn from Latin America's historical colonial subjugation and past revolutionary republican independences. In doing so, his Bolivarian revolution invoked regional identities and narratives of Latin American brotherhood by drawing upon former leaders and intellectuals, such as Venezuelan President Simón Bolívar, Cuban patriot Jose Marti, and Argentinean author Manuel Ugarte as sources for member identification and supranational policy characterizations (Angosto-Ferrández, 2013). Further supporting this anti-colonial identity was Chávez's critical stance towards the US; not only did Chávez call President George W. Bush the "devil" but also utilized the term "imperialism" to describe US actions in world affairs (McCarthy-Jones & Turner, 2011). Thus, as Cash and Kinnvall (2017) argue, post-colonial borders and the search for OS are intimately connected to a nation's "national fantasies" as political collectives' desire a sense of national wholeness and stable self. As a result, sources of ontological attachment defining one's identity include narratives anchored in providing a sense of home and past practices by drawing upon emotional memories and symbols while also seeking to define a sense of self through defining the "other" or "stranger" (Agius, 2017; Combes, 2017). Here, Chávez's Bolivarian Revolution constituted this new national fantasy drawing from highly emotive regional memories of Latin America's fight against the colonial other.

Venezuelan media

While the political and economic crises Venezuela faced throughout the 1990s created the conditions for Chávez's new narrative vision and national identity for Venezuela to take hold, he needed control over the media to institutionalize his ideological vision. In this sense, as Subotić (2016) explains, during times of great crisis, political elites can construct new narratives providing a feeling of state OS by offering autobiographical continuity, a sense of routine, familiarity, and calm; but these narratives are not left unchallenged, and are contested not only domestically but also by elites. Indeed, Chávez's remaking of Venezuelan politics did not go unchallenged with opposition parties even succeeding in creating a recall election against Chávez in 2004. Nonetheless, Chávez fought off the opposition to win the recall election through deft use of the media and political messaging demonizing leaders of the opposition as backed by the "Devil" and supported by "the biggest devil of all, George W. Bush" (Hawkins, 2010, p. 2). This narrative contestation highlights Arsenault, Hong, and Price's (2017) argument regarding the importance of the media landscape in that "it is in these mediated spaces that narratives are validated, contested, and ultimately made into reality" (p. 204).

Thus, control of the media was center stage in Chávez's struggle for hegemony within Venezuela with the state creating new laws to regulate the media market and colonize Venezuela's public sphere (de la Torre, 2017). Beyond regulating media content, Chávez also removed radio and television frequencies from critics with the state becoming the main communicator through control of 64% of television channels, leading to the public media becoming tools in the hand of the government (Corrales, 2015). In support of his populist, charismatic image of leadership, Chávez even created his own TV show and forced all media venues to air it, including his four to six hour weekly Sunday address to the nation where he sang popular songs and discussed his personal life and dreams. (de la Torre, 2017). Therefore, while under the Chávez formal pieces of participatory democracy were embraced other democratic institutions, such as the autonomy of the media, were severely challenged (Schiller, 2018).

More recently, this dismantling of Venezuela's free press, which began under Chávez's rule, has become increasingly worse (Freedom House, 2019). Currently, critics have accused today's disputed President Maduro of utilizing similar tactics as Chávez, especially when it comes to persecuting hostile and oppositional media outlets. This has led to Venezuela's media falling into a state of distress declining 27 slots from 2014 to 2017 on Reporters Without Borders World Press Freedom Index (Allsop, 2019). Indeed, by 2017 nearly 40 independent radio stations have closed, owing to state shutdowns with others going out of business, owing to economic conditions. Moreover, by 2019 most independent newspapers had closed, while some operated in an exclusively digital format but subjected to frequent blackouts and blocking via the state run CANTV service provider, which owns most of Venezuela's communications infrastructure (Freedom House, 2019). In 2019, "el Nacional" the last anti-government newspaper circulating nationally went out of print (Allsop, 2019).

Beyond the newspaper industry, the majority of the television services are state run with frequent media blackouts occurring when global news outlets spotlight current deleterious conditions in Venezuela. Even internet freedom has been in a state of decline in recent years moving from "partly free" to "not free" in reports from Freedom House in 2017. Still, despite frequent internet blackouts and underfunded web infrastructure leading to almost unusable connection speeds, networks of activists and former journalists have continued to fight back through services like "WhatsApp" thereby teaching citizens how to navigate online restrictions and maintain some oppositional support (Nugent, 2019).

Today's Venezuela and the global order

While Chávez succeeded in promoting his national vision of a Chavismo, Bolavarian Revolution during his decade and a half tenure as president, his death in 2013 and Venezuela's crumbling economic infrastructure has placed the nation in a new crisis of identity. As Romero and Mijares (2016) explain, Chávez enjoyed extra ordinary conditions enabling his foreign policy successes, including high oil revenue, the rise of emerging powers, and US geostrategic orientation away from the region. Thus, high oil prices from 2003 to 2009 fueled Venezuela's "international spending spree" with Chávez collecting allies and establishing new multilateral regional organizations undermining US authority and influence (Corrales, 2011, p. 33). However, Venezuela's "expansive and military policy" in international affairs is now unsustainable (Romero & Mijares, 2016, p. 188), especially as oil prices have collapsed to an all-time low. Moreover, these problems are exacerbated by Venezuela's domestic situation. Since Maduro's election after Chávez's death, Venezuela's economy has continued to spiral into crisis with *The Washington Post* noting, "Experts attribute the crash to a toxic mix of failed socialist policies, corruption, mismanagement and lower oil prices—the last disaster for a country with the world's largest proven oil reserves" (Krygier & Faiola, 2018, p. 1). Thus, Venezuela's influence in the global order appears at a crossroads with its foreign policy constrained by its fragile domestic situation and inability to compete in international markets.

Indeed, on the international front, whereas once Venezuela was an influential agent and leader in regional integration projects (Angosto-Ferrández, 2013), today its leadership is in doubt. Whereas Chávez was able to set up multiple regional organizations including the Bolivarian Alliance for America's (ALBA), the Union of South American Nations (UNASUR), and Community of Latin American and Caribbean States (CELAC), among others, its influence in these organizations has diminished; including its ideological appeal no longer holding sway among partner nations. For instance, Romero and Mijares (2016) point out that Ecuador and Bolivia have distanced themselves from Venezuela's economic model with Cuba, a staunch supporter of Venezuela and it's anti-US orientation, now beginning the process of rapprochement with the US. Likewise, Cusack (2018) concludes that ALBA faces significant challenges moving forward, and suggests the organization is trapped following Venezuela's "ever grander plans with ever lesser credibility, leaving both in danger of disintegration" (p. 23).

Like its multilateral relations, Venezuela's bilateral alliances have weakened. Maduro has been unable to maintain alliances with Middle Eastern partners—such as Iraq, Libya, Syria, and Algeria—while Brazil and Russia, its main political and economic partners, are weakened by their own economic and domestic political problems (Romero & Mijares, 2016). Russia in particular has been a key ally of Venezuela supplying significant military weaponry and provision of loans with Venezuela's financial debt to Russia continuing to soar. Likewise, seeking to diversify its partners for energy exports, Venezuela has turned to and become increasingly dependent on China for aid. Today, as Venezuela undergoes significant domestic turmoil, Chinese and Russian loans have managed to keep the Venezuelan economy afloat, with Venezuela owing the two nations at least $100 billion (Sigalos, 2019).

The interrelated nature of Venezuela's foreign and domestic political problems is evident by China and Russia's initial pause regarding their continued support for Maduro given the extent of Venezuela's opposition leader Juan Guido's challenge to Maduro's authority. Indeed, as Angosto-Ferrández (2013) argues, it is difficult to discern the boundaries between Venezuela's domestic and international politics and rhetoric with Chavismism manifesting itself through its resiliency in support of the political regime (Anselmi, 2016; Mijares, 2017) and continuities in foreign policy (Romero & Mijares, 2016). Although now China and Russia appear to be backing Maduro out of concern over whether Juan Guido would recognize Venezuela's debt obligations (Sigalos, 2019), nonetheless Guido has garnered significant international support for his cause with over 50 countries, including the US, recognizing his leadership (Human Rights Watch, 2019).

Thus, today Venezuela faces a perilous situation. According to Pew Research, Venezuelan public opinion of its economic situation has dropped with 44% of respondents viewing it favorably in 2013 and only 20% in 2017. In 2018 Maduro's election placed the country in crisis, met with accusations of fraud, voter intimidation, and massive uprisings as hundreds of thousands of Venezuelan protestors took to the streets led by head of the National Assembly Juan Guido who called for fair and free elections. Eventually, Guido declared himself interim president of Venezuela and demanded Maduro allow international humanitarian aid into the country as citizens faced widespread shortages of basic goods, food, and medicines. But Maduro blocked the aid and called Guido's movement an attempted coup, subsequently cracking down on the opposition (BBC, 2020) with many fearing an escalation of the crisis, including the possibility of foreign intervention into Venezuela's politics (NPR, 2019). In this case, blaming the US and its sanctions against Venezuela, Maduro's rhetoric reminiscently drew upon Chávez's own response to opposition during his 2004 recall election by claiming US influence was supporting the opposition. However, Maduro has gone further by sealing Venezuela's Colombian and Brazilian borders to prevent international interference, further disrupting US-Venezuelan relations (Specia, 2019). As Romero and Mijares (2016) explain, while Maduro himself has staked his political legitimacy on the political model inherited by his predecessor, including the same objectives and mechanisms of control, importantly Venezuela's "domestic and international conditions have changed, making the continuity of the Chávez doctrine a toxic necessity for Maduro's foreign policy" (p. 190).

What remains in store for Venezuela remains unknown. Whether the nation remains attached to the identities and narratives perpetuated by Chávez or is able to adapt its identity and secure a sense of self both at home and in the international order remains to be seen. Regardless, its relationships with the international community appears in flux with its previous routines and behaviors allowing for its rise in international influence under threat from an ideological weakening both at home and abroad, further constrained by an economy in collapse. Therefore, to determine how Venezuelan media narrates and makes sense of what the future global order holds, and Venezuela's place within it, this chapter asks two questions:

RQ1. How do Venezuelan media narrate the future global order?
RQ2. How do Venezuelan media narrate the future of global competition?

Method

For a full description of the methodology, see Chapter 2. As a synopsis, researchers employed a mixed methodological design including qualitative narrative analysis aided by the text-mining program KH coder as well as a quantitative content analysis. The study analyzed over 60 native language Venezuelan news articles across fifteen media sources provided by the Factiva data base from December 2014 until 2019. Researchers conducted a systematic random sampling at a 90% confidence interval of the articles collected by using a series of keywords (international/global influence, global order, international/global competition).

The qualitative narrative analysis applied a grounded theory approach with researchers beginning by reading through all of the sampled articles before identifying emerging patterns which were then abstracted into larger thematic categories. Focus was placed on understanding the narrative structure of the news articles in relation to their depiction of the global order and competition within it with narrative broadly conceptualized using Burke's (1969) definition of narratives including act, agents, scenes, instruments, and purpose.

For the quantitative analysis, two coders analyzed the news articles using four general categories with subsequent subtopical categories. The first two broad categories were used to determine how Venezuela narrated the nature of global competition, including mentions of Venezuela key vulnerabilities and necessary capabilities with subcategories related to the DIME instrument of power framework. Two further broad categories were included to capture Venezuela media portrayals of the global order. The first including depictions of escalation management, deterrence, redlines, competitors, and alliances; and the second, including stated viewpoints related to Venezuela's depiction of the make-up of the future global order, Venezuela's role in the global order, as well as valence of US and Western Europe's role in the global order.

RQ1. How do Venezuelan media narrate the future global order?

Figure 5.1 depicts the predominate themes in Venezuelan media discourse surrounding global order as notably including nations such as China and the US and topics including, nations-justice-law, liberal-western-other, sovereignty-interest-hegemonic-able-own, tensions-peaceful-phase-period, and America-Europe-defense-civilization. These themes coalesce within Venezuelan media narratives presenting the current and future of global order and competition

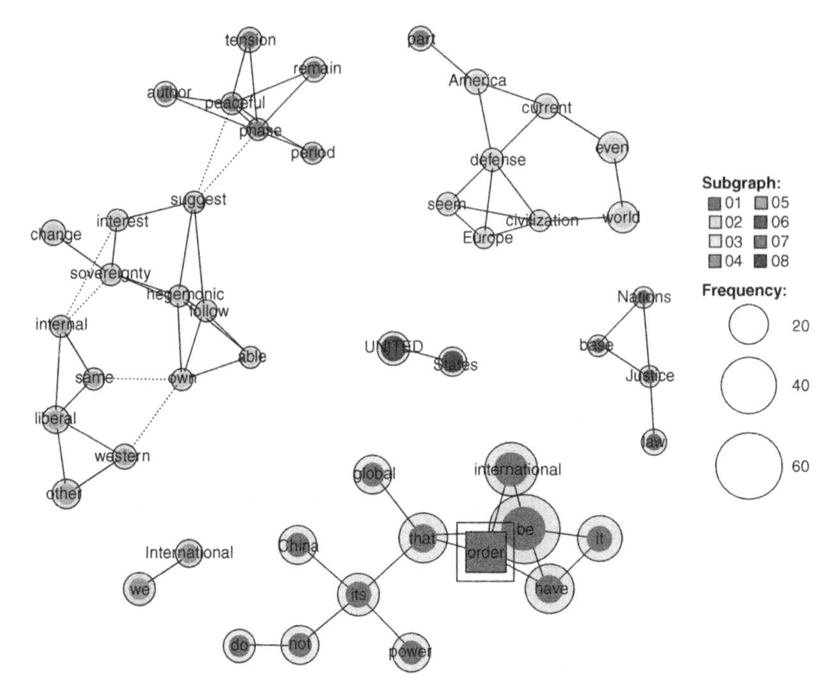

Figure 5.1 Co-occurrence Network of Venezuelan Reporting Referencing "Global Order"

within it in ideological terms whereby imperialist nations of all sorts, including the US, China, and Russia, compete for their own economic and political influence irrespective of other countries' overall wellbeing in face of international law designed to protect and safeguard nations' sovereignty. Thus, the current and future global order is a story of great power competition, of which Venezuela is not a competitor. Instead, Venezuela is viewed as weak and susceptible to negatively characterized foreign influence, especially given its weakened state from domestic turmoil.

As Table 5.1 illustrates, Venezuelan media discussions about the global order are highly negative. Venezuela's role in the global order is only discussed in slightly over a quarter of the articles (n = 17; 28%) with a

Table 5.1 Venezuelan Media Views on the Global Order and the West

	Article Mentions	*Valence (1=positive, -1=negative)*
Venezuela's Role in Global Order	N = 17 (28%)	Mean =.-.35
Perspectives of Global Order	N = 33 (53%)	Mean = -.55
Perspectives on the US	N = 35 (57%)	Mean = -.40
Perspectives on Western Europe	N = 11 (18%)	Mean = -.18

negative valence (m = -.35). The global order is viewed even more negatively (m = -.55) with perceptions of the US and Western Europe also negative, albeit the US more so (m = -.4 and m = -.18 respectively). In this sense, Venezuelan media show little optimism or a positive role for Venezuela to play on the international stage.

Global order

Venezuelan media narrate a weak global order with multilateral institutions providing the only safeguards against imperialist impulses. Imperialist nations are viewed as threatening developing countries' sovereignty and taking advantage of their natural resources, with articles explaining the routine behavior and modus operandi of imperialist nations in negative terms including their imposition of unilateral coercive measures to promote changes in foreign governments, control of developing countries' natural wealth, and subjugation of others through their hegemonic power.[1] In doing so, these unilateral actions violate the principles of state sovereignty and non-interference in the internal affairs of states, as well the freedom of international trade.[2] More specifically, the economic policies of imperialist countries are described as self-serving and predatory, all designed to augment their power. Imperialist countries and their oligopolies thus compete in the dividing of the world into zones of influence, both with the desire to expand their sources of production and the obtainment of natural resources, which allows them to expand their markets and hegemonic power in general.[3]

Beyond economic power, Venezuelan media explain imperialist nations as drawing upon their hegemonic influence to extend their power into the cultural realm through communication technologies used to support large corporations. Thus, ideological and cultural imperialist domination is promoted through modernized hegemonic control devices that include cell phones, social networks, Internet search engines, online stores and other consumerist advances of the times through their strategic offering of such technologies as voluntarily and free of charge, leading to populations giving their personal, sensitive information to large corporations.[4]

In contrast, international institutions are shown as providing the legal framework safeguarding state sovereignty. In doing so, they allow for the democratic participation and the formation of a nation's self-determination to define its own culture and values which stand in opposition to the hegemonic attempts by imperialist nations. For instance, articles note how the international order, represented by the United Nations (UN), is the indispensable foundation of a more peaceful, prosperous, and just world.[5] Specifically, the values embedded in the UN Charter are described as reaffirming the values of international law and justice through their creation of an international order based on the rule of law.[6] Venezuelan media consistently attach importance to the legal nature of the international order, which provides some normative protection from imperialist countries and defines the identity of the international order as separate from imperialist behavior. As a report from *Panorama* explains, the guiding principles of international law, supported and codified by numerous UN resolutions, emphasize the sovereign rights of states to decide their own political, economic, social, and cultural models; and yet, despite this, imperialist nations continue in their efforts to impose their own unique model of civilization.[7]

Other examples of articles juxtaposing the values of the international order with the desires of imperialist nations include those describing the international order as fair, inclusive, multicentric, and pluripolar whereas, in contrast, hegemonic powers possess unilateral tendencies.[8] While the values of the international order dictate strict respect for the people's right to self-determination, including both the institutions chosen by them and the diverse cultures that exist on the planet, unilateral actions by imperialist nations through their interventionist practices are incompatible with the principles of international law and the UN charter.[9]

While Venezuela attaches the protection of international law as its basic trust system governing international affairs, it also notes its fragility. Specifically, reports explain the normative forces required to sustain commitments to international law as including actors' abilities to agree on how to coordinate their behavior and cooperatively and consistently articulate its norms and values; unfortunately, this coordination falls into the hands of international politics, inhibiting and undermining its efficacy.[10] Indeed, as an article from *El Universal* notes, the problem posed by international politics is that politicians ignore the rulings of international bodies which eroding both the normative power of international law and the ordering of international relations in the world today.[11] Thus, the international system can only exist when states honor its main obligations; only from states' previous protection and affirmation of these rights has an international constitution composed of national and international sources been able to achieve such an international legal system. The article continues by warning how pretending to turn back on such agreements is to be on the sideline of advancing a civilized legal global order—a position held by uncivilized, imperialist nations—in contrast to Venezuela's membership and affirmation within the civilized club of nations supportive of international law.

Continuity and change in the global order: Same Imperialism but new great powers

The predominant discussion of global order revolves around Venezuelan media describing it as undergoing a transition caused by US decline with new great powers filling the void albeit still performing the similar routine behavior of imperialist nations. Articles note how we live in a historical period right before a phase of a ruptured, old international order where the US was the only great power with global disorder having generated geostrategic uncertainty.[12] The current order is shown as self-unraveling, with Venezuelan media narrating the problem in Marxist-Leninist terms and the decline of neoliberal globalization[13] illustrated by the US and Great Britain's retreat from international trade and divides among the world's financial elites. For instance, Venezuelan media report how the political forces backing Trump and Brexit took advantage of the disagreement of workers and other social sectors affected by neoliberal globalization by seizing their governments in order to destroy their global order resulting in the imperial powers financial elites and ruling classes' confusion over how this occurred.[14] Other articles attribute the bankruptcy of Lehman Brothers as creating the space for this new world order whereby galloping unemployment, harsh austerity measures, and rampant inequality catapulted extremist formations from the left, but especially the right.[15] The result was a transformation of economic political thinking where vestiges of bad policies that harmed economic growth had flourished.

Venezuelan media appear conflicted with this new economic global order. Some articles point out how officials from European nations warn against these isolationist measures. For instance, articles cite Spanish leaders who note how everyone embedded in the global order remained opposed to the departure of the UK from the European Union (EU),[16] and Germen officials warning that too much is at stake for Brexit to be taken lightly with its manifestation being a warning for others not to take for granted the rules undergirding the international order.[17] Other articles, however, are more supportive and note the need for a new mechanism for re-founding the geopolitical and economic-financial system as the global order is already in a spin.[18] These new mechanism reference stalwart institutions, including suggestions of the creation of a new Bretton Woods system with new formulas for governing globalization and restoring the multilateralism that generated the geostrategic "siesta" at the end of the Cold War.[19] Such calls reaffirm some of the values of the current neo-liberal order. Indeed the need for this re-founding comes in response to contemporary forces seen as challenging the current order, such as Trump's America first agenda described as putting the first world power, America, into a dangerous path of protectionism and international insulation.[20] Nonetheless, other articles take the opposite stance, arguing that capitalism, through its most modern form of globalization, must change or collapse.[21] The contradiction between those in support for the international neo-liberal trading order and those against reflect Venezuela's cultural past and Chávez inspired identity as a proud socialist country fighting against Western imperialism but also its relationships with other nations and the need to trade within a rules-based order.

In addition to reporting the neo-liberal global order as self-imploding, Venezuelan media describe the rise of emerging powers using a narrative of great power competition. Specifically, the rise of China as well as the reemergence of Russian influence are noted as challenging US authority with the rapid rapprochement between China and Russia leaving the US far behind.[22] This allows Russian and Chinese cooperation to continue attacking the US-led international order.[23] As another article explains, China's relationship with Russia is at an historical high point with its old struggles with the former USSR having been resolved. Thus, through their cooperative relationship the two nations have formed a similar international vision nurtured by a strong relationship further strengthened by European myopia and China's awareness of its strategic rivalry with the US.[24]

Particular emphasis is placed on China's rise and its unlikely willingness to conform to the current Western-led order. China is reported as following its own path and internal evolution while yearning to do the same internationally without renouncing its sovereignty, with Chinese resurgence becoming synonymous with Western decline.[25] Venezuelan media conclude that as there is no harmony between China's return to global prominence and the hegemony of liberal modernity, China is unlikely to conform to Western supremacy and instead act to change the management of the global system.[26] Other articles further spell out the consequences of this, noting that if China is reluctant to join the US's dependency networks, confrontation is likely.[27]

Although China, and to some extent Russia, are portrayed as challenging US hegemony with their subsequent rise in influence, Venezuelan media explains that this does not suggest an end to imperialism. Indeed, the Venezuelan media extends its great power view of world politics to China and Russia as well, describing the routine interactions of great power behavior falling along imperialist tendencies. Thus, reports state that China is following an imperialist trajectory with its aspiration to become a great power through its interests in the South China Sea.[28] Nonetheless, while China is defined as an emerging imperialist country it is also characterized as having some fundamental weaknesses and challenges before it can become a stable imperialist nation.[29] Thus, like imperialist motivations to seek out hegemony through unfair trade and resource extraction, China is narrated as promoting its China 2025 and New Silk Road projects for similar self-serving reasons. As an article from *Rebellion* explains, China's 2025 policy aims to develop their technological capacity to move up the global value chain with their New Silk Road project intended to build infrastructure throughout Eurasia in line with Chinese interests. Both projects are central to China's imperialist ambitions and are a symptom of the country's overproduction and overcapacity problems.[30]

Such referencing to China's overproduction and capacity problems is reminiscent of Lenin's explanation of capitalist countries maintaining their positions of power, despite Marx's claim of their unsustainability, by needing to seek out markets in third world nations; this further reinforces Venezuela's ideological, socialist worldview. Thus, China is seen largely in the same light as the US, albeit with some distinction. China is described as a unique power with its own version of state capitalism but with expansionist aims and an unwillingness to be a second-class partner of the US; while China is not yet on the same plane as the US, nonetheless one thing both countries have in common are that they are both capitalists and imperialists in some form.[31]

In sum, Venezuela's narrative negatively characterizing imperialist ambition as shared by all great powers is best illustrated in an article attributing twenty-first century violence as being exacerbated by imperialist wars from on all sides—not just Yankee imperialism, but also European imperialism, Russian imperialism, and Chinese imperialism.[32] Importantly, as the article continues to explain, this system of imperial rule is not just limited to the great powers themselves, but also within other nations complicit in this global pattern of behavior. Therefore, while several governments of the world raise anti-imperialist flags and make speeches against one side of a dispute, such statements only serve as trumpets hiding the surrender of those governments towards some other imperialist side—like criticisms of progressive fetishism against Yankee imperialism used simply to promote a new form of Chinese imperialism.[33]

Taken together, on the one hand Venezuelan media narrates the global order as one based on international law designed to safeguard nations' sovereignty and democratic right to self-determination and culture; on the other, it showcases how strong nations impose their will for self-gain. This pattern of imperialist behavior thus threatens Venezuela's OS in that its trust system, anchored in international law, is tenuous as best. However, to some extent it might allow for an element of OS by providing cognitive order connecting this routine behavior to larger trends of history espoused by Marxist-Leninist thought and reflective of Venezuela's self-identity as a socialist nation trying to survive in an anarchical world. Nonetheless, the extent to which this identity narrative is drawn upon to provide Venezuela agency in the global order is severely limited by its domestic turmoil.

Venezuela's role in global order

Venezuelan media depict a weak Venezuela will little international influence. Its domestic crises, both economic and political, leave the nation vulnerable to foreign countries with few, if any, articles presenting autobiographical narratives of the state's role in foreign affairs. Instead, Venezuela is seen primarily as an object, not an agent in international politics.

Venezuela's domestic turmoil is reported as not only weakening the nation but also resulting in severely limited international clout. Reports express how Venezuela is going through serious internal problems, including declining national production and hyperinflation leading to impoverished living conditions.[34] These internal struggles coincide with foreign challenges as high levels of political conflict and the deterioration of international institutions place Venezuela in a critical situation forcing it to separate itself from geopolitics given the tensions present in the international order.[35] Thus, articles note how Venezuela is in the eye of a hurricane with tense relations involving several countries.[36] Even in regional multilateral institutions Venezuelan influence is described as minimal with reporting of Venezuelan diplomacy being denunciated by members of the Organization of American States.[37] As an article from *La Patilla* aptly summarizes, some 25 years ago when Venezuela was making a place for itself within a new international order and global business community through cultural and scientific development as well as television production, today the country is but a shadow of its former vibrancy.[38]

A major challenge facing Venezuela is its political turmoil. Articles note how Maduro acts as an outlaw in violating the international order with his political battles and usurpation of the presidency causing Venezuela to become a failed state and prey to the negative agenda of global powers and international politics.[39] Consequently, Maduro's refusal to leave elected office and the subsequent chaos and humanitarian crisis resulting from this decision spark concerns that the international community might intervene into Venezuelan domestic politics. While Venezuelan media presents a mixed opinion of this, with some thanking the pressure from the international community and humanitarian organizations in denouncing the Maduro regime's abuses[40] others urge the international community to refrain from interceding in Venezuelan domestic politics and avoid coercion of any kind against the nation's territorial integrity and political independence.[41] Regardless, Venezuelan media depict a very real possibility of foreign intervention, with articles reporting that while Venezuela hopes there will not be a foreign military intervention, if the Maduro regime continues to prevent foreign humanitarian aid from entering the country, the international community has the right to act.[42]

Coverage of whether foreign nations will intervene in Venezuela's domestic crisis further demonstrate the country's lack of agency in international affairs. Articles note how Venezuela owes Rosneft approximately $2.3 billion in addition to $3.1 billion to the Russian Ministry of Finance for arms, trucks, and grain all purchased on credit.[43] This debt is described as forcing the Russian government to make a decision to either increase support for its ally—Maduro, or to begin backing his opponent and elected successor.[44] This decision is reported as ultimately deciding Venezuela's future in that Putin's chosen path will determine if Venezuela has a peaceful government transition or start a civil war consolidating the repressive model of the Maduro government.[45] As an article from *Tal Cual* explains, Venezuela is caught up in great power politics with the Putin's privileged relationship with President Trump and the complex relationship between the two administrations limiting any room for maneuver, placing the Bolivarian Revolution as a peripheral actor in this global situation.[46]

Allies, competitors, and conflict management

As Venezuela's narratives of the global order explain, great power politics and imperial ambitions significantly influence international relations. While Venezuelan allies and competitors referenced in context to global competition are roughly equal, overall the country is reported as isolated and confronted with significant conflict. As Table 5.2 shows, references to Venezuela's competitors (n = 12; 19%) are slightly more frequent than alliances (n = 10;16%), with Venezuela's alliances primarily being with Russia, owing to its economic and military trade relations, but also include the potential for multilateral cooperation with Central American and Caribbean nations and the possibility for trade with China. While its competitors include the US, doubts regarding the integrity of Russian and Chinese interests are also evident, with some media reporting favorably on the US. In sum, Venezuela's lack of a clear international identity, combined with portrayals of its current domestic turmoil and views on the natural behavior of imperialist nations, leads to a bleak and contradictory picture of the global order in relation to its OS.

Russian and Chinese relations

The most clearly articulated ally to Venezuela is its relationship with Russia. Their close partnership is evident by reports stating how Maduro is attempting to save the political system built over the past two decades by Chávez around the support of Russia.[47] Under this system Venezuela supported Russian interests by acting as a Russian ally standing opposed to US policies in the Western Hemisphere. Furthermore, Russia and Venezuela enjoyed substantial cooperation in the oil industry with Rosneft recently becoming Venezuela's largest oil partner and an emergency lender through its acquired shares in five oil production projects and $7 billion in loans to the Maduro government in exchange for petroleum.[48] This enabled Rosneft to become an escape route for Maduro by helping him skirt the harsh sanctions placed on Venezuela's oil industry by the US.[49]

Venezuelan relations with China are likewise reported as lending similar strategic advantages. Articles report US officials fearing that the Venezuelan

Table 5.2 Venezuelan Media Reporting of Conflict Dynamics

	Article Mentions
Mentioned Competitors	N = 12 (19%)
Mentioned Alliances	N = 10 (16%)
Legitimate Deterrence	N = 2 (3%)
Conflict/Escalation Management	N = 21 (34%)
Redlines to Action	N = 3 (5%)

crisis represents not just a threat to US security but also its interests in South America, owing to the geopolitical influence obtained by China and Russia with both nations utilizing the financial needs of the Maduro regime to gain privileged access to substantial oil and mineral reserves as well as entry to key regional markets.[50] Nonetheless, Venezuela media maintain that Russia and China are not well-hearted allies, but act according to Venezuelan narratives of imperialist nations desiring to augment their influence and extract resources from developing nations. Although Russia is noted at times as an ally, other articles report how Russia's defense of Venezuela is waffling as Russian officials' public statements shifted unequivocal support of Maduro to offering mediation in negotiations with the opposition party in conjunction with holding talks between Venezuela and the US in response to the political crisis on the ground.[51]

US and other actors

Other prominent actors include the US, which is frequently invoked as an enemy to Venezuela, especially with its imperialistic ambitions. Articles explain how the US wants to provoke Venezuelan society by circulating fake news and create social fragmentation; such goals are described as attacks on Venezuela motivated by the greed of US imperialism and the petty interests of Latin American oligarchies.[52] Specifically, the US is viewed as partnering with Columbia against Venezuela with Colombian fascists setting fire to supposed humanitarian aid on the Colombia-Venezuela border supported by aggressive, destabilizing actions promoted by the US government in the region.[53] As an article from *Panorama* reports, quoting Venezuelan Chancellor Jorge Arreaza, the orchestrated maneuvers by the US and Colombia against Venezuela contradicts the principles and stated purposes of the UN Charter.[54] Nonetheless, Venezuelan media critical of the Maduro regime at times call for US support. As *La Patilla* reports, Venezuelans recognizes the nation's current predicament and serious political, social, and economic instability. As a result, the situation has reached a point in which only through US military intervention, supported by US allies, can Venezuela as a nation not disappear; those supportive of democracy, freedom, and free markets know that only the US can take the initiative to restore Venezuelan institutions and the rule of law.[55]

Other potential Venezuelan allies are harder to specifically find, especially with Venezuela's reported departure from regional multilateral institutions. Nonetheless, some articles express a desire to work with other Latin American and Caribbean nations, with Venezuela having reiterated their commitment to Latin American and Caribbean unity and the search for their own, independent, sovereign destiny through the full commitment to Latin American and Caribbean integration processes through institutions such as CELAC, UNASUR, the Caribbean oil alliance (Petrocaribe), the Caribbean Community (CARICOM), or ALBA.[56]

RQ2. How do Venezuelan media narrate the future of global competition?

Reflective of its narration of global order as dominated by great power imperialism and Venezuela's weakened role in the world, references to vulnerabilities are much more frequent than capabilities, suggesting limited capacity to compete in the future global order. Indeed, Venezuelan agency appears in doubt in that its vulnerabilities, and even capabilities, are provided more in defense than promotion of its interests, especially with imperialist nations viewed as desiring to undermine its sovereignty. The most significant instrument of power discussed in Venezuelan media is diplomatic, of which Venezuela is seen as both lacking and needing in order to safeguard the nation within the emerging future global order.

Vulnerabilities

Venezuelan narratives regarding its vulnerabilities within the global order are anchored in its lack of global influence and domestic instability. These factors leave the country open to what it perceives as imperialist interference and ambitions arising from the US as well as distrust towards China and Russia. Most frequently cited are diplomatic weaknesses (n = 29; 47%) which critique Venezuela's role and declining influence in international organizations, especially trade related organizations. Informational vulnerabilities are the second most cited (n = 14; 23%) stressing concerns regarding propaganda related influences from the US and other imperialist nations which are attempting to undermine Venezuelan interests within a Leninist-Marxist ideological framework; connected to this is the rise of authoritarian practices globally, which threaten Venezuelan democracy and human rights. Military and economic vulnerabilities are mentioned both in 18% (n = 11) of the articles with concerns placed on foreign intervention and a humanitarian crisis.

Diplomatic vulnerabilities

Venezuela's diplomatic vulnerabilities come from its weaken domestic state, isolation from diplomatic institutions, and target for imperial

Table 5.3 Venezuelan Vulnerabilities and Capabilities in News Media

	Articles Mentioning Key Vulnerabilities	*Articles Mentioning Necessary Capabilities*
Diplomatic	N = 29 (47%)	N = 13 (21%)
Informational	N = 14 (23%)	N = 9 (15%)
Military	N = 11 (18%)	N = 1 (1.6%)
Economic	N = 11 (18%)	N = 3 (4.8%)

ambition. As previously noted, Venezuelan media report Venezuela's serious internal problems coinciding with its decision to separate itself from multilateral institutions despite tensions within international order that have appeared at the current moment.[57] Other articles depict Venezuela as a peripheral actor as it remains sidelined by US-Russian relations,[58] with Venezuela having lost its place in the new international order.[59] More specifically, this decline in diplomatic influence is evident in multilateral organizations that Venezuela leads. As *Panorama* reports, despite the Bolivarian Alliance for the Peoples of America—launched by Venezuela and Cuba—celebrating its ten year anniversary as a forum for political debate and international influence, this diplomatic mechanism is increasingly limited as a mode for economic integration as it is completely overshadowed by other regional mechanisms.[60] The reason for this failure is attributed to ALBA having lost its influence in the global arena, owing to its advocacy of a unique and ideological vision leading only to nations who are allies or dependent on Venezuela as having joined.[61] This causes ALBA to never hold important diplomatic weight, not even within Latin America.[62] Thus, not only does Venezuela have limited diplomatic influence, but this ideologically inspired diplomacy has lost much of its persuasive appeal, thereby inhibiting Venezuela's ability to compete in the diplomatic space.

Informational vulnerabilities

In the information space, Venezuela is viewed as vulnerable from external forces such as imperialist nations' propaganda campaigns as well as internally through authoritarian manipulation of domestic political institutions and messaging. Thus, one significant theme in Venezuelan coverage of the shifting global order includes the rise of authoritarianism globally and its implications on Venezuela. While this rise in authoritarianism is reported most often as occurring in China, Russia, Europe, and the US, Venezuelan media note that Venezuela itself is susceptible to these practices, explaining how authoritarian states exert control over foreign elections through electoral observers as well as by investing in media control enabling them to control of the flow of information while simultaneously serving the propaganda goals of the regime.[63] All of these practices are explained as well known and suffered by Venezuelans, with Venezuela at this particular moment reported as facing ever increasing dangers pouring over from their national borders opening an authoritarian tide in all its variants and extremes domestically.[64]

More frequently cited, however, are reports showcasing Venezuela as under attack by imperialist propaganda. For instance, articles note how the imperialist deploy a strategy of fomenting and demoralizing the Venezuelan people with ambitions to tire the Venezuelan populace with its constant affectation in their daily lives.[65] These actions are described as pursuing the objective of using public opinion to question the Venezuelan government, generating social malaise.[66] Likewise, another article explains that international media campaigns try to justify the use of unilateral coercive measures against developing countries with imperialists seeking to prevent Venezuelans from exercising their legitimate right to elect their president through free, universal, direct, and secret voting.[67] These campaigns' objective is to promote political destabilization in order to overthrow the legitimate government and president—in this case Maduro—through foreign military invasion.[68]

Thus, not only is imperialist domination exercised by ideological and cultural mechanisms, but also promoted through modernized hegemonic control devices[69] with new communication technologies and cyber-attacks undermining Venezuelan sovereignty. As an article from *Rebellion* explains, the recent and flagrantly aggressive cybernetic attacks against Venezuela has caused power outages, impacted mobile service, and underground transport services in Caracas, representing a new form of twenty-first century war whereby technology takes over.[70] The consequence of this new form of warfare for Venezuela is a civil battle by fascist bands to destabilize the Maduro government and promote looting and sabotage to all sorts of businesses while manipulating the facts to portray a pretend, internal crisis.[71] In essence, Venezuela is surrounded and targeted by foreign and domestic information campaigns destabilizing the nation.

Military vulnerabilities

Military vulnerabilities are inwardly focused and closely relate to Venezuela's economic and political turmoil as well as lack of diplomatic influence, manifesting in concerns regarding the possibility of foreign intervention by the international community. As a result, the turmoil and humanitarian crisis caused by the Maduro government results in discussions regarding the international community's right to protect (R2P). As *La Patilla* explains, although the international norm of R2P provides the international community with the right to put an end to the Maduro regime's serious human rights violations by force, Venezuela wishes it will not do so; and yet, as the article continues, despite Venezuela's wish, the country can do absolutely nothing to prevent it.[72] As an article from *El Tiempo* explains, the situation in Venezuela is a regional and hemispheric issue that should not be used as an instrument of any geopolitical competition, including the deployment of military force in support of the Maduro regime; such actions would jeopardize Venezuela's democratic transition and constitutional normalization as well as constitute a threat to peace, security, and stability in the region.[73] The mere discussion of the use of R2P, even if in a strictly academic fashion, is reported as dangerous for Venezuelans and others in that it creates a bad precedent for the peace and stability of humanity.[74]

Economic vulnerabilities

Economic vulnerabilities are described in relation to criticisms of the Maduro regime and its allies, but also through descriptions of how Venezuela's economy suffers from economic blockades and sanctions from other nations. Domestically, articles explain how Venezuela is now a country in ruins with towns beset by hardship. As a result, the country faces not only a serious humanitarian crisis but a moral one as well; no longer are there only a few corrupt people benefiting from bribes, but a band of outlaws has emerged with ties to drug trafficking, human trafficking, international terrorism, and money laundering all with close connections to government officials.[75] Exacerbating this situation are countries ignoring the suffering of Venezuelans wallowing in misery, hardship, and starvation caused by the imposition of a criminal regime [Maduro] that deceives the world by manipulating and distorting reality.[76] As a result, the international community is reported as turning a blind eye and deliberately ignoring the human rights violations and international crimes committed by the Maduro government exercised through its use of military, police, and security forces for years on end.[77]

Imperialist nations in particular are described as contributing to Venezuela's economic woes. The US is reported as having imposed harsh sanctions on Venezuela's oil industry[78] with other nations more broadly accused of hypocrisy. As *Panorama* reports, imperialists speak of free markets all the while excluding developing countries, such as Venezuela, from engaging in international capital markets.[79] As a result, Venezuela suffers from economic wars, financial blockades, and high levels of smuggling to which the nation requires international solidarity to solve these problems.[80]

Capabilities

Venezuelan media narratives describing what capabilities the country has or should pursue are sparse and tend to focus more on current crises, suggesting a lack of forward vision for what Venezuela needs in order to compete in the future global order. Most frequently cited are diplomatic capabilities (n = 13; 21%) stressing Venezuela's call for multilateral governance. Informational capabilities are the second highest in frequency (n = 9; 15%) and draw upon Venezuela's ideological identity as a socialist nation to call for domestic solidarity against imperial encroachment. Both economic and military capabilities are rarely reported (n = 3; 5% and n = 1; 2% respectfully), suggesting a very limited capacity for Venezuela to compete in the future global order.

Diplomatic capabilities

The closest depiction of Venezuela's diplomatic capabilities are exhortations for greater multilateral cooperation to stem the tide of imperialism.

For instance, Venezuelan media include calls to build an international order that is democratic and equitable, as such an order is necessary to overcome market fundamentals and temptations of powerful countries to economically and politically subjugate developing nations.[81] To support such efforts, Venezuela is reported as continuing its pursuit of a diplomacy of peace by advocating for a democratic and equitable international order that ends unilateral coercive measures against developing countries through multilateralism emphasizing state sovereignty.[82]

Venezuela is able to exert some diplomatic agency through ALBA, with one article noting how members of ALBA were able to ratify a decision to continue promoting the construction of a new international order through the promotion of fair, inclusive, multicentric, and pluripolar world that stands in contrast to hegemonic, unilateral tendencies based on a strict respect for all peoples and the institutions chosen by them.[83] Finally, the need for Venezuelan diplomatic capacity to avoid the spread of global imperialism is reported in an article from *Panorama* which describes imperialists and neoliberals acting to delegitimizing the main political institutions of the international order postwar—the UN—by denying the fundamental principles on which it was founded; these actions require Venezuelan support for multilateralism as a means to democratize international relations by including the participation of peoples and sovereign states in decision-making mechanisms on major world issues to which, central to this effort, is a new multilateralism that must be based on solidarity and cooperation.[84]

Informational capabilities

Information capabilities are called for in order to warn the Venezuelan populace against neo-liberal policies, which are seen as a tool for imperial ambitions with the potential to undermine Venezuelan democracy, and instead embrace Venezuela's socialist identity to regain cultural cohesion and domestic solidarity at home. For instance, articles provide a consciousness raising function, like one from *Rebellion*, explaining how the higher phase of capitalism should cause Venezuelans to seriously reflect on the idea of imperialism, especially in Latin America, and understand how it functions in today's changing world where capital continues to dominate. The article continues to note the urgency of such reflection, warning that the pincers of the world's powers hover over the innocent Venezuelan people with Venezuela potentially becoming another battlefield of imperialist war in the twenty-first century if they are unable to achieve a democratic, sovereign and, above all, peaceful solution to their own political situation.[85]

Other articles explain the solution, or Venezuela's capabilities to combat imperialist attempts to undermine the nation, by narrating how at this historical movement Venezuelans must return to the moral leadership provided by Chávez, specifically his pronouncement that socialism will save the peoples of the world from poverty, hunger, and inequality. As a result, Venezuela must consciously defend its Bolivarian Republic and construction of a socialist, twenty-first century utopia.[86] This moral, cooperative exhortation is likewise reflected in calls for Venezuelans to combat the imperialists intent on fragmenting and dividing the nation; imperialist greed and arrogance can only be stopped by Venezuelans presenting a united front based on the morals and ethics of a people determined to defend their social gains and rights.[87] In sum, Venezuela's informational capabilities come not from its technological ability to shape its information environment but from its ideological vision for the Venezuelan people.

Economic capabilities

Only three articles mentioned economic capabilities. These articles primarily revolve around advocating for enhancing Venezuela's role in multinational trade organizations. For instance, the benefit of multilateral cooperation is seen by an a report from *El National* explaining how, the members of the EU and CELAC represent 61 states, or about a third of UN members through which they can economically cooperate to become more than just the sum of their parts.[88] As a result, by cooperating together these countries can better compete in the global order, in that the partnership between these two regions is both necessary in an increasingly complex world in which the fundamental principles of international order are at stake, but also by joining forces they can address issues of common concern, like the fight against poverty.[89] Other economic capabilities are more tangentially related, emphasizing more of the potential for cooperative benefits rather than Venezuela's current successes in doing so. For instance, Venezuela is viewed as needing to, and somewhat capable of, reforming ALBA with an article reporting that the ALBA problem stems from its members and the institution's dependency relationship with Venezuela; while multilateral integration is good and desirable, for ALBA to be successful over time it must create a bond of interdependence whereby mutual benefits are shared by all its members.[90]

Military capabilities

Strikingly, only one article mentions military capabilities, and does so by vaguely calling for greater multilateral cooperation in combatting terrorism and drug trafficking. The article explains how the EU and CELAC countries have both the opportunity and the responsibility to do more together in combatting organized crime, drug trafficking, and terrorism to restore peace in post-conflict areas.[91] With this cooperation, Venezuela is reported as being able to manage some security related issues in the

Americas and beyond by stressing how security is a common challenge requiring a shared way to coordinate security forces but also collaborate in social and development measures through the creation of employment and economic growth allowing for the defense of human dignity writ large.[92] Nonetheless, given that only one article discusses military capabilities, identifying a narrative theme is difficult. Thus, perhaps the larger conclusion is that Venezuela lacks significant capabilities to defend itself, let alone exert influence in the global order.

Taken together, Venezuela appears to suffer from a lack of agency. From the perspective of OS, this lack of capacity to act is explained by its unstable environment and absence of productive autobiographical narratives depicting what role the state has in the global order. Indeed, Venezuelan media appear at times to be in opposition with itself, with some arguing in support of the Maduro regime and others against. Moreover, the domestic calamities and humanitarian crisis place its self-identity narrative as a socialist nation capable of providing security and economic benefit for its citizens in doubt. While its socialist identity might provide some element of cognitive ordering of its environment, with its foreign adversaries clearly defined, Venezuela's attachment to this identity is clearly shown as inhibiting its ability to form productive multilateral relationships, specifically in the ALBA organization, but also in its isolation from other regional institutions.

Discussion

In sum, Venezuelan media depict the global order as one dominated by imperialist ambitions with multilateral institutions providing a legal, normative influence as a restraint to imperialist impulses, albeit a fragile one. Against this backdrop, Venezuela appears unable to influence international affairs not only because of its lack of great power status, but also because of its domestic turmoil. Indeed, in the time period covered in this study, Venezuelan media rarely project narratives of Venezuela as representing even a regional power let alone an international norm shaper, marking a stark contrast to Chávez's foreign policy goals during his final years in office (McCarthy-Jones & Turner, 2011).

Whereas the identities of Chavismo and Bolivarian Revolution constructed during Chávez's tenure built Venezuela's sense of identity and international order, the articles examined in this study suggest a collapsing of this ontological ordering during the Maduro regime. As defined by Kinnvall and Mitzen (2017), OS is understood as the securing of one's sense of being, rather than focus on physical safety with Mitzen (2006) adding that actors form this sense of self by building trust in their routines and biographical narratives in a particular time and space (Mitzen, 2006). This element of time and space is of particular importance within the Venezuelan context in that Chávez was able to craft narratives of Latin

American integration and fraternal relations through a vision of a new twenty-first century democratic socialism during a period of high oil prices and American hegemony (Romero & Mijares, 2016). These narrative visions provided not only a sense of order regarding Venezuela's international environment, establishing clear relational routines through biographical narratives of Venezuela leading Latin America against the colonial, imperialist US, but also recognition and elements of success both at home and abroad as Venezuela bought regional allies and provided lush subsidies to its citizenry.

However, under Maduro, Venezuela's position within the international order and global economy has changed despite his clinging to Chávez's ideological visions. As the media reports analyzed in this study show, Venezuela's influence with its regional partners has evaporated with Venezuela becoming increasingly isolated, evident by its diplomatic vulnerabilities mentioned most frequently out of all the DIME vulnerability and capability categories. Even its bilateral partnership with Russia is reported as tenuous as Venezuela is depicted as a sideline observer of Russian-US negotiations regarding Russia's continued support for the Maduro regime, prompting real fears regarding the international community intervening in its domestic politics.

Domestically, Venezuela's conceptualization of democratic socialism likewise appears bankrupt with significant media coverage citing the humanitarian crisis unfolding in the nation. Concerns over rising authoritarian practices are prominent with overt critiques of Maduro's political leadership. Strikingly, some articles even welcomed international intervention as Venezuela was viewed as unable to fix its political system; the fact that only three articles discussed Venezuela's capabilities to compete economically further demonstrates its lack of agency. Thus, as Kinnvall and Mitzen (2017) explain, when relationships and understanding are destabilized, political collective's OS is threatened, leading to anxiety, paralysis, or violence. In the case of Venezuela, all three of these elements are present, culminating in domestic protests and violent crackdowns.

Taken together, Venezuela's basic trust system, both domestically and internationally, appears lacking. Declining support for Maduro, evident by large-scale protests in opposition to his presidency, combined with a collapsed economy and humanitarian crisis offers a harsh material reality to Venezuelan citizens making it difficult to buy into his predecessor's vision for a new socialist economy. Likewise, the shifting global order reported as including new imperialist nations such as China, in addition to the traditional imperialists powers like Russia and the US, places Venezuela as an object rather than agent in international affairs; especially as its narratives of self-serving, unilateral imperialist actions stand in contrast to international governance and law. Indeed, today's Venezuela is unable to even rely upon international law to protect itself from great power incursions as its own media, at times, report Venezuela's humanitarian crisis as justifying international intervention, owing to its humanitarian crisis.

Trajectory/self-reflection

Based on the findings of Venezuelan media reporting on the future of global competition and Venezuela's ability to compete in the global order, what does Venezuela's future narrative trajectory look like? Krolikowski (2008) explains that actors with healthy basic trust systems have the capacity to rationally deliberate, learn, and adapt to changing circumstances, but those with low trust systems are unable to reflect and engage in the self-monitoring and updating of their autobiographical narratives. Our results suggest Venezuela falls into this latter category. Not only does Venezuela's narratives of the global order provide little trust, especially as the nation finds itself internationally isolated, but also the frequencies of Venezuela's vulnerabilities and capabilities related to global competition indicates Venezuelan perceptions of its future influence and economic capacities as continuing to decline. While a political reimagining is possible, evident by Juan Guido's leading of the opposition against Maduro and the levels of domestic and international support he has garnered, past studies on OS suggests continuing paralysis might be more likely.

Our findings suggest that the challenges facing Venezuela will likely contribute to a retrenchment or polarization of its current identity. A key component of Venezuela's identity established by Chávez was the perceived economic inequalities stemming from the neo-liberal order representative of the Washington Consensus. Chávez further strengthened this narrative anchoring through invocation of Latin America's colonial trauma by imperialist countries as part of his Bolivarian revolution. As Kinnvall (2004) argues the rapid social transformations brought forth by globalization and post-colonialism provided strong motivational forces for groups to seek out and reaffirm their self and collective identities. These forces are likely to continue and even intensify as further instability caused by new narratives of nationalistic, "country-first" rhetoric polarizes the international economic landscape leading to further uncertainty and anxiety over what the global economy will look like.

Indeed, indicative of the return of nationalistic discourse on the international stage are these narrative's highly emotive nature regarding concerns over nations' ability to secure a stable sense of self within an evolving international landscape. Thus, collective emotions including hate, fear, and love for the nation, play central roles in narrative consolidation of collective identities (Kinnvall et al., 2018), with self/other demarcation providing especially forceful resources for defining one's identity (Combes, 2017). Consequently, the specter of imperialists nations threatening Venezuela's security with ideations of a global order whereby Venezuela leads its Latin American brotherhood to the salvation of its people holds a seductive suasive force even if one's material realities fail to live up to such vision. According to Cash and Kinnvall (2017), post-colonialism and countries' search for OS are intimately connected to "national fantasy" as political collectives attempt to reclaim control over their perceived lost sovereignty and historical identities (p. 269). In Venezuela's case, and from the perspective of OS, despite its fractured societal politics, the need for social actors to believe they have a sense of wholeness and mastery of self makes discarding its Chávez defined identity difficult, especially as Maduro cracks down on civil society with government control over Venezuela's media-scape preventing alternative narrative visions to take root. Moreover, Chavismo is likely to limp along as Maduro's political legitimacy remains anchored in its continuation (Romero & Mijares, 2016). As Mitzen (2006) argues, as actors become attached to certain identities or routines, it becomes hard to let go of these attachments as doing so increases their anxiety and fears requiring a sacrifice in their sense of agency. In cases where one's basic trust systems are already low, making this further sacrifice in agency proves difficult (Krolikowski, 2008). Thus, nations, such as Venezuela, can become attached to detrimental identity narratives, even attached to conflict (Mitzen, 2006). As Venezuela grapples with the conflicts unfolding within its own society and politics, it will unlikely be able to pursue long-term strategic goals as its focus is consumed by short-term necessities inhibiting its ability to influence the future global order and successfully compete within it.

Notes

1 *Panorama* (March 15, 2018). Factiva.
2 Ibid.
3 *Rebellion* (March 8, 2019). Factiva.
4 Ibid.
5 *Panorama* (February 3, 2019). Factiva.
6 Ibid.
7 *Panorama* (March 15, 2018). Factiva.
8 *Panorama* (March 6, 2018). Factiva.
9 Ibid.
10 *Tal Cual* (January 5, 2019). Factiva.
11 *El Universal* (April 15, 2019). Factiva.
12 *Rebellion* (March 20, 2019). Factiva.
13 Ibid.
14 *Panorama* (September 27, 2018). Factiva.
15 *Rebellion* (April 11, 2019). Factiva.
16 Globovisión (February 11, 2019). Factiva.
17 Radio Union (January 8, 2019). Factiva.
18 *Rebellion* (February 25, 2019). Factiva.
19 Ibid.
20 Ibid.
21 *Rebellion* (March 20, 2019). Factiva.
22 *Rebellion* (March 13, 2019). Factiva.
23 Ibid.
24 *El Viejo Topo* (January 2019). Factiva.
25 *Rebellion* (March 2, 2019). Factiva.
26 Ibid.

27 *El Viejo Topo* (September 2019). Factiva.
28 Rebellion (March 18, 2019). Factiva.
29 Ibid.
30 Ibid.
31 Ibid.
32 *Rebellion* (March 8, 2019). Factiva.
33 Ibid.
34 *Panorama* (October 25, 2018). Factiva.
35 Ibid.
36 *Panorama* (October 25, 2018). Factiva.
37 *Tal Cual* (May 5, 2019). Factiva.
38 *La Patilla* (March 13, 2019). Factiva.
39 *El Carabobeno* (February 16, 2019). Factiva.
40 *La Patilla* (January 28, 2019). Factiva.
41 *Panorama* (March 6, 2018). Factiva.
42 *La Patilla* (March 13, 2019). Factiva.
43 La Patilla (March 8, 2019). Factiva.
44 Ibid.
45 Ibid.
46 *Tal Cual* (January 5, 2019). Factiva.
47 *La Patilla* (March 8, 2019). Factiva.
48 Ibid.
49 Ibid.
50 *The National* (September 14, 2017). Factiva.
51 *La Patilla* (March 8, 2019). Factiva.
52 *Rebellion* (March 14, 2019). Factiva.
53 Ibid.
54 *Panorama* (February 23, 2019). Factiva.
55 *La Patilla* (March 13, 2019). Factiva.
56 *Panorama* (March 6, 2018). Factiva.
57 *Panorama* (October 25, 2018). Factiva.
58 *Tal Cual* (January 5, 2019). Factiva.
59 *La Patilla* (March 13, 2019). Factiva.
60 *Panorama* (March 6, 2018). Factiva.
61 Ibid.
62 Ibid.
63 *The National* (January 27, 2017). Factiva.
64 Ibid.
65 *Rebellion* (March 14, 2019). Factiva.
66 Ibid.
67 *Panorama* (March 15, 2018). Factiva.
68 Ibid.
69 *Rebellion* (n.d.). Factiva.
70 *Rebellion* (March 14, 2019). Factiva.
71 Ibid.
72 *La Patilla* (March 22, 2019). Factiva.
73 *El Tiempo* (April 3, 2019). Factiva.
74 *La Patilla* (April 2, 2019). Factiva.
75 *La Patilla* (March 13, 2019). Factiva.
76 *La Patilla* (March 1, 2019). Factiva.
77 Ibid.
78 *La Patilla* (March 8, 2019). Factiva.
79 *Panorama* (March 15, 2018). Factiva.
80 *Panorama* (February 21, 2018). Factiva.

81 Ibid.
82 Ibid.
83 *Panorama* (March 6, 2018). Factiva.
84 *Panorama* (March 15, 2018). Factiva.
85 *Rebellion* (n.d.). Factiva.
86 *Rebellion* (March 14, 2019). Factiva.
87 Ibid.
88 *The National* (January 27, 2015). Factiva.
89 Ibid.
90 *The National* (December 14, 2014). Factiva.
91 *The National* (January 27, 2015). Factiva.
92 Ibid.

References

Agius, C. (2017). Drawing the discourses of ontological security: Immigration and identity in the Danish and Swedish cartoon crises. *Cooperation and Conflict*. 52 (1), 109–125.

Allsop, J. (2019, January 25). Venezuela's war on the press. *Columbia Journalism Review*. www.cjr.org/the_media_today/venezuela_crisis_maduro_trump.php.

Angosto-Ferrández, L. F. (Ed.). (2013). *Democracy, revolution and geopolitics in Latin America: Venezuela and the international politics of discontent*. Routledge.

Anselmi, M. (2017). Post-populism in Latin America: On Venezuela after Chávez. *Chinese Political Science Review*. 2(3), 410–426.

Arsenault, A., Hong, S. H., & Price, M. (2017). Strategic narratives of the Arab Spring and after. In A. Miskimmon, B. O'Loughlin, & L. Roselle (Eds), *Forging the world: Strategic narratives and international relations*, 190–217. University of Michigan Press.

BBC. (2020). *Juan Guaidó: The man who wants to oust Maduro*. January 23, 2020. www.bbc.com/news/world-latin-america-46985389.

Burke, K. (1969). *A Grammar of Motives*. University of California Press.

Cash, J. & Kinnvall, C. (2017). Postcolonial bordering and ontological insecurities. *Postcolonial bordering and ontological insecurities*. 20(3), 267–274.

Chacko, P. (2014). A new "special relationship"?: Power transitions, ontological security, and India–US relations. *International Studies Perspectives*. 15(3), 329–346.

Combes, M. D. (2017). Encountering the stranger: Ontological security and the Boston Marathon bombing. *Cooperation and Conflict*. 52(1), 126–143.

Corrales, J. (2009). For Chávez, still more discontent. *Current History*. 108(715), 77–82.

Corrales, J. (2011). Conflicting goals in Venezuela's foreign policy. In R. S. Clem and A. P. Maingot (Eds), *Venezuela's petro-diplomacy. Hugo Chávez's foreign policy*, 32–48. University Press of Florida.

Corrales, J. (2015). Autocratic legalism in Venezuela. *Journal of Democracy*. 26(2), 37–51.

Cusack, A. K. (2018). *Venezuela, ALBA, and the limits of postneoliberal regionalism in Latin America and the Caribbean*. Springer.

De la Torre, C. (2017). Hugo Chávez and the diffusion of Bolivarianism. *Democratization*. 24(7), 1271–1288.

Freedom House. (2019). *Freedom in the World 2019: Venezuela*. https://freedomhouse.org/country/venezuela/freedom-world/2019.

Giddens, A. (1991). *Modernity and self-identity: Self and society in the late modern age*. Stanford University Press.

Hawkins, K. A. (2003). Populism in Venezuela: The rise of Chavismo. *Third World Quarterly*. 24(6), 1137–1160.

Hawkins, K. A. (2010). *Venezuela's Chavismo and populism in comparative perspective*. Cambridge University Press.

Human Rights Watch. (2019). *Venezuela: Events of 2018*. www.hrw.org/world-report/2019/country-chapters/venezuela#.

Huysmans, J. (1998). Security! What do you mean? From concept to thick signifier. *European Journal of International Relations*. 4(2), 226–255.

Karl, T. L. (1997). *The Paradox of Plenty*. University of California Press.

Kiger, P. J. (2019). How Venezuela fell from the richest country in South America into crisis. *History*. May 9, 2019. www.history.com/news/venezuela-chavez-maduro-crisis.

Kinnvall, C. (2004). Globalization and religious nationalism: Self, identity, and the search for ontological security. *Political Psychology*. 25(5), 741–767.

Kinnvall, C., Manners, I., & Mitzen, J. (2018). Introduction to 2018 special issue of European Security: "Ontological (in)security in the European Union". *European Security*. 27(3), 249–265.

Kinnvall, C. & Mitzen, J. (2017). An introduction to the special issue: Ontological securities in world politics. *Cooperation and Conflict*. 52(1), 3–11.

Krolikowski, A. (2008). State personhood in ontological security theories of international relations and Chinese nationalism: A sceptical view. *Chinese Journal of International Politics*. 2(1), 109–133.

Krolikowski, A. (2018). Shaking up and making up China: How the party-state compromises and creates ontological security for its subjects. *Journal of International Relations and Development*. 21(4), 909–933.

Krygier, R. & Faiola, A. (2019). A humanitarian crisis in Venezuela? Nothing to see here, government says. *The Washington Post*. October 13, 2019. www.washingtonpost.com/world/the_americas/a-humanitarian-crisis-in-venezuela-nothing-to-see-here-government-says/2018/10/12/6ebd1aa6-c2ac-11e8-9451-e878f96be19b_story.html.

Levitsky, S. & Roberts, K. (2011). Conclusion: Democracy, development, and the left. In S. Levitsky & K. Roberts (Eds.), *The resurgence of the Latin American left*, 399–429. Johns Hopkins University Press.

McCarthy-Jones, A. & Turner, M. (2011). Explaining radical policy change: The case of Venezuelan foreign policy. *Policy Studies*. 32(5), 549–567.

Mijares, V. M. (2017). Soft balancing the titans: Venezuelan foreign-policy strategy toward the United States, China, and Russia. *Latin American Policy*. 8(2), 201–231.

Mitzen, J. (2006). Ontological security in world politics: State identity and the security dilemma. *European Journal of International Relations*. 12(3), 341–370.

NPR. (2019). *All Things Considered*. Venezuela Hovers On The Brink Of Conflict — Many Fear The Situation Will Escalate. March 28, 2019. www.npr.org/2019/03/28/707722484/venezuela-hovers-on-the-brink-of-conflict-many-fear-the-situation-will-escalate.

Nugent, C. (2019). 'Venezuelans are starving for information.' The battle to get news in a country in chaos. *Time*. April 16, 2019. https://time.com/5571504/venezuela-internet-press-freedom.

Pérez, J. O. (2019). Venezuela and its neighbors: The discursive struggle for Latin America. *Relaciones Internacionales*. 28(57), 53–69.

Pew Research. (2020). *Global Indicators Database*. www.pewresearch.org/global/database/indicator/5/country/ve.

Romero, C. A. & Mijares, V. M. (2016). From Chávez to Maduro: Continuity and change in Venezuelan foreign policy. *Contexto Internacional*. 38(1), 165–201.

Schiller, N. (2018). *Channeling the state: Community media and popular politics in Venezuela*. Duke University Press.

Sigalos, MacKenzie (2019). *China and Russia loaned billions to Venezuela - and then the presidency went up for grabs*. CNBC. February 7, 2019. www.cnbc.com/2019/02/07/venezuela-china-and-russia-owed-debts-as-presidential-fight-rages.html.

Smilde, D. (2015). The End of Chavismo? *Current History*. 114(769), 49–55.

Specia, M. (2019). What is happening in Venezuela and why it matters. *The New York Times*. April 30, 2019. www.nytimes.com/2019/04/30/world/americas/venezuela-crisis.html.

Steele, B. J. (2008). *Ontological security in international relations: Self-identity and the IR state*. Routledge.

Steele, B. J. & Homolar, A. (2019). Ontological insecurities and the politics of contemporary populism. *Cambridge Review of International Affairs*. 32(3), 214–221.

Subotić, J. (2016). Narrative, ontological security, and foreign policy change. *Foreign policy analysis*. 12(4), 610–627.

Tarver, H. M. (2018). *The History of Venezuela*. ABC-CLIO.

Vieira, M. A. (2016). Understanding resilience in international relations: The non-aligned movement and ontological security. *International Studies Review*. 18(2), 290–311.

6 Ontological Security Narratives in Iranian Media

Narrative Plurality and Moral Righteousness in Defense of a Regional Islamic Order

Introduction

The ambitions of Iran regarding its regional neighbors and the prevailing global order have been long-discussed and oft misunderstood by academics, policy experts, and military strategist alike since the Islamic Revolution of 1979. While the rise of challengers to the Western-led global order, toward Zakaria's (2008) "post-American world," most often contemplate the roles of states like Russia (Mead, 2014) and China (Kastner & Saunders, 2012), Iran has more readily been seen as a "rogue state" (Chase, et al., 1996; Pompeo, 2018); memorably labeled as part of the "Axis of Evil" by President George Bush in his 2002 State of the Union address (Glass, 2019). Indeed, Iranian antagonism is evident and consequential amid an increasingly nationalistic and dynamically shifting global system with questions about US global leadership. As a result, there have been long standing reports by outside observers, as well as statements by Iranian leaders, noting that Iran is increasing its regional presence and aligning itself with China, Pakistan, Turkey, and Russia toward a new, anti-Western, global order (Kredo, 2014; Frantzman, 2018). Yet others claim that Iran's posturing in the global order are more so indicative of larger trends, such as regional players having increased military capabilities, decreased tolerance by world powers to engage in outright conflict, declining value of territorial-bound states as economic or strategic footholds, and the growing international trend to prioritize domestic socioeconomic policies over foreign policy (Trenin, 2020).

Either way, Tehran remains a major regional power, critical to stability in the Middle East and South Asia with its ability to find common ground with the US and a normative role within the larger US-led global order remaining elusive. What is increasingly clear from recent Iranian and US confrontations is that the shifts taking place in the global order exacerbate friction points placing Iran in an outsider or revisionist role in international affairs (Katzman, et al., 2020; Behravesh, 2018) with its complicated political and economic objectives creating strong contrasts to the West making cooperation difficult (Bahgat, 2017). What remains unclear,

DOI: 10.4324/9781003197478-6

however, is the efficacy and sustainability of this role; specifically, whether it will significantly influence the global order to the extent to which it provides space and support for Iran's domestic stability, prosperity, and growth.

As identities of political actors are the basis from which they form their interests, which in turn informs their actions (Wendt, 1992), the construction of Iran's national identity becomes crucial in international and domestic politics. As Willmott (1986) explains, the concept of the nation state both binds and limits human social interaction; allowing our cultural "selves" to be maintained in structured unison with others, reducing our anxieties yet limiting our cooperative potential with outsiders. In ontological security (OS) terms, state agency rests on its function as an institution capable of patterning and reinforcing identity to individual citizens both in alleviation of the fear of the unknown-non-being and through the ordering of state's social relations with others to create a level of certainty to abstract fears allowing for action (Mitzen, 2006; Krolikowski, 2018).

The consequences of state identity on state policies are significant, especially so in Iran when the binding identity of the state is made in contrast to the prevailing system powers. This is not to say Iran has one, immutable identity. Its conservative, theocratic notion of self provides important sources of cognitive stability regarding the nation's identity. But revolving, and at times, competing with this narrative is its historical past as a great Persian empire and its more progressive sense of self, reflective of its political reformers and young population (Barzegar & Divsallar, 2017). The balancing and sustainability of such identities, when placed in opposition to Iran's regional and global competitors and its own domestic tribulations, has the potential to create OS and *in*security as well if the challenges facing the nation leads to an overwhelming number of perceived threats eroding the state's legitimacy and function as an OS supplier (Krolikowski, 2018).

Thus, this chapter examines how the unique complexities of Iranian identity, seen through the lens of OS, manifest through media narratives depicting the future global order and competition within it. We argue these narratives represent performances of Iranian state identity and one important means by which it communicates a binding cultural self for its citizens in the face of a shifting global order. In doing so, we find Iranian narratives taking a regional focus with the US placed in direct contestation against Iran, but also include the construction of the international community as a normative body whose values and interests are in contrast to those of the US and its regional allies. The global order therefore gets presented as a competitive diplomatic landscape, with various coalitions jockeying for influence. While the US is recognized as the only single nation possessing the power necessary for global leadership, Iranian narratives highlight how resistance to such power is possible by envisioning Iran as a state with the moral and religious beliefs capable of protecting those living in the Shia Crescent as the future order moves into one of greater multi-polarity.

Ontological security and a revisionist state

Over the past 50 years, Iranian society has experienced significant domestic and political turmoil. From the fall of the Western-back Shah to the rise of the Iranian theocratic state, Iranian society has faced multiple economic shocks, political protest movements, and foreign policy crises shaping its cultural identity. Such moments of turbulence and transition require political communities to maintain a sense of biographical continuity while simultaneously providing opportunities for state officials to selectively activate certain aspects of narrative identity over others, providing the cognitive bridges smoothing out otherwise incongruent state policies and actions (Subotić, 2016).

In Iran's case, such narratives revolve around and integrate its history as a great Persian empire of antiquity and, more recently, its unique interpretations of Shia Islam as well. However, additional challenges, like those of modernity—and its claims of universal democratic and Enlightenment principles—crash upon Iran's unique cultural codes and native traditions, pushing progressive reforms as part of broader social and political change (Tazmini, 2018). Internationally, this appears to have resulted in the manifestation of a revisionist Iranian identity with Iran emerging, at times, as xenophobic, dogmatic, and threatening to the global order or as offering well-reasoned advice toward a more moral and fair international system, depending upon one's perspective.

From the perspective of state's as OS suppliers (Steele, 2008; Krolikowski, 2018; Chacko, 2014), the balancing of Iran's historical, traditional, and more modern narratives in providing a coherent sense of self becomes crucially important in maintaining state legitimacy (Krolikowski, 2018; Huysmans, 1998) and understanding of how it conceives the global order, especially within the context of Iran's revolutionary politics. As Silverstone (1993) explains, OS is an equation of "trust, security, and the capacity to act both individually and socially" with media in modern societies functioning cathectic-ally and culturally as transitional objects in realizing one's "self" (Silverstone, 1993, p. 584). Media, as a transitional object, thus offers a space where "self" can be recognized in contrast to "other" with news media in particular offering a clear dialectical articulation of social anxiety and security, as well as fostering trust of the state system, critical to OS.

As Tazmini (2018) explains, the complex identity present in Iranian media when projecting OS relies on multiple elements and continuums that pivot around one another. These include Iraniyat discourses involving Iranian-Persian history and culture as a great civilization from antiquity; Islamiyat, discourses on Iran's Islamic past values, dogmas, traditions, and classic revolutionary themes of Islam; and Shia discourses on Iran's revolutionary revivalism, nationalism, and populism within the Islamic world. More specifically, the Islamic Republic can be seen as performing its state identity by using these three cultural narratives across four pillars: 1) Republicanism and participation—emphasizing civil society, popular sovereignty, and pluralism; 2) Economic development—emphasizing state projects aimed at reviving the economy; 3) Economic justice—emphasizing the redistribution of wealth and tackling of corruption; and 4) Independence/freedom—emphasizing resistance of foreign interference and encroachment. Taken together, these pillars, when wedded to Iraniyat and Islamiyat continuums, mark key pivot and amplification points utilized by Iranian leaders to narrate the performance of the state over time, bridging its past to the present and projected onto the future, forming a sense of continuity amid a sea of change.

On the global stage, the result is Iran's presentation as a revisionist actor. As Behravesh (2018) argues, the various elements and continuums of Iranian state identity manifest in action as that of a "thin revisionist" actor in the international arena. Thin revisionist actors pursue policies and practices of defiance intended to unsettle or take advantage of established norms and structures in such a way as to force reconsideration. Behravesh (2018) draws out the importance of understanding the relationship between OS and revisionist state actors by highlighting how revisionism (which itself is often based on moral codes, political principles or ideologies opposed to the ruling order) generally defines "relations with the outside 'Others' primarily in terms of dissatisfaction and thus self-extending change" (p. 841). While revisionist states have a firm sense of identity to inform action, the nature of that action entails isolation from the status-quo ruling-order, setting the potential for escalatory conflict as normative and essential to understanding how the "self" of the state is supposed to engage with powerbrokers. Consequentially, actions performed in securing self-identity by a revisionist state actor can have predictably toxic outcomes both domestically and internationally; yet are undertaken anyway for reasons of OS management. In this sense, the Iranian state provides OS by fixating on and performing its Iraniyat, Islamiyat, and Shia cultural elements within a broader revisionist identity (Behravesh, 2018). It does so by reinforcing sharp ideological contrasts between itself and the Western-led global order, as well as monarchial manifestations of Islamic states, fueling conflict between Iran and the West.

And yet, experts note that the complexity behind Iranian revisionism is not well understood, making it difficult for external observers to make sense of Iranian actions toward the global system. Whereas Edelman and Takeyh (2020) argue that Iran's narratives are not sufficiently flexible, contending that Iran's cobbled revisionist identity as guarantor of OS destines it for conflict and failure as its narration is bent against the status quo, Maloney (2008) believes that Iran should be considered more as a pivotal state in relation to US interests in that the potential for success and failures of the regime carry significant regional implications. Thus, the complexities of Iranian identity require more nuanced understanding in order for the US to more successfully engage Iran as something more than a rogue state (Maloney, 2008; Chase et al., 1996). In other words, an understanding of Iranian OS constructions as a revisionist actor is needed to comprehend why certain foreign policies, and their associated performances, are pursued, both at domestic and international levels. Before doing so, however, one must understand how Iran's cultural narratives have evolved during its modern history, specifically their expressions within the lived realities and politicized social movements of its people and its mediated depicted performative actions.

Iranian history and cultural narratives

Experts have examined Iran's cultural narratives from a variety of viewpoints. Here we outline how such perspectives have influenced Iran's historical identity and their implications on Iran's current relations in the international order. We start broadly by discussing the contending elements of Iran's Iraniyat and Islamiyat cultural narratives before outlining how its Pahlavi and Iraniyyat identities functioned prior to its revolution, moving into discussions of its Khomeini and Islamiyyat narratives shaping its understanding of the world today.

Iraniyat and Islamiyat cultural elements

Critical to having agency, and one of the greatest challenges for the Iranian state, is embracing the full complexity of historical Iranian identity and coming to terms with pre-Islamic and Islamic aspects of the Iranian sense of self. According to Davaran (2010) Iranians navigate daily a complex back and forth shift between pre-Islamic and Islamic identity as they move throughout society. Thus, close examination of Iran's attempt to consistently describe Iranian social mores and beliefs transcend a purely Islamic description of Iran to include Persian perspectives in understanding its social, cultural, political, and economic understandings of society. In this sense, Holliday (2007) argues that there exists a binary of Iranian national identity between cultural elements of Iraniyat—identifying Iranianism with pre-Islamic Iranian heritage to the exclusion of Islam, and Islamiyat concepts—identifying Iranian-ism in terms of Iran's Islamic heritage to the exclusion of the pre-Islamic legacy. Importantly, having two discourses of national identity creates inherent social and political tensions that limit the power of the Iranian state as a binding monolithic institution as there is an ever-present fractionalization between the people and the regime. The result is that any overarching, Islamist-Iranian discourses of inclusion grapple with dichotomies of Iranian Shi'ism within Islam as well as the appropriation of Iranian culture into political constructs for the purpose of the state (Holliday, 2007).

Thus, in conveying OS to Iranian audiences, state-backed narratives wrestle with and tie together three very distinct, and historically rich cultural elements when grappling with its positioning on the global stage. As Akbarzadeh & Barry (2016) argue, central to understanding Iranian foreign policy is a triangulated identity of nationalism revolving around Iran-ism (Iraniyat), Islam (Islamiyat), and Shi'ism. None of which can be entirely divorced from one another with each element having an idealized, or pure form that allows Iranian leaders to pivot toward more useful elements in explanation of given a policy. The consequences of these complex identity continuums thus implicate Iran's source of autobiographical continuity, especially as it relates to its theocratic revolution in 1979 and relations to others on the international stage.

Pahlavi & Iraniyyat

Prior to today's anti-US theocratic regime, Iran was a key Western ally. Supported by covert US forces, Mohammad Reza Pahlavi became Iran's leader in 1953 in a coup, replacing Mohammad Mosaddegh (Kinzer, 2011). Entering into a controversially close relationship with the US, the Pahlavi regime modernized Iran, including shaping it into a secular state (Cordesman, 1999) but with the Shah becoming increasingly autocratic and sultanistic (Keddie & Mathee, 2002). As Holliday (2016) explains, the Iraniyat-prioritizing Pahlavi regime embraced Westernization not simply for the technological and developmental visions of a "modern" Iran, but more principally to reclaim Iran as a "great civilization" of antiquity.

Thus, under the Pahlavi regime, Iran experienced tremendous economic growth and modernization across education, technology and healthcare sectors with the rise of an upper and modern middle classes and integration into the larger global political order (Parsa, 1989). However, the regime's implementation of the "capitalist method of modernization" under the banner of Iraniyat revitalization created gross inequalities between elites and the rest of society driving Iranians, albeit reluctantly, toward the only functional and traditionally understood powerbrokers left in Iranian society, the anti-regime clergy (Abrahamian, 1980, p. 23). Here the fractured elements of society, feeling trampled upon by a modernizing state, found unity within the foundational counter elements of Islamiyat and Shi'ism. Whereas the Shah's Westernization was thought of as a dialectic exchange between East and West, Old World and New World, toward a fresh synthesis in which Iran might play a leading role, perceptions of the Shah as Westernizing to the exclusion of Islamiyat contributed both to his downfall as well as to the radical reconstruction of traditionalist Islamiyat nationalism and its post-revolutionary revisionist identity (Holliday, 2016).

The Iraniyat prioritization of the Shah had lasting impacts on the ways in which Persian nationalism has manifested through to the present day (Soleimani & Mohammadpour, 2019). Under Pahlavi, non-Persian Iranian elements of Iranianism were suppressed, criminalized, and accused of being manufactured by the Persian intelligentsia and literary classes so that a singular Persian-Iranian identity could be grafted onto the state. The consequence post-revolution has been a consistent internal colonization of non-Persian "others" within Iran. While the fall of Pahlavi initiated an anti-American and anti-Western turn by the Iranian state, it did not do away with the Iraniyat identity. The tensions of the two dominant cultural Iranian binaries, along with the complexities of the Shi'ism element, simply took on a new form with the construction of Iran as an Islamic Republic.

Khomeini & Islamiyyat

Beginning in October 1977, demonstrations and protests against the Pahlavi regime coalesced into a campaign of civil resistance incorporating both secular and religious elements of Iranian society (Abrahamian, 1982, 2009; Afkhami, 2009). As protests intensified, Iran's Shah went into exile while Ayatollah Khomeini was invited to return to Iran. Upon arrival, military forces quickly overthrew those loyal to the Shah, ushering Khomeini into power and forming today's Islamic Republic (Graham, 1980; Kurzman, 2004). As Amuzegar (1991) notes, Iran's revolution was unique in that Iran was not in a state of financial crisis or possessed a disgruntled military. Indeed, as Abrahamian (1980) explains, the revolution was an internal movement unaided by outside forces. As such, it did not graft new political parties, ideologies, or societal classes onto Iranian politics and society but offered a radically new understanding of self in relation to other. In doing so, it harnessed aspects of Jihadi Islamiyat traditionalism as a backlash against societal equity with religious leadership seen by many as capable of protecting the people from foreign influence, exerting power over elected officials, examining the activities of domestic social groups, and guiding the nation toward virtue (Abrahamian, 1980).

Therefore, under the leadership of Ayatollah Khomeini, Iranian identity was reformed by centering itself along Islamiyat notions harkening back to a "radical reinterpretation of Islamic social standards dating back 1,300 years" (Ansari, 1999. p. 8). Such prioritization of its Islamiyat identity created internal suppressions in pursuit of Iran as a theocratic-great civilization with Khomeini advocating that the "government derives its legitimacy from God" with "proper government requir[ing] a radical Islamic reconstruction of society" (Stempel, 1981. p. 47). In this sense, embedded in the revolutionary nature of Khomeini's movement was a narrative highlighting injustices perpetrated against the Iranian people as well as linking the collapse of Iranian society and self-rule to its deviation from its Islamiyat traditionalist interpretation of Islamic laws and ordinances in favor of the materialism and sciences of the West. In doing so, Khomeini successfully wove an Iranian identity along a theocratic, Shia Islamiyat interpretation of Iranianism that retained distinctive Iraniyat cultural elements, bonding Islam to the state. Such linkage marshalled the state's instruments of power as enacting laws that creates, fosters, and protects Islamic identity and harmony in diametric opposition to any other form of outside rule with military, economic, and diplomatic losses depicted as failures of properly enacting Islamic ordinances indicative of Islamic identity (Algar, 1981). Thus, the revolution was an effort towards home-grown modernity through the prioritization of Islamic inheritance behind the rhetoric and practices of Shia revolutionary activism, critically rejecting the West, its institutions, and its secularism, while attempting to find balance between the competing aspects of its own extraordinarily complex identity (Tazmini, 2018).

Iranian media in service to the state

As the brief history of Iran's post-World War II experience demonstrates, the strategic interweaving and contestation of Iran's cultural narratives have played important roles justifying and legitimizing the state, supplying its people with a sense of identity. Such processes are not unique to Iran with elites from other nations found to strategically incorporate past narratives during times of crisis, including their adaption to larger societal master narratives (Subotić, 2016; Hagström & Gustafsson, 2018). Indeed, Silverstone (1993) locates media as an integral part of such constructions, defining one's social reality into the fabric of our daily lives with Krolikowski (2018) emphasizing how states supply OS through the transmission of state policy and ideology through media to one's citizenry. The continuing tension between Iran's Islamiyat and Iraniyat identity has led to Iranian leaders strategically controlling its media to maintain control of its cultural narratives; according to Koo (2017) while old media helped produced the symbols and recognitions contributing to the Islamic Revolution's success, new media is leading discourses that threaten the current Islamic authority.

Thus, today's Iran is a state with a relatively unfree media system with Iranian leaders attempting to constrain and influence public discourse in significant ways. Reporters Without Borders ranks the state nearly at the bottom of its World Freedom Index, falling at 173 out of 180; for the past 40 years, Iran has exercised extensive control over its media landscape including targeting of international media (Reporters Without Borders, 2021) with authorities aggressively pursuing mastery of its public sphere, including its emerging digital realm (Faris & Rahimi, 2015). And yet, despite such attempts, the Iranian-regime is unable to prevent the total exclusion of liberal and oppositional elements within society (Rubin, 2019). Mazrooei et al. (2017) summarizes the Iranian media landscape as reflective of the contradictions of Iran's complex political and institutional architecture with media heavily censored with journalists and bloggers facing high risks of imprisonment. While all TV and radio stations are controlled by the state, print media includes reporting from centrist, moderate, and conservative viewpoints, albeit within the limits of state dictates. The Iranian media market, similar to the rest of the Iranian political economy, retains the massive state-owned corporate media required to propagate Islamic values and culture in maintenance of its identity while tolerating small-scale production of alternative, more liberal, voices.

More specifically, Rahimi (2015) argues that Iranian leaders regulate and manipulate its media ecology in both reactive and proactive measures aiming to control the "production of ideas, information, images, values, and emotions in the public sphere" (p. 359–360). Reactive measures include censorship designed to manage ideas and information to suppress domestic opposition and a litany of bureaucratic control and regulation of various media and cultural outlets, with other reactive features including unofficial censorship carried out by pro-government pressure groups and quasi-official censorship regulating research and academic activities. Importantly, such measures aren't total or always unified. Iranian media control include "competing policies and strategies, designed at times by factions within Iran's political order" (2015, p. 359).

Proactive measures, according to Rahimi (2015), are about soft power elements "shaping perceptions, behavior, and sentiments of solidarity and prosperity" (p. 371), especially important with the expansion of global media technology. Such efforts include propagating state ideology, but importantly go further in attempting to build perceptions of legitimacy and trust in the state. Proactive measures comprise of building resources, institutions, platforms, and legal frameworks expanding social control through various media technologies. In support of these endeavors, the Iranian government has pursued narratives of "soft war" portraying foreign-directed media initiatives as implicitly and explicitly attempting to undermine Iranian cultural norms and values, placing the state as its protector.

In this sense, post-revolution Iran has been creative and adaptive in the use of technologies and media in maintaining support for the current government. Such control is particular noteworthy given the current climate of economic devastation wrought from US sanctions, as the poorer Iranians social classes that form the backbone of support for the theocratic state grow discontented with the regime (Edelman & Takeyh, 2020). With state power resting on the ability to construct, project, regulate and manipulate ideas, information, images, and values to citizens in ways that link foundational identities as dependent upon the state for survival, Iranian media and the narratives circulating and reported within it, play important elements in sustaining the state's legitimacy, including its visions of the current and future global order and the means by which Iran understands in ability to compete therein.

The rouge state of the global order

Like its cultural history, Iranian foreign policy presents a mix of both continuity and change with elites attune to developments in Iran's international environment as well as domestic concerns. Such shifting priorities influence Iran's position in the global order and how it sees competition moving forward, evident by changes in national priorities from the Ahmadinejad presidency to Rouhani. As Barzegar and Divsallar (2017) explain, during President Ahmadinejad's tenure in office (2005–13) ideology and conflictual relations with the US and West took center stage. However, such antagonism proved ineffective, resulting in a nuclear stalemate between Iran and world powers with the Ahmadinejad government perceived as unable to successfully manage the costly economic sanctions placed against the country. Thus, under President Rouhani, Iran has taken a more balanced position, pursuing a pragmatic-centrist vision of Iranian foreign policy emphasizing rational assessment of its resources and strategic limits in order to optimize Iranian power (Barzegar & Divsallar, 2017; Golmohammadi, 2019).

Nonetheless, today's Iran still faces significant global challenges. According to Haghgoo et al. (2017), during Rouhani's ascension to power, Iranian foreign policy has been exposed to tremendous developments characterized by the prevalence of conservatism over a revolutionary mindset, nationalism over trans-nationalism, and structuralism over agent-oriented trends. Such shifts occurred as Iran's international environment presented a variety of challenges, including the deteriorating situation in Syria, increased sectarian tensions in the Middle East, enduring security issues in Afghanistan, hardening of Israeli opposition against Iran (Akbarzadeh & Conduit, 2016), and conflict with Saudi Arabia in Yemen and the international community over its nuclear program (Barzegar & Divsallar, 2017). To meet these challenges, the basic principles of Iran's foreign policy include: 1) development of its economy and preserving its territorial integrity and national sovereignty; 2) defense of Muslims and liberation movements specifically against attacks from Israel and the West; and 3) establishing an Islamic society based on Shi'a principles (Sariolghalam, 2005, 2020). Despite shifts in Iran's posture towards others under President Rouhani, scholars note that many of Iran's policy principles and practices have remained stable—emphasizing self-sufficiency, indigenization, exceptionalism, and resistance—intensifying Iran's isolation in the international arena (Golmohammadi, 2019) and contributing to its outsider identity as a revisionist state (Behravesh, 2018).

No more is this evident than by Iran's troubles with the US under the Trump administration with the US withdrawal from the Iranian nuclear deal. While US-Iranian antagonism is mutual and reciprocal in nature, hardline stances taken by the Trump administration has escalated tensions. Data from IranPoll, a Canadian-based polling company notes that, during the Trump administration, "unfavorability" of the US among Iranians increased from 71% in January of 2016 to 86% in May 2019. In 2019 a total of 66% of Iranians believed the US to be a dangerous international actor seeking confrontation and control, as opposed to 46% in 2005 (Datta, 2020). Similarly, Mohseni, et al. (2017), surveying Iranians following the first year of the Trump administration and the 1-year anniversary of the Joint Comprehensive Plan of Action (JCPOA)'s implementation, found that Iranian support for the nuclear deal was declining with appetite for renegotiating terms virtually non-existent among a majority of Iranians believing the US would not live up to its obligations outlined in the nuclear deal and would continue to find ways to impose sanctions and restrict other nations from having normalized relations with Iran (Mohseni, et al., 2017).

Indeed, by May 2018 the Trump administration had abandoned JCPOA and by November reinstated sanctions targeting Iran and its trade partners. The consequence was a massive shock to the Iranian economy: quadrupling annual inflation rates, devaluation of its currency to historic lows, investor abandonment, and civic protests (BBC, 2019). US Secretary of State Pompeo, in a 2018 *Foreign Affairs* article, described Iran as part of a resurgence of "outlaw regimes-rogue states that defy international norms" failing to respect human rights, acting against US interests, and endangering the world in pursuit of conflict and weapons (Pompeo, 2018; p. 60). As reports in January 2020 showed, the US and Iran almost went to war after the downing of a US drone and the US assassination of Iran's Major General Qassim Suleimani (Baker et al., 2020).

Iran's relations with the US reached a nadir with the Trump administration, and its regional position remains tenuous at best. As Barzegar and Divsallar (2017) note, Iran's alliances have diminished over the years. Although its state and non-state partners can project some hard power, they are nonetheless limited in helping Iran achieve its foreign policy objectives, lacking soft power potentials and deeply dependent on Iranian aid while experiencing their own internal divisions. Furthermore, Iran remains largely unable to define strategic initiatives with global allies, like Russia and China, who have differing global objectives and a wider environment to operate within. Managing rival alignments too poses challenges. Shared perception of Iran's growing regional influence, especially after the nuclear deal, has led to a common containment policy against Iran by competing regional powers. Saudi Arabia in particular has shaped opinion of Persian Gulf Sunni states, but also Arab people against Iran, establishing an "Islamic coalition" to battle Iranian influence and terrorist networks (Barzegar & Divsallar, 2017). Thus, Iran's international environment has largely proven inhospitable to Rouhani's planned détente, implicating his domestic support. As Akbarzadeh and Conduit (2016) argues, Rouhani's legacy in Iranian politics is a poor one with mounting pressures from conservative factions within Iran.

This is not to say Iran has no foreign policy resources. It remains capable militarily, combining geography with highly trained fighters and asymmetric technologies allowing it to survive a first strike attacks while ensuring significant deterrence capabilities. Likewise, its economy holds significant potential for growth, if able to escape US sanctions. Culturally the nation enjoys significant resources as well, but only if able to manage the conflicting forces of modernity and its more traditional cultural beliefs (Barzegar & Divsallar, 2017). How then Iran balances its domestic and international pressures in its pursuit to revise the current global order remains an open question. Across economic, diplomatic, military, and informational domains, Iranian competition in the global order requires careful consideration, especially as such policy narratives are communicated to Iranian society in support of its theocratic regime amid the variety of threats and changes in global power. To determine how Iranian media narrates to its citizens what the future global order holds, and the implications of these narratives to its identity, relational attachments, and routine behaviors, this chapter asks two questions:

RQ1. How do Iranian media narrate the future global order?
RQ2. How do Iranian media narrate the future of global competition?

Method

For a full description of the methodology, see Chapter 2. To summarize, researchers employed a mixed methodological design including qualitative narrative analysis aided by the text-mining program KH coder, as well as a quantitative content analysis. A total of 134 Iranian news articles were examined across seven Iranian news media publications. Data were collected using the Factiva platform, which aggregates and stores international news media. Researchers conducted a systematic random sampling at a 93% confidence interval on the articles collected by using a series of keywords (international/global influence, global order, international/global competition).

The qualitative narrative analysis applied a grounded theory approach with researchers first reading through the entire corpus of articles before identifying emerging patterns in creation of larger thematic categories. Emphasis was placed on understanding the narrative structure of the news articles in relation to their depiction of the global order and competition within it. As with all the chapters in this manuscript, narrative was broadly conceptualized using Burke's (1969) definition of narratives including act, agents, scenes, instruments, and purpose.

For the quantitative analysis, two coders analyzed the news articles using four general categories with subsequent subtopic categories. The first two broad categories were used to determine how Iranian media narrated the nature of global competition, including mentions of Iranian key vulnerabilities and necessary capabilities with subcategories related to the DIME (diplomatic, informational, military, and economic) instrument of power framework. Two further broad categories were included to capture Iranian media portrayals of the global order, including depictions of escalation management, deterrence, redlines, competitors, and alliances; and stated viewpoints related to Iran's depiction of the make-up of the future global order, Iran's role in the global order, as well as valence of US and Western Europe's role in the global order.

RQ1. How do Iranian media narrate the future global order?

In sum, Iranian narratives construct the global order as a competitive diplomatic landscape, with various coalitions jockeying for influence. While the US is recognized as the only single nation possessing the power necessary for global leadership, Iranian narratives highlight how resistance to such power is possible by drawing from past and present examples to showcase how US influence is contested, and weakening—especially through the actions of President Trump—pointing towards a future order of greater multi-polarity, affirming the importance of diplomacy and multilateralism. The international community is constructed as a normative body whose values and interests are in contrast to those of the US and its regional allies with Iran depicted as a defender of the people in the Shia Crescent, placing emphasis on regional dynamics of competition. As the co-occurrence figure demonstrates, key terms regarding Iranian media reporting on the global order include: having a say in the international order, presenting the global world order as "other" (i.e. they, its), war; American, collapse, system, hegemony, military, action, prevent, Syria, Soviet, Russia; Dialogue, accords; Strategic; Political Presence; More, Power; Trump, President; United States.

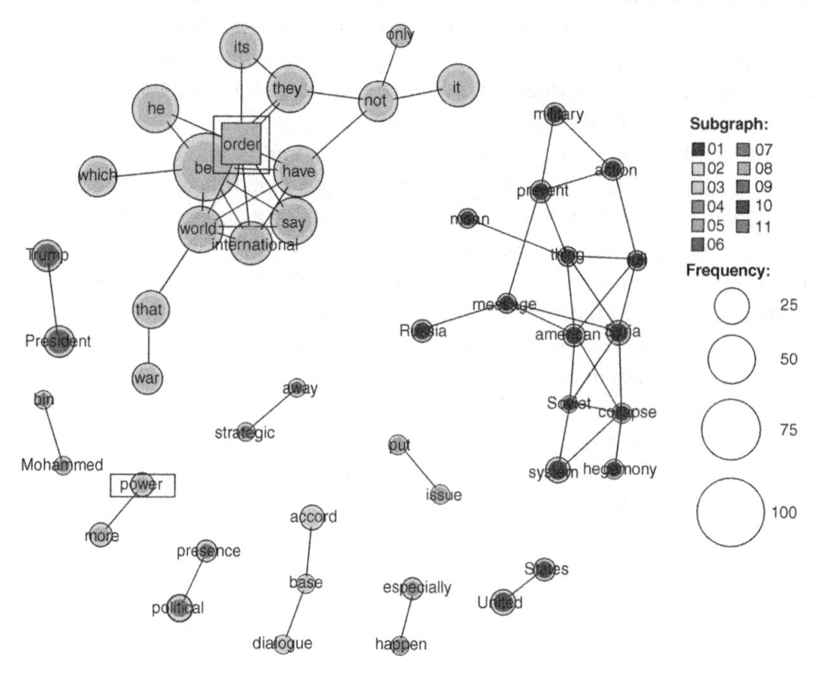

Figure 6.1 Co-occurrence Network of Iranian media Reporting Referencing "Global Order"

These narrative themes reflect the quantitative measures of Iran's view of the global order as well as itself, the US, and Western Europe. As Table 6.1 shows, Iranian media perceive the US in highly negative terms (m = -.74) with the US dominating Iranian media reporting with its presence in over 75% of articles. As the qualitative results show, the presentation of the US as a negative actor draws out the more extreme elements of the Iranian identity performance with US actions viewed as immoral and untrustworthy, leading to conflict destabilizing the global order. Such narratives support those identifying Iran as revisionist actor in the global order (Behravesh, 2018) with Iran's identity in the global order as one tied to the US in opposition to its policies, values, and character, emphasizing Iran's cultural narratives of Jihadi Islamiyat principles of revolution and Iraniyat negation of others. In contrast, Western Europe and the global order as a whole are presented in less, but still negative terms (m = -.16 and -.24 respectfully), reported in only one-third of the articles with a more moderate version of Iranian revisionism incorporating some elements of Iran's Ejtehadi Islamiyat narratives advocating for shared international norms and equitable international laws.

Both coalesce to varying degrees, however, in locating the Shia Crescent as the key scene of competition with portrayal of Iranian stewardship of the region as tied to the state's aspirations as a political and moral power in the world order, reflective of its highly positive view of its own role in the global order (m =.60). In this case, the overarching narrative present in Iranian media discussions of the global order place Iran as the protagonist with the US and its allies as antagonists, affirming Iran's perceived need to take action and provide leadership, with Iran's internal development and cohesion emphasizing Iran as a model and unifier for the greater Muslim world. Thus, Iranian narratives reveal both some simplicity in defining its identity in black and white opposition to the US, but also significant complexity with its historical, cultural narratives accentuated and integrated in important ways depending upon the narrative contexts, or scenes of global competition.

Global order

Iranian media narrate the global order as one centered upon immoral US leadership and its attempts to actively marshal diplomatic partners against

Table 6.1 Iranian Media Views on the Global Order and the West

	Article Mentions	*Valence (1=positive, -1=negative)*
Iran's Role in Global Order	N = 67 (50%)	Mean = .60
Perspectives of Global Order	N = 99 (74%)	Mean = -.24
Perspectives on the US	N = 104 (77.6%)	Mean = -.74
Perspectives on Western Europe	N = 44 (33%)	Mean = -.16

the interests of, and in threat towards, Iran and the Shia Crescent. Importantly, while the US is recognized as the preeminent global power, Iranian narratives describe the US actions and principles as leading towards its decline, moving the future global order into one of greater multipolarity.

First, Iranian media frequently and consistently construct the US as an untrustworthy, immoral, and self-interested actor with presentation of the global order tied specifically to US actions. Such negative characterizations are especially interwoven with President Trump's leadership, described as paranoid and seeking to establish a global dictatorship and accused of intentionally undermining global security.[1] Likewise, his policies are pointed out as being corrupt and as having undermined America's credibility[2] with Iranian media framing him as the great danger to the world and thus calling on the world to save multilateralism in the international system.[3] Indeed, time and again, Iranian media portray the US as an actor that, cannot be trusted in that an agreement with the US is only a proposition as US leaders can at any time renege upon such agreements.[4] This is evident not only by the US's withdrawal from the Iranian nuclear accords, but also its treaties with its own allies, like Canada, with Iranian media explaining how no one can trust the US, so why tire yourself by holding trade negotiations with a country willing to impose sanctions on its best allies while lying out the reasons for imposing punishments?[5] This storyline is extended to a variety of US positions, including US policy in Syria, the Paris climate agreement, Israeli settlements in the Golan Heights, the US embassy in Jerusalem, the treatment of Canada and Mexico concerning NAFTA, the economic trade war with China, and the Iranian nuclear deal.

Second, embedded in Iran's negative characterization of the US are claims of US immorality contributing to US decline and the rise of a multipolar world order. As *Al Alam* states, the US deals in practices of injustice and discrimination, the destruction of human dignity, and the promotion of arrogance resulting in moral decay and the corruption of culture.[6] Quoting Iranian leaders, an article from Mehr News notes how there has never been a time easier to explain to the world the extent of the White House's racist, anti-Muslim, anti-international law, and anti-Palestinian policies.[7] The consequence of such values depict the US empire as collapsing under the weight of its own corrupt political elite with attacks on Trump not just representing one instance of failed leadership but representative of a larger failure of the US system extending across US administrations; as *Al Alam* explains, Trump is not only a fundamentally unfavorable president, but that Trump himself is the product of a collective failure going back to more than just one US presidential administration.[8] This behavior is portrayed as impacting the US politically and internationally, in that America, by weakening the international system, harms itself and all other parties with the hour of payment coming.[9] As another article warns, empires collapse when they become high-cost, placing a political burden on their ruling elites; and that this is exactly what is occurring now in Washington as the ball of fire and anger that is Trump forces the world to rethink what the global order looks like without the US.[10]

While the US is presented as the predominant actor within the global order, Iranian media warns that the world is in transition and must prepare for a turbulent era as, in every period of transition, there are points of ambiguity with this era experiencing a new, systemic chaos going further than past periods of transition.[11] As Mehr News reports, a multi-polar world is the reality of today, evident by China and India having steadily increased their strength with the European Union (EU) stronger than ever before under the leadership of Germany and France; nonetheless, any country other than the US will not have the willingness to lead the international order.[12] Thus, Iranian media suggest the future global order will be one requiring greater multilateral diplomacy as US leadership is not only in decline but resulting in crisis, with the most effective solution to this crisis being that of diplomatic action through multilateral negotiations.[13]

Third, beyond merely criticizing US global leadership, Iranian media construct a threat narrative comprising of the US as bringing together a coalition of actors undermining Iranian interests and those living in the Shia Crescent, albeit one that can be defeated. Here the normalizing of relations between Arab monarchies with the US and Israel are critiqued as creating an imaginary enemy[14] consisting of Iran and those living in the Shia Crescent; as *Al Alam* explains, US and Zionist machinations are pitted against the axis of resistance in the Shia crescent from Tehran to Azza in response to the emergence of Iran as a regional power: economically, scientifically, politically, militarily.[15] Articles note how those living in the Shia Crescent face threats of colonialism that continuously try and sow division among them[16] with others explaining how unity is needed among Islamic countries and peoples now more than ever as Westerners are the terrorists promoting violence and raising political differences in Muslim societies responsible for the region's problems.[17] Within this threat narrative, Iran identifies itself as representing and protecting those targeted by US and its regional allies, like the people of Palestine,[18] Yemen,[19] and Bahrain.[20] In doing so, the Iranian state is described as rational and calling for peace while committed to protecting the region against the ruthless and belittling extremism of the ugly triangle made up of the US, Israel, and some Arab governments.[21]

Furthermore, whereas the US and its coalitional partners are narrated as posing a threat to Iran and the region's interests—increasing Iranian anxiety over its international position, Iranian media importantly assuages such fears by emphasizing US failures and Iranian successes in resisting the US and its allies. For instance, the *Iran Daily* reports generally about US retreat, citing that the US military is pulling out of Iraq three months after its defeat in Iraq and Syria[22] with other articles portending that the US will soon be forced to leave West Asia, Syria, Iraq, Afghanistan, and the Persian Gulf to escape its ultimate failures.[23] An article from Fars News Agency specifically attributes US failures as a result of Iranian supported coalitions, explaining that the allied forces of Iran, Syria, Russia, and Hezbollah defeated the foreign-backed goons led by the US in Syria.[24]

This, in conjunction with the negative characterizations of the US as the dominant actor shaping international events places attention to the importance of regional power balances in the creation of a new world order. Drawing on the importance of Iranian Shi'ism, Iranian media report the victories of Shia Muslims as marking a new dimension of the resistance movement against Israeli occupation of Arab lands and US influence in the region.[25] The Shia Crescent is shown as a vital power bloc needed to legitimately challenge US domination with Iran placed in opposition to the US as a protector, unifier, and leader of resistance. In doing so, Iranian media draws upon Iranian religious and intellectual principles to justify Iran's position, illustrating Islamiyat and Iraniyat elements of the Islamic Republic's revisionists identity, evident by a Mehr News article explaining how even Western strategists admit they cannot contain Iran's rapid and growing movement in the international order; despite decades of US conflict with Iran's people and government, Iran remains strong, owing to its legitimate religious and intellectual principles.[26]

Finally, in addition to reaffirming Iran's commitment to resisting US coalitions, Iranian media highlight the role of the international community as a normative body legitimizing state actions by narrating Iran's views as internationally accepted in contrast to the US's actions against it. As Mehr News reports, the US tries to secure support from other countries for its illegal pressures against the Iranian nation with the article citing statements from other leaders to support Iran's view; the Malaysian Prime Minister is reported as stating, as far as they can see, the US is the country making all the provocation.[27] Likewise, another Mehr News articles explains how Iran will take its case to the UN to prove US lies[28] with Fars News Agency reporting President Rouhani as underscoring the opposition made by all countries, even the Europeans, against the US's brutal pressures against Iran.[29] Iran is thereby depicted as a victim of inappropriate US actions evident by the international community's siding with Iran and in opposition to the US.

This international narrative is also applied to the Shia Crescent more specifically, again emphasizing Iran's peaceful position calling for stability and peace and calling for diplomatic unity against US actions. As one article explains, in order to preserve the international order and its stability, Iran demands that all countries declare a unified position against the policies threatening the interests of the people in the region, including the rejection of nations imposing the status quo by force onto others; such actions will resolve the outstanding problems between countries in a wise, realistic, and productive manner in accordance with international resolutions—specifically those that stand against the use of force by parties to intimidate, besiege and starve others.[30]

Iran's role in the global order

As Iranian media construct a dangerous global order, one under threat by US values and leadership, such dangers risk overwhelming the Iranian state. In maintaining support for Iran's positioning in contrast to US power, Iranian media weave elements of its various cultural narratives to provide cognitive stability for its populace while imbuing a sense of Iranian importance, and thus direction or resolution of the world's problem, particularly in the Shia Crescent. The US then, becomes a key source of ontological *in*security, but one which Iranian media utilizes in securitization of its own sense of self, providing it with the capacity to act in resistance to US pressure.

First, Iranian media describe its role in the global order by demonstrating itself as a regional power, maintaining the axis of resistance in the Shia Crescent, and propagating its legitimacy as a center of Islamic authority. In doing so, Iranian media highlight Iraniyat and Ejtehaid Islamiyat elements of its identity as a regional power amid an uncertain and changing global system. These narratives are evident by *Al Alam* reporting how the world is passing an historic turning point towards a new civilization based on justice to which the Islamic Republic has proved through its experience that it is possible to withstand, resist, and triumph over hegemonic regimes to achieve development.[31] Similarly, Mehr News notes how Iran has emerged as unified Islamic power center, despite the world's historical colonial past, reporting how the Muslim world understands and agrees that Iran is an essential part of the Arab world and the region, especially as colonial powers attempt to sow discord among Arab nations, requiring Iranian partnership to combat such attempts.[32]

Second, Iranian media claim the state to be a positive role model for other countries attempting to displace the yoke of Western rule, imbuing Iran as a nation with a sense of prestige and importance. As Mehr News reports, despite all the conspiracies purported by the West against Iran, the Iranian state has still managed to preserve its independence and identity with the Iranian people proving their existence and thereby becoming role models for the entire world.[33] Here, the notion of resistance and the importance of Iran as a genuine challenger to US authority, despite its victimization by US policies for decades, stressed through incorporation of Jihadism and negation of others, presents a more aggressive revisionism around resistance to the US. As one article explains resistance is the only way to confront the unjust and arrogant practices of global system that seeks domination, especially from the US.[34] Such resistance is noted as coming at a cost, but one worth paying; as another article from Mehr News explains, although today's political situation might make things harder for the Iranian people, it has also made it easier for Iran to bring more countries to their side.[35] Put more plainly, a report from *Al Alam* argues that Iran has successful combatted US interests, noting how the schemes of its enemies have been thwarted so far,[36] thus demonstrating that the role of the Islamic Republic of Iran in the global system, and its presence as a major player in the region, cannot be ignored.[37]

Third, Iranian media characterize Iran as a fair international actor committed to peace and the global order while unwilling to compromise its self-ascribed status as a regional power no matter the pressures applied from the US. As one article explains, political observers note that Iran's security and peace concept for the region and globe is no different from what is being discussed at the 18th Doha Forum, but with Iran being the first to call for it.[38] Others note how the logic and rationality of Iran's foreign policy comes from its calls for peace and its commitment to its commitments.[39] Iranian media even claim that the state has played an active role in supporting the international community over time, beginning with the start of the Islamic revolution as occurring during the collapse of the world's bi-polar system and the emergence of regional players; since then, Iran has played a very prominent role in the fight against terrorism, violence and extremism, and thus, no serious change in the region can occur without considering the position, role, and place of the Iranian state.[40]

This notion of history helps present both a sense of autobiographical continuity even when facing challenges regarding present day circumstances and their subsequent implications. Other examples of this include reporting on the US's withdrawal on the Iranian nuclear accords, explained at length by an article from *Al Alam*, noting how the US withdrawal from the Iranian nuclear accords is unimportant for the Rouhani government as Iranians are an independent people with great capabilities and competencies who have managed the country for the past 40 years despite the wars, embargos, and sanctions placed against them. As a result, they have never trusted the US, with the Iranian people having the experience, willingness, and leadership to continue successfully running the country under any circumstances without any problem.[41]

Through resistance and in light of Iranian exceptionalism, Iranian media claim the state to be the most powerful force among the Islamic countries in the world[42] in part because of its being the first modern religious state successfully founded upon principles combining science and reason with determination.[43] Here again we see how Iran's cultural narratives are brought together to explain the state's power, making it as the essential part of unifying the Arab world and the Middle East as a region through its rise as a unified Islamic power center. In projecting its role in the global order Iran is seen as one building a regional power bloc of resistance against the powers of the larger order, namely the US, with the Islamic Republic's narratives contributing to its revisionist identity through inclusions of Iraniyat elements tied to a sort of credibility through its longevity and initiator and its Islamiyat elements linking state and religion while combining doctrine with reason with Jihadi elements also present with Iran's resistance to the US emphasized as successfully humbling its attempts to contain Iran, forcing US recognition of Iran's strength.

Partnerships, competitors, and conflict management

Iran's depiction of a hostile environment reflects its discussions of conflict and competitors. Here, mentions of competitors (n = 80; 60%) occur almost twice as much as any of the other categories with the nearest categories being mentions of conflict/escalation management (n = 47; 35%) and mentions of alliances (n = 43; 32%). Conflict and escalation management are discussed slightly more than alliances with redlines to actual military action discussed the least (n = 14; 10%), though clear lines are drawn across these occurrences and still reported in some frequency. These results feed into presentation of Iran demonstrating its oppression at the hands of external powers with the Iranian state shown as committed to standing against such oppressors, reinforcing a larger narrative depicting the world as divided between Zionist supporters and the interests of those living in the Shia Crescent.

First, in discussing alliances and competitors, qualitative assessment shows the US, Israel, and Saudi Arabia as the most often mentioned competitors, along with states seen as under direct influence and/or pressures of those three, including: the UAE, Turkey, and the UK. Allies or partner nations include Palestinians, Yemen Houthi, Syria, Lebanon and Hezbollah, the Shanghai Cooperation Organization, and more generally those living in the Shia Crescent and the larger global Muslim community. In describing its allies, Iranian media most often report itself as representing and defending their interests broadly against Zionist forces represented by the US and Saudi Arabia. Thus, articles note how the Saudi Zionist lobby is a threat to the world[44] with others charactering the Saudi Arabian regime and its attacks against Yemen as supported by the same Zionists attacking Palestinian resistance groups, including those giving large amounts of money and arms to support terrorists and Takfiri groups.[45] Likewise, reports explain how, in addition to the US, Russia and Britain, new Zionist players have emerged over the past five years in West Asia with the UAE acting alongside Saudi Arabia in its aggression against Yemen and Qatar supporting Saudi terrorists. Zionists are thus exploiting these opportunities by attempting to provide security through them, while merely augmenting their own influence.[46] In this sense, the Shia Crescent

Table 6.2 Iranian Media Reporting of Conflict Dynamics

	Article Mentions
Mentioned Competitors	N = 80 (60%)
Mentioned Alliances	N = 43 (32%)
Legitimate Deterrence	N = 23 (17%)
Conflict/Escalation Management	N = 47 (35%)
Redlines to Action	N = 14 (10%)

and the greater Muslim community are loosely depicted as the allies of the Iranian regime with Iranian media speaking of alliances in terms of an Iranian regional area of influence, constructing itself as a protectorate of this region, rather than making claims of alignment or alliance with more traditional world powers, such as the West.

Second, in discussing conflict management and Iranian redlines, the theme of resistance is highlighted, showcasing Iranian success in combatting its competitors, but also reinforcing Iran's positive image as a moral and rational actor. In doing so, Iranian media commits to the protection of itself and its regional interests while careful to note that Iran itself is not a nation seeking escalation; rather it is the victim of US-backed hostilities. Articles note how, Iran doesn't seek war, but will nonetheless zealously defend their skies, land, and waters[47] with *Iran Daily* expressing that Iran is ready to defend its interests in the region in the wake of US aggression.[48] Such defense arises from Iranian notions of resistance, including its support of allies, like in the preservation of the Assad regime, and in opposition to the US. *Al Alam* describes the goal of Iran's resistance forces as preventing the overthrow of the Syrian government in Syria—to which it succeeded. Nonetheless, the struggle continues with hostile groups attempting to siege Iranian allies in the region day after day; to which Iran's forces of resistance are not expected to retreat, but rather expand and protect them no matter what.[49]

Narratives of Jihadi and extreme negation are further evident in Iranian media presentations of the US as its chief competitor. As *Iran Daily* notes, Iran faces unending, provocative, and sustained attempts by the US to crank up political, psychological, economic, and military pressure on Iran, and claims such actions cannot be assessed as anything but a conscious decision to provoke war.[50] In facing such aggression, Iranian media warn that any conflict with the US will result in a long drawn out conflict in which Iran would ultimately emerge as victorious due to costs and lack of political will for conflict in the US. As an article, quoting Bernie Sanders on the possibility of war between the US and Iran explains, this will be an asymmetrical war in the Middle East that never ends, making the Iraq war look like a cakewalk.[51] Others emphasize the point further, stressing Iran's ability to disrupt the global economy as half of the world's oil exports are described as at the mercy of Iran, its allies, and missiles.[52]

Despite such military warnings, Iranian media also demonstrates a more conciliatory approach when discussing conflict by appealing to the international community for rational evaluation of the escalations and demonization of Iran by the US. As Mehr News explains, actions designed to escalate tensions in the region through drums of war and confrontation, accompanied by the imposition of unilateral economic sanctions by the US against Iran, are contrary to international laws and customs.[53] Thus, Iranian media describe US sanctions as illegitimate as they stand in opposition not only to the Iranian nuclear accords, but also UN Security

Council resolutions and decisions made by the International Court of Justice.[54] The unilateral nature of US actions is further emphasized in articles describing the US as strong-arming Europe into punishing Iran with the consequence of the US decision to nullify the Iran nuclear deal causing the escalation of relations between Europe and America.[55]

Finally, Iranian media present a sense of calm and a notion of Iran's maturity in wake of President Trump's rhetoric. Despite portrayals that Iran would again face pressures from the Great Satan, evident by Trump's anti-Iranian rhetoric, Iranian media note that they don't want to be pessimistic regarding the Trump administration, and instead will judge US actions rather than its words as Iran does not want to place barriers between them and anyone in the world. Supportive of this position, the Iranian people are described as open, and wanting to deliver their messages to the world in a safe and reasonable manner by applying international laws.[56] In sum, Iranian media showcase how, in the face of openly hostile rhetoric from the US administration, Iranian leaders, and thus the state as a whole, is a mature, rational actor willing to observer and respond to US actions, not just its antagonistic messaging.

RQ2. How do Iranian media narrate the future of global competition?

In discussing what global competition is comprised of, Iranian media, despite facing significant threats depicted within the global order, focus less on military dimensions of global competition and more on the importance of diplomacy. When reporting both its competitive vulnerabilities and capabilities, diplomatic elements are cited most frequently, with a combined average of 29.4%, compared to informational elements (10.9%), military (6.7%), and economic (6%). Appealing to diplomatic agents, such as the EU, as well as emphasizing a common cultural coalition of people in the Shia Crescent, appear to mark Iran's chief concern reported in its media while relatively downplaying the military and economic risks of standing in opposition to the US, Saudi Arabia, and Zionist forces broadly defined. In doing so, Iranian capabilities are, on average, more often reported than vulnerabilities with about 11% of articles emphasizing the later and 16% the former with its described vulnerabilities tending to go hand in hand with its capabilities, providing a sense of trust in Iran's ability to meet the challenges required of competing in the global order while also placing the country in a state of anxiety.

Vulnerabilities

Iranian vulnerabilities are most frequently cited in diplomatic competition (n = 27; 20%) focusing on its competitors' attempts to diplomatically isolate the nation and form coalitions containing it. Informational vulnerabilities are the second most often in occurrence (n = 17; 12%) with military and economic weaknesses discussed least frequently (n = 5; 5% and n = 8; 6% respectfully). Narration of Iran's vulnerabilities primarily revolve around elements of its Jihadi Islamiyat morality and Iraniyat negation in portraying the US and its coalitional partners as undermining unity within the Shia Crescent as well as Iran's revisionist identity decrying the current system as one dominated by the US. Nonetheless, Ejtehadi Islamiyat and shared cultural aspects of its Iraniyat narratives are present too, especially in calling for the international community to stand up against US unilateralism.

Diplomatic vulnerabilities

Diplomatic vulnerabilities play a key role in Iranian media descriptions of its ability to compete in the global order, often taking the form of narrating the Iranian state as an outside actor victimized by US leadership, but also in making appeals to international law. Thus, White House officials are described as acting globally through a criminal international gang[57] abusing their position on the Security Council with US sanctions specifically designed to directly and adversely affect economic relations with Iran by intimidating third parties and pressuring other states to abide by its political aspirations.[58] In contrast, Iranian leadership is shown as stressing upon the international community the need to resist US domination, calling on the international community to define its position in relation to US unilateralism, and whether it wants to live under a law-based system or to submit to the pressures and threats of Trump.[59] In facing diplomatic pressure from the US, Iranian media repeatedly note the illegality of US actions, stating that the US threat against Iran is a flagrant violation of international law not just to its own sovereignty, but also representative of an open aggression against Muslim people who refuse to bend, bow, and surrender.[60]

While Iranian media presents the state as an actor whose leadership, rationality, and moral correctness are recognized by the international community, it notes that such behavior is now uncommon in the region. As an article from *Al Alam* explains, the wits of the Iranians and their values of pride, dignity, and self-respect are now less commonly shared in

Table 6.3 Iranian Vulnerabilities and Capabilities in News Media

	Articles Mentioning Key Vulnerabilities	*Articles Mentioning Necessary Capabilities*
Diplomatic	N = 27 (20%)	N = 52 (39%)
Informational	N = 17 (12%)	N = 13 (10%)
Military	N = 7 (5%)	N = 11 (8%)
Economic	N = 8 (6.0%)	N = 8 (6%)

the region.[61] Furthermore, the US and its allies are viewed as preventing Iran's emergence as a truly global leader with forces set against it shown as significant impediments to the Iranian state as Trump and his so-called Arab North Atlantic Treaty Organization allies—comprised of Saudi Arabia, UAE, Kuwait, Qatar, and Israel—are shown as disingenuously offering dialogue without preconditions yet wishing to wage war on Iran.[62] Here the US and its allies are linked to the suppression of Iran and cast as forming a coalition of enemies around it. Competition, then, is breaking Iran's diplomatic containment with diplomatic leverage an area where it recognizes itself as vulnerable.

Informational vulnerabilities

Iran's diplomatic concerns are reflected in its informational vulnerabilities, presented as US-led attempts to isolate Iran and disrupt potentials for Muslim unity. Iranian media emphasize the weaponization of rhetoric by the US and Israel in demonstration of their attempts to sow internal and external divisions among Iranians and the larger Muslim community while the US is shown as inhibiting Iran's voice in the international order. Thus, informational vulnerabilities include Western-led stoking of internal political disputes via information campaigns and online social networks. As *Al Alam*, reporting on Iranian domestic protests in 2017, explains, although Iran's constitution recognizes the right of expression and the demand for other rights more broadly, when legitimate political demands turn into masks for disrupting security and public order and attacks on public and private property, this leads to suspicions and misgivings surrounding the movement with Iran's enemies grabbing popular movements to incite violence.[63] Indeed, the US and Israel are often accused of running global media campaigns to discredit the Iranian regime in the eyes of its own people and the rest of the world, as well as other Middle Eastern nations; like reports stating how the US is leading the conspiracies of Iran's enemies across military, economic, and social dimensions raising political tensions and discontent[64] with such actions described as intending to discredit Iran in the international system.[65] Gulf nations too are viewed as conducting informational campaigns weakening the Islamic identity of the region with Gulf media playing the dirty role of diluting Arab identity and creating a culture of religious and sectarian antagonism that flattens the Arab dream.[66] Other concerns include US attempts at using terrorism as a pretext to justify military infiltration into Iran with articles warning that Iranians should be prepared for such actions.[67]

Military vulnerabilities

Military vulnerabilities are rarely explicitly mentioned, largely because the conversation on vulnerabilities are seldom shown in the context of just the

Iranian state. Rather, vulnerability is seen within a larger regional context that focuses on military actions from Iran's enemies related to the region as a whole with little discussion highlighting the extent to which such actions directly threaten the Iranian state. Thus, the general concern is the militarization of Gulf Arab regimes combined with US and Saudi support against Iranian interests in Syria, Iraq, Algeria, Yemen, and Sudan. For instance, articles cite Iran's Foreign Minister as having criticized the US's military presence in the Persian Gulf as illegal and creating tensions in the region[68] with Saudi Arabia also being interested in increasing tensions in the region through its blockade of Qatar and the military operations in Yemen.[69] Western support for Saudi Arabia is described as complicit in escalating tensions, as a number of Western countries—including the US and UK in particular—supporting ongoing aggressions by supplying Saudi Arabia with advanced weapons and military equipment as well as logistical and intelligence assistance.[70]

More specific concerns arise from US threats to conduct military strikes against Iran, with *Iran Daily* noting how many in Washington expected President Trump to take military actions against Iran in response to Iran shooting down a US drone; the article reports that Trump had already sent an aircraft carrier strike group and several long-range bombers, in addition to additional US troops into the region.[71] Nonetheless, Iranian media presents such threats as more statements of fact rather than describing in detail how such threats undermine Iran's security specifically.

Economic vulnerabilities

Economic vulnerabilities are explained as stemming primarily from Iran's dependency on oil exports with US sanctions reported as threatening Iranian economic development. An article from *Tehran Times* notes how the Iranian economy has struggled since Trump pulled out of the 2015 nuclear accord, re-imposing sanctions and restrictions on oil sales[72] with others characterizing the intent of US sanctions as a threat to squeeze Iran's economy until it squeals.[73] Likewise, FARS News reports how the US withdrawal from the nuclear agreement left Iran dealing with problems in banking relations and oil as foreign companies that had previously invested in Iran have become skeptical about continuing their business, impacting its economy.[74]

While the emphasis on Iran's economic vulnerabilities comes from US sanctions, Iranian media also note how the Islamic world more generally suffers from a lack of economic development, resulting from internal and external conflicts; as *Al Alam* reports, unfortunately, the Islamic world today remains weak as it suffers from poverty, internal conflicts, and conflicts caused by the pressures made by ignorant regimes.[75] Such vulnerability is presented in line with Iran's depiction of the US and Israel more broadly as corrupting Islamic unity in exchange for money and power in partnerships with untrustworthy enemies, with Trump bullying and extorting the Arabs in the Gulf region until they obey his orders and meet all his financial demands.[76] Other themes include the US and Israel as attempting to colonize a divided Islamic world by exploiting Arab monarchies in order to control their natural resources, as well as insidious attempts to control the Palestinian territory and the use of financial bribery among Muslim communities.[77]

Capabilities

Iranian capabilities for competing in the global order involve narrating itself as a moral and rational revisionist pushing for justice, independence and republicanism. The promise of victory over the power brokers of the status quo in unity with others allows Ejtehadi Islamiyat and shared culture Iraniyat aspects of Iranian revisionism to be projected in relation to competition while its military capabilities stress its Jihadi Islamiyat elements placing resistance to the US and its allies as crucial to competition. Thus, diplomatic capabilities are by far most occurring (n = 52; 39%) followed by information (n = 13; 10%), military (n = 11; 8%), and economic (n = 8; 6%) with Iranian news suggesting that Iran is able to weather confrontation, both militarily and economically, from those seeking to contain it.

Diplomatic capabilities

To successfully compete in the current and future global order, Iran emphasizes the need and benefits of diplomacy as well as accentuating its diplomatic resources in combatting US attempts to contain and pressure it. First, articles explain the importance of economic delegations and diplomacy to mitigate US sanctions against Iran. *FARS News* specifically explains how special attention to economic diplomacy and paying attention to public confidence is the biggest back up for countering foreign pressures and sanctions.[78] Nonetheless, the importance of diplomatic capabilities extends beyond just economic considerations and includes potentials for mitigating conflict in the Middle East more broadly. As *Al Alam* explains, through their successive visits of economic delegations, European leaders have expressed as openness to economic cooperation with Iran, but with political cooperation being no less important; EU leaders have thus also demonstrated a desire to engage Iran in dialogue with such cooperative efforts playing an important and distinctive role in strengthening security and stability in the region.[79]

Thus, Iranian media stress not only the importance of diplomacy, but also European nations' desire to engage Iran in discussions. This sentiment is echoed in other reports, including relations with the US, with an article citing and affirming Iraqi President al-Maliki's call for an end to the crisis between the US and Iran by engaging in dialogue and ending military escalation in the region, as well as and the renunciation of states attempting to impose a fait accompli on others.[80] Even Iran and Turkey are reported as capable of cooperating with an article noting that both nations have also called for comprehensive efforts to protect the nuclear deal while confirming it as an example of how multilateral diplomacy can bear fruit.[81] Further support of Iran's commitment to diplomatic efforts is evident in an article from *Mehr News,* stating Iran's belief in solving outstanding problems between countries in wise, realistic and productive ways and in accordance with international resolutions in contrast to the use of force and intimidation.[82]

Second, Iranian media, despite describing the pressures of US diplomatic attempts at isolating the nation and undermining its economic growth, make sure to point out how such attempts are failing, thereby highlighting Iran's diplomatic capabilities vis-à-vis the US. A report from FARS News Agency most explicitly makes this clear, noting that Iran's economic cooperation with other countries is increasing with such developments proving that US plots against Iran's economy will remain unrealized.[83] Others note how the multipolarity of the global order, specifically with the rise of Chinese and Russian influence, undermine US influence and support Iran's position in that US sanctions against Iran are doomed to fail as the world's major economic players—Russia and China—are on Iran's side.[84] As FARS News Agency reports, the irresponsible conduct of the US requires a collective response by the international community to uphold the global system's rule of law and protect multilateralism from US efforts to undermine diplomacy.[85]

Informational capabilities

To combat Iran's competitors from dominating the information space, Iranian media narrate the importance of its religious and moral beliefs. Here, the strength and unity of the Shia Crescent, the ability to demonstrate the injustices of the US-led global order, and showcasing Iran as an exemplar of Koranic modernity are described as critical to successful global competition and creating a balanced multi-polar world order. Articles note how the only way to confront the weaknesses of the Islamic world today, caused by internal and external conflict, is to implement Koranic teachings and move forward towards achieving its lofty goals.[86] Likewise, while Iran's livelihood and economy is being targeted by some Westerners, with the US economic war against Iran going hand-in-hand with psychological operations meant to divide Iranian officials from ordinary people, nonetheless through the prudence of Iranian authorities in combination with the insight of the people, Iran can proudly continue its journey as a modern theocratic state and neutralize their enemy's conspiracies against their political system grounded in freedom and moral and religious values.[87]

Additional capabilities arise from Iran's ability to provide a legal defense to the international community demonstrating the illegality of US actions. As an article from Mehr News, reporting on Iran's downing of a US military drone upon entering Iranian airspace explains, Iran responded by sending a letter to the United Nations (UN) Secretary General and Security Council president providing sufficient legal evidence proving the US's provocative and intrusive aggression.[88] Such articulations of Iran's legal rights thereby function as combatting US diplomatic isolation while undermining US credibility and upholding Iran's commitment to global governance norms.

Military capabilities

Iranian military capabilities are described in defensive terms, specifically in relation to US military threats against the Iranian nation. Iranian media thus demonstrate that, despite US sanctions, Iran has managed to develop sufficient deterrent capabilities in response to US provocation making war a costly endeavor that Iran can, and will, succeed in. For instance, an article from Mehr News comments on Iran's military preparedness, expressing how Iran's military regularly holds war games and drills to maintain its military preparedness allowing it to deliver the heaviest blows to its enemies in the case of any possible attack.[89] In addition to war games, Iranian media states it is in possession of a significant arsenal of missiles, developed despite US sanctions with the achievements by its missile defense and nuclear industries having astonished the world.[90] As another article notes, four decades of US imposed sanctions on Iran has only led to its progress in the development of missile defense and promising that a new round of sanctions will only lead to become stronger in this field.[91] Nonetheless, Iranian media explain that its missiles are defensive in nature in that they need them for deterrence, and that Iran uses them far less for military action compared to anybody else in the region; this is why, from the beginning, Iranian leaders have stated that their missile program is non-negotiable.[92]

Economic capabilities

Iran's stated economic capabilities primarily revolve around steps it is taking to combat US economic sanctions. For instance, *Tehran Times* reports Iranian experts as pointing out the country's oil-reliant economy as susceptible to pressures from US sanctions with the only way to combat US sanctions being to strengthen Iran's non-oil exports by supporting medium and small industries in need of government support to grow their presence in the global markets.[93] Likewise, another article from *Tehran Times* explains to its readers that although the nation is an oil producer with an oil-reliant economy dominated by petrodollars, Iranian leadership plans to reduce its dependence on petrodollars by seeking other currency tools like cryptocurrencies and blockchain technology to make up drops in oil revenues resulting from economic sanctions designed to cut its oil sales.[94]

Iranian media also describe its economic capabilities by reporting how the state plans on improving Iran's economy more broadly by tapping into its national potentials to make the country sanctions-proof.[95] Such efforts are described as eventually improving Iran's economy, promising that after a period of crisis the dreams of Iran's enemies to hurt the nation economically will not come true and lead to Iran's economic situation improving.[96] In the meantime, Iranian leaders are reported as offering a package of policies involving social and cultural measures to reinvigorate the nation's economy and infrastructure against the US sanctions seeking to mitigate their effects and allowing for Iran's economy to improve step by step.[97]

Discussion

This chapter set out to determine how the Iranian state, through its narratives of global order and competition, supply Iranians with OS regarding its geopolitical position. In sum, Iranian narratives stress the rise of resistant regionalism as a the form of multi-polar world power by weaving religious narratives pitting the morality of the Iranian state against the US, Saudi, and Zionist forces while projecting an imagined, but also real, Islamic homeland in the Shia Crescent. Within this, and on a macro-level, Iranian Islamic ideology and revisionist narratives bent against the US form important identity markers essentializing Iran's sense of self against its external "others" while nonetheless also including some elements of a shared international community accentuating Iran's depiction of immoral US leadership standing in contrast to the global system's values upon which the international community should rally against. This latter element plays out even more so on a regional level, with Iranian leadership emphasizing commonality among nations and the people living within the Shia Crescent. Thus, Iranian visions of the future of the global order involves a compilation of regional powers contending, resisting, and reaffirming the status-quo, which Iran views itself as capable of maneuvering within given its history of resistance towards dominant powers and the moral correctness of its actions.

As the OS literature related to state systems argues, the underlying motivational anxiety to solidify identity amid a transforming international system is central to how and why populations understand their own agency as a unified civic-body within the confines of the nation-state (Mitzen, 2006; Krolikowski, 2008). Thus, in response to rapidly changing socio-economic and political realities, religious and nationalist discourses have increasingly dominated public debate among nations with religious nationalism becoming a driving force for identification within societies (Kinnvall, 2007). This is particularly important for Iran as its theocratic state and traditional Islamic values come in competition internationally with Western and progressive values of modernity and its own internal, pre-Islamic narratives and pressures from reformists.

However, the clarity of Iran's identity, amid these alternative, competing elements create pressures on Iran's OS, especially given its tenuous geopolitical position with rising confrontation with global and regional powers and its domestic instability. Indeed, President Rouhani came to power as a result of Iran's elites viewing his predecessor's antagonistic and ideologically driven rhetoric and actions as undermining Iran's security (Golmohammadi, 2019; Barzegar & Divsallar, 2017; Haghgoo et al., 2017) with Rouhani pledging to de-securitize and normalize Iran's foreign relations while focusing on improving Iran's economy (Akbarzadeh & Conduit, 2016). And yet, Iran's deteriorating international position and the US election of President Trump undermined Iran's attempted shift, highlighting how external relations can significantly influence domestic identity constructions. Thus, the bulk of the articles analyzed in this study showed an overwhelming focus on the US's pulling out of the Iranian nuclear deal and subsequent antagonistic actions taken against Iran. The result appears to be Iran falling back on its previous identity and routinized relationships in opposition to US leadership.

Within Iran's depiction of the global order, Iranian media thus depict its aspirations as involving a confrontation with the US on the global level while involving itself as competing and solidifying its dominance of the Shia Crescent toward an export of a righteous-resistance mentality in response to its regional competitors. Iranian confrontation with the US is narrated as a diplomatic campaign highlighting US injustice to others in prevention of US dominance within the normative and informational sphere while the regional exportation of Islamic unity under Iranian guidance is narrated as a demonstration of its own cultural, intellectual, and moral excellence. In sum, competition amid a multi-polar world order is seen as an endeavor of diplomatic positioning under moralistic terms as new regional powers arise and alliances form.

Trajectory/refection

While a strong sense of who one is provides the self with the capacity to act, when such identities become overly fixed around conflictual relations with others, one's security might actually become undermined (Mitzen, 2006). In Iran's case, its identity appears to largely become essentialized into binaries posed against the US and broadly defined "Zionist" forces drawing upon the isolationist and xenophobic elements of its Iraniyat and Islamiyat cultural narratives. Thus, in response to US antagonism, Iran is primarily placed into an Islamiyat/Jihadi mindset with Iran narrated as ready and willing to fight a war of attrition in order to defeat the US. Such a plotline provides little reflection on the possibility of mutual shifts toward a common middle. While describing the US as a weakened enemy and Iran as a defiantly strong regional power willing to sacrifice all if necessary provides a compelling narrative for Iran's role in the global order, it also makes it difficult for the Iranian state to back away from conflictual actions if provoked. The strength of such narrative, especially in providing legitimacy for Iran's theocratic government, calls into question its ability to build a truly cooperative relationship within a US-led global system with Iranian antagonism toward the US appearing critical to its performance of "self" with its projected trust system remaining anchored in religious narratives of resistance. Nonetheless, Iran's international narrative of a multipolar order characterized by diplomacy provides some element of reflection and adaptability. It's drawing upon shared norms and calling upon global leaders, including European nations, to admonish US actions provides a potential pathway avoiding conflict; only if such a pathway proves incapable is Iran ready to rely upon its ability to resist and fight against US provocations.

A key question then, regarding Iran's future narrative trajectory is what happens to its identity if the US vacates its role as the leader of the global order or takes a more conciliatory approach to relations with Iran? Indeed, a rapprochement between the US and Iran appeared to be occurring under President Obama and with Rouhani's election, diverted, however, with the surprising election of Trump. Our findings suggest a more cooperative tone is possible, although difficult, and perhaps coming in a more marginal manner. While much of Iran's narratives against the US focused on Trump's policy and leadership, the US as a whole was still represented as Iran's chief global competitor. Such symbolic formulation of an outside enemy resonates well with Iran's cultural narratives and sense of self, with the OS literature suggesting this to be of crucial significance when the state faces substantial challenges and doubts regarding its basic trust systems and routines over its ability to provide security and development for its domestic populace (Krolikowski, 2008; Huysmans, 1998). Thus, only if Iran's material conditions improve, including the competitive dynamics it faces in the Middle East and with a relaxation of sanctions allowing for Iran's economy to grow, may the Iranian leadership be able to scale down its antagonistic rhetoric.

Likewise, although Iranian narratives demonstrated a willingness to engage the broader global community on more cooperative terms through diplomatic means, this cooperative posturing still occurs within a thin revisionist mindset comprised of creating contrasts and folding in of the rules against the US and its affiliated allies. In other words, some cooperative elements map onto Iran's Ejtehadi Islamiyat and Iraniyat elements of self-identity allowing for a more mild form of an ethical global system with adjustments amid a multi-polar world order. However, competing with such narratives is a level of ethnocentrism within Iran's Shi'ism and Jihadi Islamiyat understanding of the world contributing to Iran's identity as a revisionist state, making it difficult to imagine Iran taking on a genuinely cooperative role within any global system.

Furthermore, it's important to note that the US is not Iran's sole competitor. The foundational aspects of a non-cooperative Iranian state identity runs deeper than US contrasts, with Saudi Arabia and Israel posing additional competing value systems. Iran's regional competitors feed into its Shia and Jihaid Islamiyat elements internalizing a self at odds with its neighboring countries, contributing to a non-cooperative sense of self pitted against its "outsiders."

That said, the Iranian state has shown itself as a pragmatic performer of role when the stage demands. Indeed, over the past 40 years Iran has demonstrated itself as capable of blending a complex identity into that of a stable revisionist actor able to withstand bouts of extreme external pressures while flexible enough to pivot when practicality and utility demand. How this unfolds amid an evolving global order with US predominance declining remain to be seen, especially as Iranian society reflects on how its identity roles help or hinder its domestic development in a globalized economy.

Notes

1 *Al Alam* (October 14, 2017). Factiva.
2 *Al Alam* (March 6, 2019). Factiva.
3 Mehr News (May 16, 2018). Factiva.
4 *Al Alam* (March 16, 2019). Factiva.
5 Ibid.
6 *Al Alam* (May 27, 2014). Factiva.
7 Mehr News (July 22, 2018). Factiva.
8 *Al Alam* (January 7, 2018). Factiva.
9 *Al Alam* (March 16, 2019). Factiva.
10 Al Alam. (January 7, 2018). Factiva.
11 Mehr News (January 22, 2017). Factiva.
12 Mehr News (August 29, 2017). Factiva.
13 *Al Alam* (August 13, 2017). Factiva.
14 *Al Alam* (February 19, 2016). Factiva.
15 Ibid.
16 Mehr News (November 13, 2016). Factiva.
17 *Al Alam* (April 7, 2018). Factiva.
18 Mehr News (September 17, 2016). Factiva.
19 *Iran Daily* (December 15, 2018). Factiva.
20 Mehr News (October 9, 2018). Factiva.
21 Al Alam (July 24, 2018). Factiva.
22 *Iran Daily* (June 22, 2019). Factiva.
23 Fars News (November 11, 2018). Factiva.
24 Fars News (December 31, 2018). Factiva.
25 *Al Alam* (June 1, 2017). Factiva.
26 Mehr News (June 3, 2015). Factiva.
27 Mehr News (June 22, 2019). Factiva.
28 Ibid.
29 Fars News (November 23, 2018). Factiva.
30 Mehr News (May 11, 2019). Factiva.

31 *Al Alam* (September 30, 2014). Factiva.
32 Mehr News (November 13, 2016). Factiva.
33 Mehr News (July 4, 2016). Factiva.
34 Mehr News (February 13, 2019). Factiva.
35 Mehr News (July 22, 2018). Factiva.
36 *Al Alam* (February 6, 2019). Factiva.
37 Ibid.
38 *Al Alam* (December 15, 2018). Factiva.
39 *Al Alam* (July 24, 2018). Factiva.
40 *Al Alam* (January 28, 2018). Factiva.
41 *Al Alam* (May 7, 2018). Factiva.
42 *Al Alam* (April 20, 2018). Factiva.
43 *Al Alam* (February 9, 2015). Factiva.
44 *Al Alam* (September 18, 2018). Factiva.
45 Mehr News (June 21, 2019). Factiva.
46 *Al Alam* (November 21, 2016). Factiva.
47 Mehr News (June 21, 2019). Factiva.
48 *Iran Daily* (June 19, 2019). Factiva.
49 *Al Alam* (June 1, 2017). Factiva.
50 *Iran Daily* (June 18, 2019). Factiva.
51 *Iran Daily* (June 19, 2019). Factiva.
52 *Al Alam* (August 1, 2018). Factiva.
53 Mehr News (May 11, 2019). Factiva.
54 *Al Alam* (November 3, 2018). Factiva.
55 Mehr News (November 1, 2018). Factiva.
56 Mehr News (November 13, 2016). Factiva.
57 *Al Alam* (September 18, 2018). Factiva.
58 FARS News (November 17, 2018). Factiva.
59 *Al Alam* (September 18, 2018). Factiva.
60 Mehr News (May 11, 2019). Factiva.
61 *Al Alam* (August 1, 2018). Factiva.
62 Ibid.
63 *Al Alam* (January 5, 2018). Factiva.
64 *Al Alam* (August 1, 2018). Factiva.
65 *Al Alam* (April 21, 2016). Factiva.
66 *Al Alam* (February 19, 2016). Factiva.
67 *Al Alam* (January 5, 2018). Factiva.
68 *Iran Daily* (December 29, 2018). Factiva.
69 *Iran Daily* (December 15, 2018). Factiva.
70 Ibid.
71 Ibid.
72 *Tehran Times* (January 8, 2019). Factiva.
73 FARS News (November 14, 2018). Factiva.
74 FARS News (November 17, 2018). Factiva.
75 *Al Alam* (May 23, 2015). Factiva.
76 *Al Alam* (August 1, 2018). Factiva.
77 Iran Daily (6/23/19). Factiva.
78 FARS News (12/24/18). Factiva.
79 Al Alam (2/9/16). Factiva.
80 Mehr News Agency (May 11, 2019). Factiva.
81 *Tehran Times* (December 21, 2018). Factiva.
82 Mehr News (May 11, 2019). Factiva.
83 FARS News (January 6, 2019). Factiva.
84 *Iran Daily* (November 30, 2018). Factiva.

85 FARS News (November 17, 2018). Factiva.
86 *Al Alam* (May 23, 2015). Factiva.
87 FARS News (24 December 2018). Factiva.
88 Mehr News (June 21, 2019). Factiva.
89 Mehr News (June 22, 2019). Factiva.
90 *Tehran Times* (December 17, 2018). Factiva.
91 FARS News (November 15, 2018). Factiva.
92 *Iran Daily* (December 15, 2018). Factiva.
93 *Tehran Times* (December 14, 2018). Factiva.
94 *Tehran Times* (January 16, 2019). Factiva.
95 FARS News (November 23, 2018). Factiva.
96 FARS News (January 6, 2019). Factiva.
97 Ibid.

References

Abrahamian, E. (1980). Structural causes of the Iranian Revolution. *MERIP Reports*. (87), 21–26.

Abrahamian, E. (1982). *Iran between two revolutions*. Princeton University Press.

Abrahamian, E. (2009). Mass Protests in the Islamic Revolution, 1977–79. In A. Roberts and T. G. Ash (Eds.), *Civil Resistance and Power Politics: The Experience of Non-violent Action from Gandhi to the Present*, 162–178. Oxford University Press.

Afkhami, G. R. (2009). *The life and times of the Shah*. University of California Press.

Akbarzadeh, S. & Barry, J. (2016). State identity in Iranian foreign policy. *British Journal of Middle Eastern Studies*. 43(4), 613–629.

Akbarzadeh, S. & Conduit, D. (Eds). (2016). *Iran in the world: President Rouhani's foreign policy*. Palgrave Macmillan.

Algar, H. (1981). *Islam and revolution, writings and declarations of Imam Khomeini*. Mizan Press.

Amuzegar, J. (1991). *Dynamics of the Iranian revolution: The Pahlavis' triumph and tragedy*. SUNY Press.

Ansari, I. (1999). Maulana Maududi's revolutionary message not allowed to reach masses by Jama 'at-e-Islami. *Dalit Voice*. September 8, 1999.

Bahgat, G. (2017). US-Iran relations under the Trump administration. *Mediterranean Quarterly*. 28(3), 93–111.

Baker, P., Bergman, R., Kirkpatrick, D. D., Barnes, J. E., & Rubi, A. J. (2020). *Seven Days in January: How Trump Pushed U.S. and Iran to the Brink of War. The New York Times*. January 11, 2020. www.nytimes.com/2020/01/11/us/politics/iran-trump.html.

Barzegar, K. & Divsallar, A. (2017). Political rationality in Iranian foreign policy. *The Washington Quarterly*. 40(1), 39–53.

BBC. (2019). Six charts that show how hard US sanctions have hit Iran. *BBC*. December 9, 2019. www.bbc.com/news/world-middle-east-48119109.

Behravesh, M. (2018). State revisionism and ontological (in) security in international politics: The complicated case of Iran and its nuclear behavior. *Journal of International Relations and Development*. 21(4), 836–857.

Chacko, P. (2014). A new "special relationship"?: Power transitions, ontological security, and India–US relations. *International Studies Perspectives*. 15(3), 329–346.

Chase, R., Hill, E., & Kennedy, P. (1996). Pivotal states and U.S. Strategy. *Foreign Affairs*. 75(1), 33–51.

Cordesman, A. H. (1999). *Iran's military forces in transition: conventional threats and weapons of mass destruction*. Greenwood Publishing Group.

Datta, M. (2020) What Iranians think of the US and their own government. *The Conversation*. https://theconversation.com/what-iranians-think-of-the-us-and-their-own-government-129400.

Edelman, E. & Takeyh, R. (2020). The next Iranian revolution: Why Washington should seek regime change in Tehran. *Foreign Affairs*. 99(3), 131–145.

Davaran, F. (2010). *Continuity in Iranian identity: Resilience of a cultural heritage* (Vol. 7). Routledge.

Faris, D. M. & Rahimi, B. (Eds.). (2015). *Social media in Iran: Politics and society after 2009*. SUNY Press.

Frantzman, S. J. (2018). Who Are Iran's 80,000 Shi'ite Fighters in Syria? *Jerusalem Post*. August 28, 2018.

Glass, A. (2019). President Bush cites "axis of evil" *Politico*. January 29, 2019. www.politico.com/story/2019/01/29/bush-axis-of-evil-2002-1127725.

Golmohammadi, V. (2019). The foreign policy of the Islamic Republic of Iran: Prospects for change and continuity. *All Azimuth: A Journal of Foreign Policy and Peace*. 8(1), 93–102.

Graham, R. (1980). *Iran, the illusion of power*. St. Martin's Press.

Haghgoo, J., Hashjin, Z. G., & Aghaei, M. (2017). A review of the turnaround in Iranian foreign policy during president Hassan Rohani's administration. *Journal of History Culture and Art Research*. 6(3), 245–263.

Hagström, L. & Gustafsson, K. (2019). Narrative power: How storytelling shapes East Asian international politics. *Cambridge Review of International Affairs*. 32 (4), 387–406.

Holliday, S. (2007). The politicisation of culture and the contestation of Iranian national identity in Khatami's Iran. *Studies in Ethnicity and Nationalism*. 7(1), 27–45.

Holliday, S. (2016). *Defining Iran: Politics of resistance*. Routledge.

Huysmans, J. (1998). Security! What do you mean? From concept to thick signifier. *European Journal of International Relations*. 4(2), 226–255.

Kastner, S. L. & Saunders, P. C. (2012). Is China a status quo or revisionist state? Leadership travel as an empirical indicator of foreign policy priorities. *International Studies Quarterly*. 56(1), 163–177.

Katzman, K., McInnis, K., & Thomas, C. (2020). U.S.-Iran conflict and implications for U.S. Policy. *Congressional Research Service*. https://fas.org/sgp/crs/mideast/R45795.pdf.

Keddie, N. R. & Matthee, R. (Eds.). (2011). *Iran and the surrounding world: Interactions in culture and cultural politics*. University of Washington Press.

Kinnvall, C. (2007). *Globalization and religious nationalism in India: The search for ontological security*. Routledge.

Kinzer, S. (2008). *All the Shah's men: An American coup and the roots of Middle East terror*. John Wiley & Sons.

Kinzer, S. (2011). *Reset Middle East: Old Friends and New Alliances: Saudi Arabia, Israel, Turkey, Iran*. I.B. Tauris.

Koo, G. Y. (2017). Constructing an alternative public sphere: The cultural significance of social media in Iran. In N. Lenze, C. Schriwer, & Z. A. Jalil (Eds), *Media in the Middle East*, 21–43. Palgrave Macmillan.

Kredo, A. (2014). Iran supreme leader: 'Prepare for the new world order.' *Business Insider*. www.businessinsider.com/iran-supreme-leader-prepare-for-new-world-order-2014-9.

Krolikowski, A. (2008). State personhood in ontological security theories of international relations and Chinese nationalism: A sceptical view. *Chinese Journal of International Politics*. 2(1), 109–133.

Krolikowski, A. (2018). Shaking up and making up China: How the party-state compromises and creates ontological security for its subjects. *Journal of International Relations and Development*. 21(4), 909–933.

Kurzman, C. (2004). *The unthinkable revolution in Iran*. Harvard University Press.

Maloney, S. (2008). *Iran's long reach: Iran as a pivotal state in the Muslim world*. US Institute of Peace Press.

Mazrooei, A., Sabahi, F., & Zanconato, A. (2017). Iran – Media landscapes. *European Journalism Centre*. https://medialandscapes.org/country/iran.

Mead, W. R. (2014). The return of geopolitics: The revenge of the revisionist powers. *Foreign Affairs*. 93(3), 69–79.

Mitzen, J. (2006). Ontological security in world politics: State identity and the security dilemma. *European Journal of International Relations*. 12(3), 341–370.

Mohseni, E., Gallagher, N., & Ramsay, C. (2017). *Iranian attitudes on Iranian-US relations in the Trump era*. School of Public Policy, University of Maryland.

Parsa, M. (1989). *Social origins of the Iranian revolution*. Rutgers University Press.

Pompeo, M. R. (2018). Confronting Iran. *Foreign Affairs*. 97(60), 60–71.

Rahimi, B. (2015). Censorship and the Islamic Republic: Two modes of regulatory measures for media in Iran. *Middle East Journal*. 69(3), 358–378.

Reporters Without Borders. (2021). *2020 World Press Freedom Index*. https://rsf.org/en/ranking.

Rubin, M. (2019). Evolution of Iranian Surveillance Strategies toward the Internet and Social Media. In S. M. Khasru (Ed.), *The Digital Age, Cyber Space, and Social Media The Challenges of Security & Radicalization*, 191–210. The Institute for Policy, Advocacy, and Governance.

Sariolghalam, M. (2005). *The Foreign Policy of the Islamic Republic of Iran: A Theoretical Revision and the Coalition Paradigm*. Center for Strategic Research, CSR Press.

Sariolghalam, M. (2020). Iran and the West. *Horizons: Journal of International Relations and Sustainable Development*. 16(Spring), 160–167.

Silverstone, R. (1993). Television, ontological security and the transitional object. *Media, Culture & Society*, 15(4), 573–598.

Soleimani, K., & Mohammadpour, A. (2019). Can non-Persians speak? The sovereign's narration of "Iranian identity". *Ethnicities*, 19(5), 925–947.

Steele, B. J. (2008). Ontological security in international relations: Self-identity and the IR state. Routledge.

Stempel, J. (1981). *Inside the Iranian revolution*. Indiana University Press.

Subotić, J. (2016). Narrative, ontological security, and foreign policy change. *Foreign policy analysis*. 12(4), 610–627.

Tazmini, G. (2018) Rouhani redux: Iran on the edge of change. *Middle East Review*. 5(3).

Trenin, D. (2020). *A storm in January: Implications of the recent U.S.-Iran crisis for the global order*. Foreign and Security Policy. Carnegie Moscow Center. https://carnegie.ru/commentary/80963.

Wendt, A. (1992). Anarchy is what states make of it: The social construction of power politics. *International Organization*. 46 (2), 391–425.
Willmott, H. C. (1986), Unconscious sources of motivation in the theory of the subject; An exploration and critique of Giddens' dualistic models of action and personality. *Journal for the Theory of Social Behaviour*. 16(1), 105–121.
Zakaria, F. (2008). *The post-American world*. W. W. Norton & Company.

7 Quantitative Comparisons and Drivers of Global Competition and Narratives of Global Order

Introduction

Whereas existing ontological security (OS) research has examined in-depth individual cases or broader social trends such as post-colonialism and globalization, our project takes a comparative lens to explore how four nations aligned against the West imagine both their individual places and roles within the global order as well as their common constructions of the competitive global landscape. Our mixed-methods approach, specifically the inclusion of quantitative data, provides further empirical insight into OS sustainment and formation. Thus, this chapter reports the comparative analysis of Chinese, Russian, Iranian, and Venezuelan media narratives regarding visions of the future of global competition, including their instruments of exerting power, purported vulnerabilities and necessary capabilities, projected allies and adversaries, views on the future of global order, the US, and the European Union (EU), as well as the available means by which global competition should be managed.

Because the means by which actors manage their identities in an anxious world is an inherently subjective experience, we contextualize the quantitative findings with the qualitative themes in which they emerge. Although scholars are rightly concerned with quantitative attempts at capturing OS dynamics, including artificial bracketing of identities, we maintain that measurement of broad quantitative trends, when taken in context, can provide useful insight into foundational elements related to OS management.

In sum, our quantitative findings demonstrate the following: First, the key to the future of global competition is one of diplomatic and economic contestation rather than military. In all four cases, military vulnerabilities and capabilities are discussed least frequently while diplomatic concerns are mentioned most, followed by economic. Second, while Russia, China, and Iran all note more capabilities than vulnerabilities, China appears the best positioned to compete and contribute to the global order, whereas Venezuela is the least so. As such, only China has a positive view on the global order, with Russia, Iran, and Venezuela all decidedly negative.

DOI: 10.4324/9781003197478-7

Regardless, with the exception of Venezuela, all three countries still view themselves as nations with a positive role in our global order while viewing the US and Western Europe in negative terms, albeit with the US depicted three times more negatively than Western Europe. The US, then, is seen not as a supporter of the current international system, but one playing a detrimental, often hypercritical, and self-serving role. This is not to suggest that all four nations similarly view the global order. Russia and Iran view themselves as most distinctly under siege by US and Western norms and actions and are most likely to include deterrence messaging when reporting on global order while Iran and Venezuela report higher levels of potential conflict escalation. China, on the other hand, tends to draw more from within current norms advocating for continued free trade and avoidance of conflict through multilateralism and mutual cooperation.

Taken together, predictors regarding all four nations' reporting on the future of the global order include positive correlations with discussions of diplomatic and economic capabilities while negatively correlated with mentions of competitors and diplomatic vulnerabilities. Moreover, positive perspective of one's role in the global order is linked to increases in discussions addressing informational vulnerabilities and military capabilities of the nation. This suggests that the more secure a nation feels at home, that is their ability to maintain cultural cohesion and fend off informational attacks from abroad while also feeling confident with their military resources, the more likely they perceive themselves as having a leadership role in the global order. This sense of security is also tied to their relationship with the US in that the US is viewed more positively as discussions of competitors and conflict escalation/management decrease. When discussions of alliances and inclusion of foreign sources were present within news stories, the perspectives on Western Europe were more positive as well.

Sentiment analysis

Figure 7.1 summarizes the valance scores related to the global order and key actors within it. In sum, all of the nations, with the exception of Venezuela, view the role of their nation in the global order as strong. China presents itself as an emerging superpower, while Russia and Iran view themselves as necessary regional counter-balances to the US and the West. Only Venezuelan media present their nation as weak and ineffectual within the current global order. However, China holds the only positive outlook on the global order with the others reporting a pessimistic view on how changes to the global order and competition within it manifest. All four nations share a negative view of the US within their media, however Iranian media statistically holds the strongest. Likewise, all four countries view Western Europe negatively, though far less negatively than the US.

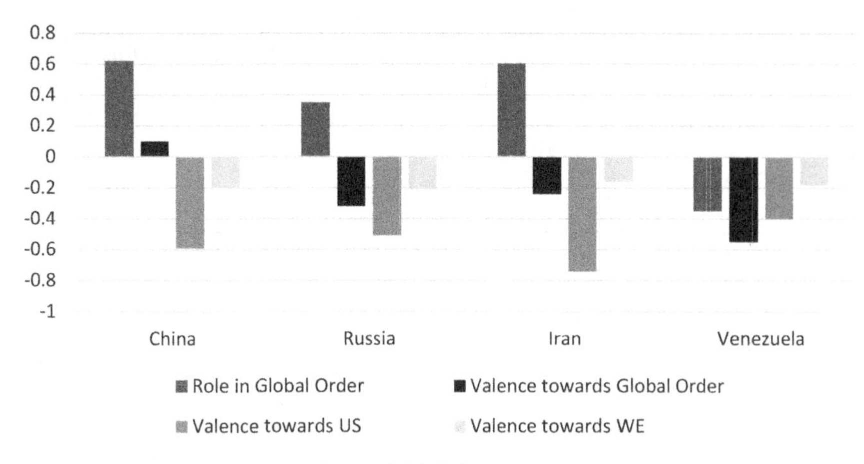

Figure 7.1 Sentiment Comparison of Global Order and Actors

Views on global order

Only China reports a slightly positive view of the global order (m =. 10). From the qualitative data, this view arises from Chinese media presenting their nation as standing in for US global leadership, given the US's global retreat over the past few years. As a result, China describes its role as supporting the post-World War II international architecture, which, according to Chinese narratives, the US is now undermining. Chinese media warn against isolationism and nationalism and advocate for a doubling down on globalization policies and multilateral institutions, thus providing some support for its current ideation.

The media from Iran, Russia, and Venezuela all present the global order in a negative light. For Russia (m = -.32) and Iran (m = -.24), immoral behavior and leadership from Western nations highlights the unfairness of the current system as the US and West are able to act in contrast to the values of the international community. Venezuelan media reports the most negative view of the global order (m = -.48) and perceives imperialist nations, including not only the US but also China, Russia, and the Europe, as violating international law specifically and, like Russia and Iran, view these actors as pursing their own self-interests to the detriment of others. Thus, while Iran, Russia, and Venezuela view the global order negatively, this comes not from disbelief in the importance of international institutions and norms, but from their lack of efficacy in constraining others' behavior. China, meanwhile, holds a positive view while seeing international institutions as still capable of promoting trade and cooperative relations, albeit threatened by isolationist and nationalist currents.

Table 7.1 Comparative Portrayals of Global Order

	Russia (N = 166)	*China (N = 270)*	*Venezuela (N = 62)*	*Iran (N = 122)*
Article Mentions	N = 94 (57%)	N = 203 (75%)	N = 33 (53%)	N = 95 (78%)
Valence (Mean) (1=positive, -1=negative)	-.32	.10	-.48	-.24

Role in global order

Russia, China, and Iran are all presented by their respective media as having an established and important role in the global order, although representing three distinct directions. Russia presents the least positive view (m = .35), but still quite high. Russia is reported as a sort of swing actor—affirming its own sense of global importance, whose commitments to alliances with one party over another can sway the balances of power in the international system—thus not necessarily beholden to the current order; with Russia increasingly identifying its Eurasian identity over its European one as the community most likely to support its future aspirations. China, on the other hand, presents itself as a rational global power committed to the global order and building a fairer international system; here China sees itself as a much needed force affirming many of the underlining beliefs of our international, rules-based trading system marking a highly positive role for itself in the global order (m = .61). Iran too presents itself as a holding a highly positive role in the global order (m = .63) through its narratives depicting itself as the preeminent regional power in one of the most important areas in the world; Iran's role as unifier and leader of the Shia Crescent, and its various coalitions to challenge the US and Israel, provide further support of its self-ascribed importance.

Venezuela's reported role in the global order stands in stark contrast as it is the sole country to report a negative perception of its role, as well as a highly negative view (m = -.35). As the qualitative data shows, Venezuelan media report a threatening global order coupled with an alarming inability to defend its interests both at home and abroad. Thus, despite US decline, new emerging powers are arising; all of which have an eye for augmenting their self-interest within nations unable to hold them at bay. Venezuela's domestic tumult and self-perceived international failures leaves it with little capacity to shape its environment. Rising authoritarianism around the world is also viewed as potentially creeping into its domestic politics while foreign nations are reported as contemplating intervention in Venezuela's electoral politics. Thus, Venezuela is shown as largely unable to influence the global order, and is rather subjected to, and victimized by, the disruptions to that order.

Table 7.2 Comparative Portrayal of Host-nation's Role in the Global Order

	Russia (N = 166)	*China (N = 270)*	*Venezuela (N = 62)*	*Iran (N = 122)*
Articles Mentioning Russia's Role	N= 55 (33%)			
Valence (Mean) (1=positive, -1=negative)	.35			
Articles Mentioning China's Role		N= 219 (82%)		
Valence (Mean) (1=positive, -1=negative)		.61		
Articles Mentioning Venezuela's Role			N= 17 (27%)	
Valence (Mean) (1=positive, -1=negative)			-.35	
Articles Mentioning Iran's Role				N= 60 (49%)
Valence (Mean) (1=positive, -1=negative)				.63

Perspectives on the US

All of the national media examined in this study present the US in a negative manner. For Venezuelan media (m = -.40), that negativity involves a distrust of the authoritarian tendencies it sees in US politics, as well as concerns over US imperialism both past and present. In Russian media (m = -.51), negativity towards the US revolves around historical animosities of US cultural and diplomatic encroachment. This includes opposing geopolitical interests pitting the US against Russia, as well as more recently invoked sanctions on the Russian economy. Chinese media (m = -.58) focus on the retreat of the US from the very international organizations it helped establish in the creation of the modern global system. Chinese frustration at the US most specifically comes from what it views as an unfair reshuffling of international rules and trade agreements in order to prevent less prosperous nations, such as itself, from rising and modernizing into new international powers. Iranian presentations of the US are much more damning (m = -.74), and largely aims its criticisms squarely at the Trump administration; which it depicts as hypocritical, dangerous, and desperate for a demonstration of political solvency as it isolates Iran and goes back on the Iranian nuclear agreement. Across all four countries are themes of US decline, both materially and ideationally, resulting in decreasing abilities to influence and dictate terms to the larger international community.

Table 7.3 Comparative Portrayals of US

	Russia (N = 166)	*China (N = 270)*	*Venezuela (N = 62)*	*Iran (N = 122)*
Article mentions	N= 98 (59%)	N= 108 (40%)	N= 35 (56%)	N= 92 (75%)
Valence (Mean) (1=positive, -1=negative)	-.51	-.58	-.40	-.74

Perspectives on Western Europe

Russian media negatively perceives the Western Europe (m = -.21) with its narratives more often than not coalescing discussions on Western Europe and the US into that of the West in general. While nuance is present in some instances, largely Western Europe is seen as generally amenable to the positions dictated by the US. Venezuelan media does much of the same when discussing Western Europe more broadly (m = -.18), but European nations are also, at times, more specifically mentioned as actors supporting the larger wishes of the international community. China offers even more subtlety, particularly in relation to trade. While negative evaluations of the EU (m = -.22) come from concerns regarding rising isolationist and nationalism, especially in the wake of Brexit—concerns about which China also critiques the US—the EU is still viewed both as a potential ally and competitor with Chinese narratives positively stressing the importance of EU–Chinese trade relations and the role of the EU in supporting multilateral diplomacy.

Iran offers the least negative depiction (m = -.14) with much more distinction in its discussions of Western Europe in relation to the global order. This largely stems from its views of some states within Western Europe as capable of breaking with the US in support of sanction relief towards Iran and reestablishing the framework of the Iranian nuclear agreement. Iranian media often present Iranian officials as appealing to leaders of Western Europe to be cognizant of US hypocrisy and to remove, or ignore, unfair penalties placed on Iran by the US and its coalition partners. Thus, the EU is recognized as an important pillar of the international community, one to appeal to in order to drive a wedge between its US ally through rhetoric emphasizing the current values embedded in the global order.

Instruments of power within the DIME framework

When examining how our four cases discuss their instruments of power related to competing in the global order, military considerations are the least mentioned whereas diplomatic concerns occur most often. On

Table 7.4 Comparative Portrayals of Western Europe

	Russia (N = 166)	*China (N = 270)*	*Venezuela (N = 62)*	*Iran (N = 122)*
Article Mentions	N= 72 (43%)	N= 49 (18%)	N= 11 (18%)	N= 43 (35%)
Valence (Mean) (1=positive, -1=negative)	-.21	-.22	-.18	-.14

average across all four nations when reporting both vulnerabilities and capabilities military concerns exist in 18.25% of the articles, informational concerns in 28.75%, economic concerns in 37%, and diplomatic concerns in 56.5%. Thus, our data suggests that the future of global competition is one of diplomatic and economic contestation rather than military.

When comparing each nation's average number of capabilities to vulnerabilities, Venezuela is clearly the weakest positioned to effect change with vulnerabilities cited over twice as often as capabilities. China, however, is best positioned not only with the highest frequency of capabilities but also in referencing these capabilities more than twice as often as vulnerabilities. The same ratio is witnessed in Russian reporting, although the frequency of references both to capabilities and vulnerabilities are fewer. While the ratio of referenced capabilities to vulnerabilities in Iranian media is not quite as high as Russia or China, Iranian media still more often reports capabilities to vulnerabilities at a ratio of 3:2.

Vulnerabilities

Chinese narratives on vulnerabilities concerning global competition primarily revolve around economics (n = 20%); specifically, maintaining a

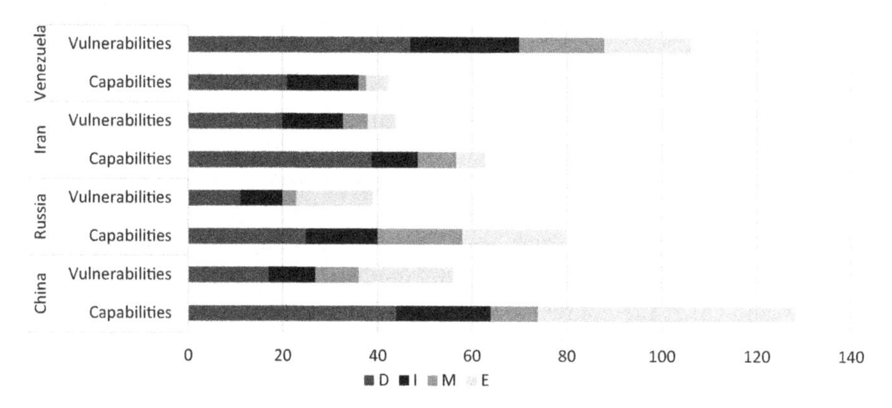

Figure 7.2 Comparative References of Instruments of Power

stable global order where countries continue policies promoting globalization and free trade. Free trade is viewed as necessary in China's domestic policies promoting technological innovation, which is attributed to helping fuel its economic growth. Isolationism and nationalism are seen as the key threats to globalization, with China calling for nations to reaffirm their commitments to multilateral institutions supporting free trade—marking diplomatic influence an area of concern (n = 17%) if China is unable to marshal support for trade and its Belt and Road Initiative (BRI). Militarily (n = 9%), Chinese vulnerabilities arise from Japanese and US militarism in the Asia Pacific. US and Japanese actions are viewed as attempts to contain China stemming from misunderstandings of China's peaceful rise. Informational concerns (= 10%) occur regarding Chinese brands, lack of voice broadcasting its own story to the world, and perceived misinformation purporting a "China threat theory."

Similar to China, Russian vulnerabilities relate to economics (n = 16%), but emphasizes the nation's lack of competitive economic advantages. According to Russian media, the country lacks resources for new investment projects and modern technologies. Russia also has weaknesses in human resource management approaches and its ability to compete in global industries; while experiencing weak economic diversification with a dependency on oil exports, suggesting an overall poor economic outlook moving forward. Thus, there is a shared understanding within Russia that its lack of technological expertise has resulted in a stagnant economy with Russian leaders often quoted as urging new economic initiatives and projects, as well as pointing out the need for foreign investments and support of national production. Nonetheless, Russian narratives often contextualize its economic decline in relation to sanctions imposed by the West, with additional concerns over diplomatic isolation (n = 11%). Furthermore, Russian media expresses worries over Western propaganda and information warfare (n = 9%), characterizing both as causing societal disruptions, with Western cultural influence viewed as intentionally undermining Russia's unique and distinct societal progression away from the West towards the East. Military concerns are rarely discussed (n = 3%).

Iranian media also highlights diplomatic (n = 21%) and informational (n = 12%) vulnerabilities as the principal concerns of the state. Iranian media points to US-led attempts to isolate Iran as the causes for its noted vulnerabilities. Iran is reported as under siege from an onslaught of US rhetoric with the US leveraging the international community in support of its goals. Military (n = 6%) and economic vulnerabilities (n = 6%) are rarely mentioned, largely because the conversation on vulnerabilities are rarely shown in the context of just the Iranian state. Rather, it is placed within a larger regional context that focuses on vulnerabilities to political and religious unity/identity of the Shia Crescent.

Venezuela was a significant outlier in discussions related to vulnerability when contrasted to the other three cases. Venezuelan narratives regarding its vulnerabilities are anchored in the nation's own lack of global influence and domestic instability, which leave the country open to what it perceives as intentional interference from the US and distrust towards both China and Russia. The fragility of the Venezuelan state is notable in the expressed concerns for Venezuela's role and declining influence in international organizations, especially economic and trade-related organizations; as well as concerns for foreign propaganda intentionally disrupting Venezuelan society. Thus, Venezuelan vulnerabilities are reported more frequently nearly across all elements of power: diplomatic (n = 47%), informational (n = 23%), military (n = 18%), and economic (n = 18%).

Capabilities

Chinese narratives regarding necessary capabilities are used to define Chinese strengths in affirming its continued growth in global leadership, including its promotion of multilateral mechanisms for coordinating global economic policies and dispute resolution mechanisms premised on dialogue and resolution within the UN. China's global preeminence and growing international influence require continued diplomatic (n = 44%) and economic (n = 54%) partnerships, especially in promoting its BRI. Importantly, military capabilities are less emphasized (n = 10%). Instead, deepening domestic and international economic development is needed to aid in China's description of its "peaceful rise" and the self-ascribed benefits such actions provide to other nations (economic development, diplomatic stability), with informational capabilities (n = 20%) reflective of its strong cultural and technological resources.

Russian media too focuses on domestic economic capabilities (n = 22%) with competitiveness in science and technology reported as more important than that of traditional military developments (n = 18%), which it general feels are already adequately strong. However, whereas China highlights its economic capabilities in more forward looking and constructive manners, Russian economic capabilities appear more reactive; as

Table 7.5 Comparison of Articles Mentioning DIME Vulnerabilities

	Russia (N = 166)	*China (N = 270)*	*Venezuela (N = 62)*	*Iran (N = 122)*
Diplomatic Vulnerabilities	n=19 (11%)	n=45 (17%)	n=29 (47%)	n=25 (21%)
Informational Vulnerabilities	n=15 (9%)	n=26 (10%)	n=14 (23%)	n=15 (12%)
Military Vulnerabilities	n=5 (3%)	n=23 (9%)	n=11 (18%)	n=7 (6%)
Economic Vulnerabilities	n=27 (16%)	n=54 (20%)	n=11 (18%)	n=7 (6%)

government officials are shown as attempting to convey a cogent strategy of domestic economic growth in relation to how the state will address its economic struggles. Thus, initiatives aimed at countering potentials for the economic decline are major drivers of its positive reporting of economic competitiveness. Likewise, Russian media reports considerable diplomatic influence (n = 25%), especially through collaborative partnerships with China, but also couches such influence within discussions of the need for improved US-Russian relations to avoid diplomatic isolation, reduce military tensions, and support to its economy. Russia's informational capabilities (n = 15%) at times include its cyber resources, but more predominantly emphasize the potential for its cultural attractiveness.

For Iran, diplomatic capabilities are overwhelming the most frequently reported (n = 40%) and take a unique focus in emphasizing its regional influence as the unifier and defender of the Shia Crescent. Thus, its immediate focus is on Iran's ability to wield its version of Islam as a relational tool supporting its claim to regional leadership capable of addressing the political failures of the region. However, it also takes an international focus through its emphasis on the current order's claims to respect territorial sovereignty and prevent unilateral action, such as steps by the US to intercede in Iranian and Middle Eastern politics. In doing so, it also calls for Iran's appropriate international behavior and rights to bolster its relationship with European nations. Relatedly, Iran's religious-cultural claims also make up a key informational resource (n = 11%) both in defense of cultural encroachment by the West and a tool for regional leadership. Military (n = 7%) and economic capabilities (n = 7%) are less frequently discussed, focused on mitigating the effects of sanctions on its economy and its ability to resist US attacks.

Venezuelan narratives describing what capabilities the country currently enjoys, or should pursue, are sparse and tend to focus more on current crises. Thus, little is offered in terms of a forward-focused vision for what Venezuela needs to compete in the global order. Nonetheless, Venezuelan media reflect Chinese, Russian, and Iranian in emphasizing its diplomatic resources (n = 21%). Here Venezuelan reports stress the importance of the current order's legal protections against foreign intervention as well as the value of regional trade networks. Venezuelan media describes diplomacy as part of a grander pursuit of a fairer, more cooperative, and multinational order to promote economic growth and protect itself against foreign intervention. Although few claims are made regarding its economic (n = 5%) and military capabilities (n= 2%), Venezuela media reaffirms its political ideology as a resource to withstand foreign propaganda and influence campaigns (n = 15%).

Conflict management

Our data reveals two key findings regarding reports of conflict management. First, the two nations most in conflict with the current order, Russia

Table 7.6 Comparison of Articles Mentioning DIME Capabilities

	Russia (N = 166)	*China (N = 270)*	*Venezuela (N = 62)*	*Iran (N = 122)*
Diplomatic Capabilities	n=42 (25%)	n=120 (44%)	n=13 (21%)	n=49 (40%)
Informational Capabilities	n=24 (15%)	n=53 (20%)	n=9 (15%)	n=13 (11%)
Military Capabilities	n=30 (18%)	n=27 (10%)	n=1 (2%)	n=8 (7%)
Economic Capabilities	n=36 (22%)	n=147 (54%)	n=3 (5%)	n=8 (7%)

and Iran—evident by their qualitative narrative themes, are also the most likely to signal some element of deterrence when discussing global order or competition (n = 13% and n = 17%, respectively). Second, those with the least international influence or power, Iran and Venezuela, are more likely to mention plans, policies, or pathways to deal with escalating tensions (n = 35% and n = 34% respectively) with Iran reporting the largest number of competitors (n = 60%), as well as allies (n = 32%). Figure 7.3 displays each nation's references to conflict management dynamics and competitors.

A further distinction comes from China's low level of deterrence messaging. Whereas Russian and Iranian media both express concerns for the defense and maintenance of their own regional power and national sovereignty, coinciding with more frequent conversations on deterrence (n = 13% and n = 14%, respectively), China's placement of itself within the current international system appears to lessens its need for deterrence messaging regarding discussions of global competition (n = 1%). Thus, China's focus on the diplomatic and economic areas of competition largely

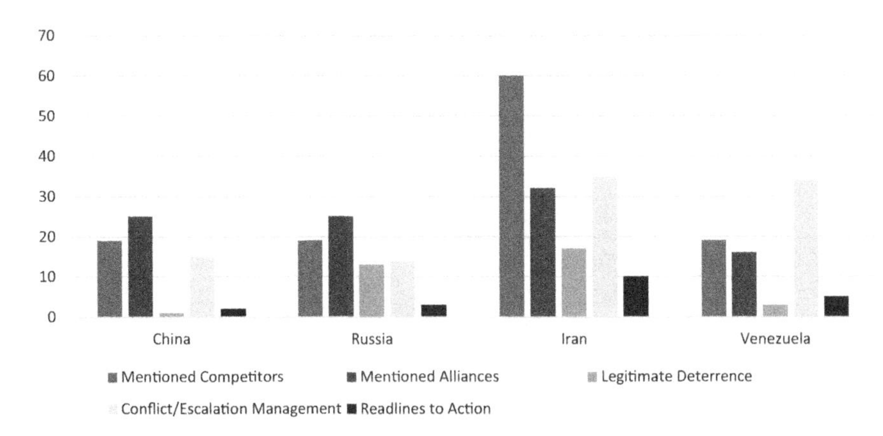

Figure 7.3 Comparison of Reported Conflict Dynamics

from within current norms furthers its appeals to follow mutual cooperation and peaceful resolution of disputes.

Taking into account the qualitative data, differences between Russian (n = 14%) and Iranian (n = 35%) conflict management to that of China (n = 15%) appear to revolve around differing conceptions of regional versus global areas of influence. Russian news media frequently stresses cultural roots, historical ties, and common religion with former Soviet states. Thus, Russia views former Soviet states countries as areas of their regional influence and urges both the US and China to avoid intervention activities towards these states. Similarly, Iran sees its areas of regional influence, and its own state sovereignty, as being under attack by US strategists. Iranian media express numerous scenarios whereby Western intervention in Iranian domestic politics and the Middle East should be deterred and countered. Iran's focus on conflict management is largely a direct commentary on actions taken by the US that are viewed as requiring some form of conflict management and reciprocal action. China's reporting focuses most on global issues, specifically trade related disputes, and stresses the need for multilateralism and resolution within international norms of reciprocity.

Venezuela, on the other hand, addresses conflict management in relation to what is described in the media as necessary multilateral cooperation in order to manage global conflict and curtail imperial ambitions of the US, Russia, and China. Venezuela's weak domestic circumstances not only fuel concerns for greater conflict as its weakened state is viewed as inviting foreign intervention from China, Russia, the US, and the international community, but also leaves it with little capacity to deter such actions, having to rely on appeals to international law and norms.

Predictive models

So far, the discussion has detailed the descriptive differences among Chinese, Russian, Iranian, and Venezuelan media reporting on the global competition. In this section, we go further in exploring how these variables correlate both within and across all four nations.

Table 7.7 Comparison of Articles Mentioning Conflict Dynamics

	Russia (N = 166)	*China (N = 270)*	*Venezuela (N = 62)*	*Iran (N = 122)*
Legitimate Deterrence	n=21 (13%)	n=3 (1%)	n=2 (3%)	n=17 (14%)
Conflict/Escalation Management	n=23 (14%)	n=40 (15%)	n=21 (34%)	n=38 (31%)
Redlines to Action	n=5 (3%)	n=5 (2%)	n=3 (5%)	n=8 (7%)

Perspectives on the future of the global order

The significant predictors on the future of the global order include mentions of necessary diplomatic capabilities (B = .174), mentions of competitors (B = -.095), mentions of necessary economic capabilities (B = .101), and mentions of key diplomatic vulnerabilities (B = -1.02). R^2 = .063, F = 7.11, (p = .000). Thus, the data suggests that perspectives on the future of the global order became more positive as mentions of diplomatic and economic capabilities increase, and mentions of diplomatic vulnerabilities and competitors decrease.

Within Russian media, as discussions on competitors decreased, outlook on the future of the global order became more positive. This could be attributable to Russian insecurities about its material capabilities to compete internationally with its current labor pool and manufacturing abilities as well as security and diplomatic concerns regarding potential isolation.

Within Iranian media, as mentions of economic vulnerabilities increased, perspectives on the future of the global order became more positive. This result is attributed to mentions on economic vulnerabilities in Iranian media being made as appeals to the larger international community to fairly evaluate Iranian actions.

Within Venezuelan media, increased mentions of necessary military capabilities lead to more positive outlooks on the future of global order. The basic ability to defend Venezuelan territorial integrity from imperial-minded powers is the driver for projections of how a weakened Venezuela can navigate the changes happening within the international system. No predictive model was able to be formed with the data from Chinese media.

Perspectives on role in the global order

Significant predictors of perspectives of role in the global order include mentions of necessary military capabilities (B = .135) and mentions of key informational vulnerabilities (B = .115). R^2 = .033, F = 5.96, (p = .003). Having a positive perspective of their nation's role in the global order is linked to an increase in discussions addressing informational vulnerabilities and articulating the necessary military capabilities of the nation.

Within Russian media, as discussions on informational vulnerabilities increased, Russia's role in the global order is presented as more positive. This variable had a specific cultural link to former Soviet states and concern for protecting a Russian sphere of cultural influence. The Russian role in the global order is thus connected to protecting its regional influence against encroachment. Within Iranian media, more positive perspective of their role within the global order occurs when mentions of larger regional culture and Shia unity are discussed. The Iranian role in the global order thus is related to regional leadership and as a unifying force of Islamic culture. Within Chinese media, as discussions on diplomacy increased, and mentions of competitors decreased, Chinese media presented a more favorable perspective on their role within the global order. This suggests Chinese garnering of more diplomatic influence increases its confidence in its ability to succeed in the current order. No predictive model was able to be formed with the data from Venezuelan media.

Perspectives on the United States

Significant predictors of perspectives of the US include mentions of competitors (B = -.200) and mentions of conflict management (B = -.131). R^2 = .072, F = 12.87, (p = .000). Here, the US is viewed more positively as discussions of competitors and conflict management decrease.

Within Russian media, the model of perspectives of the US included mentions of competitors (B = -.329) and necessary information capabilities (B = -.215). R^2 = .175, F = 10.09, (p = .025). Thus, the US is viewed more positively in Russian media as discussions of competitors and needed information capabilities decrease. In this sense, the US is most often seen as an aggressive competitor and wielder of disinformation tactics or cultural encroachment, absent these characteristics the presentation of the US becomes more favorable.

Within Chinese media, the model of perspectives of the United States included mentions of necessary information capabilities (B = .324) and key information vulnerabilities (B = -.224). R^2 = .080, F = 4.55, (p = .013). Here the US is viewed more positively in Chinese media as discussions of information capabilities increase, and discussions on information vulnerabilities decrease. Therefore, the ability of China to match US information narratives and present itself to the world in its own terms creates a more balanced presentation of the US within Chinese media.

Within Iranian media, the model for perspectives on the United States included only one variable, mentions of competitors (B = -.417). R^2 = .174, F = 18.94, (p = .000). Here the US is viewed more positively in Iranian media as discussions of competitors decrease. This is likely due to the tremendous negative coverage of the US in Iranian media, which suggests that the US is considered almost exclusively through a lens of competition from Iranian media.

Within Venezuelan media, the model for perspectives on the United States also included only one variable, mentions of necessary military capabilities (B = .351). R^2 = .123, F = 4.62, (p= .039). Similar to other findings related to Venezuela, security is the principal concern of the state when engaging foreign actors within the international system.

Perspectives on Western Europe

Overall, the significant predictors of perspectives of Western Europe include discussions of alliances (B = .235) and inclusion of foreign political sources within media (B = .168). R^2 = .074, F = 6.92, (p = .02). When discussions of alliances and inclusion of foreign sources were present within news stories, the perspectives on Western Europe were more positive. The importance of Western Europe as a potential committal ally is represented by these nations as demonstrative of declining US influence in the global order and as legitimating grievances toward the US.

Within Russian media, the model for perspectives of Western Europe was the same as the overall model with discussions of alliances (B = .266) and inclusion of foreign political sources within media (B = .227). R^2 = .114, F = 4.42, (p = .016). Within Chinese media, the model of perspectives of Western Europe included the following predictors: mentions of key economic vulnerabilities (B = -.358), key diplomatic vulnerabilities (B = -.291), and key information vulnerabilities (B = -.288). R^2 = .281, F = 5.87, (p = .002). As discussions on these vulnerabilities decreased, the Chinese media perspectives of Western Europe were more positive, suggesting that Chinese perceptions of vulnerability drive its views on Western Europe as a potential economic and diplomatic partner. Within Iranian media, the model of perspectives of Western Europe included the following predictors: mentions of conflict management (B = .502) and mentions of competitors (B = -.341). R^2 = .196, F = 4.88, (p = .013). In other words, as discussions of conflict management increased and mentions of competitors decreased, perspectives on Western Europe were more positive, suggesting Iranian media views Europe as an important partner when feelings of insecurity arise. No predictive model was able to be formed with the data from Venezuelan media.

Conclusion

The findings presented in this chapter show important media trends among US competitors. Trepidation about information vulnerabilities, concern for maintaining spheres of cultural influence, and the importance of access to the global economic system all loom large. The necessity of fairness across the international system and the need to construct a new global system with more equitable leadership are important commonalities in the media coverage especially as they point to a perceived decline in US status. Thus, if global order rests on nations' perception of its legitimacy, then the global order will need to accommodate these voices (Acharya, 2018), or face more severe contestation.

Our findings suggest that belief in one's role in the global order is an important dynamic tied to agency and political cohesion. Regardless of the nation's relative strength in global affairs, all but Venezuela see themselves as actors with a positive role. This is especially true as conflict arises from perceptions of inappropriate US behavior. Seeing the world as one embedded with conflict thus calls for white knights to ward off such challenges, imbuing nations with a sense of importance. However, a stable kingdom, or domestic situation, is required; when one's home is embroiled in domestic upheaval, both symbolically and materially—such in the case of Venezuela—perceptions of being able to effect international change is diminished.

Furthermore, the data suggest that as states see themselves as capable of competing in the global order they are more likely to support it. Whereas anxieties regarding the number of competitor nations rises and perceptions of reduced diplomatic resources occur, the global order loses its sense of efficacy. This has important implications on the future global order in that some revision appears necessary for others to gain greater voice and participation, but if threatened they might fall back on conflictual routines, particularly those with the US and to a lesser extent Western Europe. Thus, anxiety over one's relationship with the US rises with states feeling threatened when faced with conflict and larger numbers of competitors.

In theorizing positive change of the global order (Browning & Joenniemi, 2017), a relatively peaceful international environment will more likely allow for nations to express their needs for its alterations, but a more conflictual world will result in ossified negative identity-relations, primarily vis-à-vis the US. Rising perceptions of conflict could result in essentialized views (Agius, 2017) of the US as one's enemy, shoring domestic identity constructions but preventing international change. This reflects Kinnvall and Mitzen's (2017) distinction between notions of "security in being" to "security of becoming" with greater perception of threats and conflict leading to identity retrenchment, resulting in the former. The latter, however, could be more possible when one has confidence in their ability to compete. The role of diplomatic capacity suggests some evidence of this in that diplomacy assumes a degree of give and take. Countries then might be better equipped to enter a state of "becoming" by recognizing they lack total control over a desired outcome, albeit maintaining some influence, furnishing greater flexibility in how they perceive others and their relations to them moving towards some cooperative action. This can occur economically as well. As the data on China shows, its confidence in being able to compete economically through global trade coupled with its anxiety over its capacity for domestic innovation provides just enough push to take on a greater international leadership role in the face of US and European nationalism and isolationism. In doing so, China showcases how anxiety can create a positive springboard for new forms of political resistance and agency (Rumelili, 2011).

The emphasis on diplomatic dimensions of competition provides an additional bright spot regarding the future global order. As the category most often referenced, it suggests that China, Russia, Iran, and even Venezuela, still see multilateral cooperation as the primary form of international interaction within the global order, especially in contrast with the few discussions of military capabilities. Thus, the international order is still seen as the medium for peacefully negotiating relations with others to which, if continued over time, could formulate important pathways for OS stability management serving a constitutive role for cooperative relations, and enhancing the durability of cooperation (Browning & Joenniemi, 2013; Mitzen, 2006).

Finally, all four nations' claim that the international order should represent a degree of morality provides insight into what Hom and Steele (2020) call third image analysis of OS—stories told about what constitutes the international system as a whole. Negative perceptions of the US, while shared by all of our cases under analysis, primarily arise from claims of the US as acting in opposition to international values. Thus, Chinese, Russian, and Iranian beliefs in their nation as serving a positive role in the global order stem largely in part from their ability to offer alternative visions and interpretations of behavior in support of the values of the global order. While reflective of Steele's (2008) findings regarding state agents favoring moral actions in describing their foreign affairs, it also suggests nations share a common ideation of a just global order needing affirmation and protection from individualized, self-serving interests. Global institutions then represent the material embodiment of these abstract principles from which nations garner a sense of stability and order their understandings of what the international community at its base stands for.

The future of global competition, then, is one where economic and diplomatic contestation is of primary importance with international norms and institutions still held in high regard, once separated from US actions. While the spheres of economic and diplomatic relations could shift, based upon one's belief in their ability to successfully compete—such as China's affirmation of global, international trade in contrast to Russia's movement away from the West towards the East—states appear to desire maneuverability within it. Nonetheless, cultural or informational dynamics too play an important role. As participation in the global system requires some degree of openness to competing ideas and cultural values, maintaining a sense of unique socio-political cultural identity enabling the nation to provide economic prosperity and cognitive stability remains a driving force.

References

Acharya, A. (2018). *Constructing global order: Agency and change in world politics.* Cambridge University Press.

Agius, C. (2017). Drawing the discourses of ontological security: Immigration and identity in the Danish and Swedish cartoon crises. *Cooperation and Conflict*. 52 (1), 109–125.

Browning, C. S., & Joenniemi, P. (2017). Ontological security, self-articulation and the securitization of identity. *Cooperation and Conflict*. 52(1), 31–47.

Hom, A. R. & Steele, B. J. (2020). Anxiety, time, and ontological security's third-image potential. *International Theory*. 12(2), 322–336.

Kinnvall, C. & Mitzen, J. (2017). An introduction to the special issue: Ontological securities in world politics. *Cooperation and Conflict*. 52(1), 3–11.

Mitzen, J. (2006). Ontological security in world politics: State identity and the security dilemma. *European Journal of International Relations*. 12(3), 341–370.

Rumelili B. (2011). What Turks and Kurds 'make of' Europe: Subversion, negotiation and appropriation in the European periphery. In O. P. Richmond & A. Mitchell (Eds), *Hybrid Forms of Peace: From Everyday Agency to Post-Liberalism*, 226–241). Palgrave Macmillan.

Steele, B. J. (2008). *Ontological security in international relations: Self-identity and the IR state*. Routledge.

8 Efficacy of Alternative Visions of Global Order

Agency, Reflexivity, and the Limits of Change

Introduction

The goal of this project was to provide insight into the future of global order by understanding how competitor nations to the US narratively construct their abilities to compete within it. We argued that, as support for a global order requires a belief in its legitimacy (Kissinger, 2014; Acharya, 2018), actors must come to see its effectiveness in affording them with the ability to provide for their populace. Consideration of global order then draws first upon domestic political legitimacy before international. Both of which, however, comes from the expression of political communities to form some level of agreement regarding who they are at a specific moment in time and what they collectively desire to move towards, especially when grappling with anxiety present in an ever changing world (Arendt, 1972; Crick, 2014; Berenskötter, 2020; Hom & Steele, 2020). Thus, power, or the ability to influence one's environment, comes from the strength of one's sense of self as established through the ability to act in concert through communicative understanding, situated within one's material resources. Mobilizing one's domestic populace in concerted action, especially within today's new authoritarian-leaning states, highlights the importance of narratives as the means by which domestic populations come to make sense and order their world. Not only do these narratives furnish actors with a sense of biographical continuity tying together in their past, but also directs them towards more forward looking actions and beliefs.

From this, our project advances research on global order in two important ways. First, instead of assuming a level of shared interests represented by the state, we looked at how each nation discusses their anxieties within the global order as the means by which they become agentic. Thus, whereas the OS literature has persistently been critiqued for its "status quo bias" taking *fear* of change as its predominate driver (Kinnvall & Mitzen, 2020), our broader examination of state's sources of *anxiety* along diplomatic, economic, informational, and military spheres showcases how adaptive changes are possible as states narrate solutions to these concerns.

DOI: 10.4324/9781003197478-8

Second, we argued that states' level of support of the global order is based on their perceptions of their ability to successfully compete within it. In this sense, those who hold confidence in their ability to compete within certain dimensions of competition are more likely to uphold and influence those areas of the international order with the spaces where they are unable to compete contributing to negative perceptions. Taken together, our project revealed not only how these nations narrate their own insecurity but also the manner in which they situate themselves within an ontologically *in*secure global order—including how they seek to contribute, or fail to contribute, to restoring or reshaping that order.

Furthermore, our mixed methods approach allowed for the identification of each nation's unique situationally-defined perceptions of the global order and their role within it, as well as broader quantitative generalizations. Our findings suggest that the future of global competition, and thus contestation over future defining of the global order is one predicated not on military confrontation, but one based instead on a need for diplomatic and economic capabilities with a further driver being that of cultural cohesion, specifically drawn in contrast to the West. These findings provide both some support for as well as revision of the global order, at least within the short and medium term; long-term projections of what the future global order holds, however, could be in doubt based upon the narrative trajectories presented.

This final chapter integrates our results across all four cases and summarizes its contributions and implications. We begin by comparing our four cases first and second-image relations, that is their narratives about themselves as international agents and stories constituting the international system before extending our analysis to third-image considerations, that is consideration of the international realm not just as actors' environments but a collective project in its own right (Hom & Steele, 2020). In doing so, we focus on how this imagining ties into constructions of self and agency in an anxious global order. Finally, we discuss the level of reflexivity in each nation's narratives and the implications of their trajectories as it relates to the future.

First image: Defining of one's self

As changes in global order evolve, political communities are faced with new challenges regarding who they are. As key supplies of OS, providing a sense of continuity amidst the sea of these changes falls primarily upon national governments if they are to maintain their claims on legitimacy (Krolikowski, 2008; Huysmans, 1998). No more so is this true than for authoritarian-leaning states whose lack of democratic participation results in expectations of economic growth and stability (Huntington, 1991). However, in an era of open communication with economic growth predicated on global trade and technological innovation these states face additional challenges from Western informational and cultural encroachment. Narratives, then, become key resources for states to provide cognitive order within a chaotic world as well as means of maintenance of one's cultural identity. How these nations come to see themselves as agents bound together in common action, specifically what goals they are to pursue and what obstacles threaten their obtainment, play important, albeit different, functions depending upon their past and present circumstances. Here we compare these different constructions before discussing their manifestations within the global order.

China's image of itself is high, but contradictory. Foundationally, Chinese media narratives place the Chinese Communist Party (CCP) as the primary agent defending and marshaling Chinese resources successfully towards greater wealth and prosperity. Historical narratives of past Chinese trauma at the hands of the West and Japanese militarism from the early twentieth-century remain important benchmarks of what China could look like without CCP leadership. These narratives, taking into consideration concerns regarding the need for continued economic development, fuel CCP efforts to continue economic reforms and mark China's greatest vulnerabilities and capabilities regarding competition. The CCP accentuates anxieties of foreign agents seeking to hold it down and contain it while stressing the difficulties of overcoming its middle-income trap if unable to innovate. In turn, these concerns are utilized to further motivate its populace to support efforts to modernize the nation despite the socio-economic uprooting of continued economic growth through globalization while providing a scapegoat to deflect criticism from the government to external actors. Chinese media also project positive visions of the nation supplying its citizenry with ontological stability. Chinese media reports the growth and prestige of China's domestic development and current role in the world both economically and diplomatically. Lending credibility to these narratives, foreign nations are cited as calling for and inviting greater Chinese global leadership with Chinese culture and normative vision of its China Dream and BRI reported as shareable to other nations who want peaceful economic prosperity. Such presentations allow Chinese citizens to envision their nation as one contributing to humanity more broadly. China's identity is portrayed as moral, fair, and as a benevolent actor with this conception of self often contrasted to the US. China's cultural identity is thus further affirmed, with many of these leadership qualities reflected in its Confucian culture—a contrast to debates present in Chinese society at the start of the 20th century.

Russian depictions of itself are driven by a desire for recognition and agency. Memories of its importance during the Cold War in combination with its failed attempt at Westernizing its economy and political system remain the predominant factors bringing the nation together under Putin's leadership. Its imagined loss in international prestige coupled with material concerns over its economy's ability to grow and keep up with other great powers results in an anxious environment to which Russia copes by flexing its military muscle and investing in cultural sources to affirm its sense of importance and define a new civilizational identity, albeit one woven from its past. Russia thus appears attached by its old identities defining itself in opposition to the West with its military adventures further isolating the nation diplomatically and economically, continuing the cycle of Russia as a nation besieged by the West. Nonetheless, this securitization of self appears to provide Russia some agency in moving the nation towards a New Russia while affirming its citizens' ability to persevere and practice self-reliance.

Iran's characterization of its identity draws from its competing cultural narratives to portray the nation as a moral actor and protector of Islam in the Shia Crescent. While the state is shown as a rational and fair actor committed to justice and diplomacy, its identity is primarily drawn in contrast to the US, viewed as representing untrustworthiness, immorality, and self-interested hypocrisy. US actions thus appear to significantly implicate Iran's identity, specifically through its religious narratives emphasizing resistance to Western leadership and values, despite Iranian overtures for rapprochement with world leaders. Thus, while attempting to adapt its identity in relation with others, Iran, beset by a host of coalitions aimed against it, falls back onto its revisionist, resistant identity. Portrayal of the manifold threats the nation faces places Iran in a state of anxiety over its international and regional position, or ontological *in*security, but simultaneously secures the nation's sense of self as its media draws from past and present examples whereby its commitment to its Islamic principles has allowed the state to survive and succeed in resisting US power. Its calls for regional leadership and resistance to Western and Zionist forces imbues the nation with a sense of righteous agency, but places the nation in conflict with its regional and global competitors.

Venezuela's depiction of itself is one in turmoil. The nation remains attached to its Chavismo identity, which problematically stands in contrast to its current material realities. Internationally, whereas it once proudly claimed leadership of Latin America's fraternal brotherhood defined in opposition to US imperial encroachment, today Venezuelan media recognizes it no longer has the ideological or economic support to do so. Likewise, domestically under Hugo Chávez, the nation had a clear political identity as one representing a unique, truer form of political participation through its vision of socialist-democracy. However, the internal pitting of the nation's rich elites against the masses has run its toll on the economy resulting in humanitarian disaster. Unable to enact a revised or new identity, the nation has failed to effect political change at home coupled with fears from foreign intervention abroad. The country is placed in a state of collapsed agency whereby its past attachments and routines no longer are able to bring its people together towards coordinated, collective action for the common good.

Second image: Defining the global order

While domestic factors take center stage in states' constructions of themselves, such manifestations occur not in isolation but in relation with their larger environments (Hom & Steele, 2020). Here one must come to terms with how their nation exists in relation to others in an ontologically *in*secure global order. How states comes to see the international order, including its institutions and norms, lay the foundation for its system of trust implicating their capacity to compete, participate, and change. Through these understandings nations come to imagine the nature of competition, how agency is practiced, and what steps they should take to reach their goals. The nature of global competition comes to be defined differentially depending upon one's capacity and level of trust in the global order and the role they see their identity in relation to others playing out. However, common beliefs in the importance of global institutions remains, as well as shared negative depictions of the US and to a lesser extent Western Europe.

For China, the global order is represented by international institutions, anchored by the United Nations and the World Trade Organization. These institutions provide much needed stability by defining the rules in which states can cooperate economically while promoting steady growth of the global economy; they also place important constraints on international behavior through principles of mutual respect, sovereignty, and cooperation. In sum, the international order is rule-based and draws its legitimacy from values of equality and multilateralism, including participation from all nations, small and large, who wish to pursue peaceful economic development. Agency, then, is derived from one's ability to economically compete and build international trade relations and diplomatic partnerships largely outside of concerns for military conflict, marking the contours of global competition. However, the global order remains tenuous with Chinese anxieties reported as arising from fears of nationalism and protectionism broadly, and Cold War mentalities specifically. Taken together, these factors have the potential to undermine the economic rationale undergirding the international system and the diplomatic-security dimension providing the foundation for cooperative relations. In light of these concerns, China appears to have more trust than ever in the foundational principles of the current order, even suggesting revisions not so much to overturn its ideation, but to maintain its legitimacy by calling for the global order to live up to its ideals by making more space for nations to participate. Thus, the reported decline in US power marks a global order in transition, but one that requires greater participation and voice to new emerging nations. While China appears to believe these revisions will benefit itself, the reverberance of such shifting power dynamics also poses new challenges to navigate if the order is to maintain its legitimacy before China obtains enough power to sustain its own economic innovation and secure its sense of place in the world. This anxiety over eclipsing support for international trade motivates the Chinese state to affirm its values, and at times take a greater leadership role.

Russian media depicts the most agent-centric narrative of the global order. While noting the emergence of a multipolar world order, for Russia this appears to suggest that the US, China, and itself are the predominant forces on the international stage, making the relationships between these nations and their perceived power and interest of paramount importance. Projections of declining US power and ineffective global leadership are the causes for a new global order to emerge. Russian media accentuates the concerns of furthering global anxiety but does so in a way that creates space to support its own role of providing stability as an indispensable counter weight to Western global influence. Thus, within this shifting landscape, Russia defines itself in cultural opposition to the West, characterizing US and Western values as immoral, decadent, self-serving, and corrupt while Russia represents the opposite. Agency, then, is conceptualized primarily in terms of power with the ability to carve out spheres of influence becoming an important project in defining the global order; this leads to more cultural polarization defining a Western camp as distinct from Eurasia. Nonetheless, anxiety over relative power differentials comes to define Russia's worries of the international order, specifically worries over its competitiveness within the economic, cultural, and diplomatic realms. In response, Russia's ordering of the world appears to fall back on its Cold War memories where these components of global competition played out, although the military nature of conflict is relatively muted suggesting a somewhat new nature of global competition today. Importantly, however, when decrying US-led economic sanctions against Russian society, such actions are explained less by some transcendent narrative of global cooperation along international norms and more so in terms of West vs Russian relations. Along this narrative of power, Russia views China as an important actor to cultivate relations with, especially as an alternative to ties with Europe. While international norms are used to support Russian claims of US and Western hypocrisy and immoral leadership, Russia's narratives suggesting alternative multilateral bodies provides a stronger revisionist vision of the future global order while still drawing upon its current values.

Iranian media depict the global order as under threat by US values and leadership. Although viewing the US as the only nation capable of global leadership, US actions, specifically under the Trump administration, are explained as eroding international diplomacy by turning to conflict and aggression leading to a multipolar order whereby diplomatic maneuvering becomes key. The international community thus represents a normative and legal body whose values are in opposition to the US, highlighting the moral correctness of Iran's behavior and justifying its interests. Equally important though is the regional order whereby Saudi Arabia and Zionist forces broadly defined are shown as corrupting and acting against the interests of those living in the Shia Crescent. Thus, whereas Iranian narratives describe the global order in oppositional terms contrasting US and Iranian values, on the regional level Iranian media take on a more explicit religious tone emphasizing its legitimacy as the center of Islamic authority caring for people of the Shia Crescent. For Iran, agency becomes tied to its Islamic principles expressed through resistance but also more constructively by reaffirming and calling for the following of such principles allowing for unity and cooperative relations among its area of influence, enabling Iranian leadership.

Venezuelan media order international affairs by constructing two opposing forces. The first draws from ideological beliefs reminiscent of colonialism, whereby imperialist nations exert power and influence to extract economic benefit from weaker nations and flexing their military might and intervening in local politics when necessary. The second opposing force is that of international law embodied and upheld by the UN. The later provides a legal framework safeguarding state sovereignty and allowing for democratic participation and self-determination. The international system's legitimacy, then, draws from its provision of a peaceful, prosperous, and just world; with Venezuela particularly concerned with political and cultural self-determination. These values stand in contrast to anxiety producing effects of great powers capable of unilateral pursuit of self-interest and their carving out spheres of influence dictating the economic and cultural conditions of weaker nations. Importantly, Venezuela's past experience as a former colony of the West, and more recent history resisting US influence in Latin America, bolster its narrative construction of the global order, but its continuation is reflected in its current weak state in relation to emerging powers such as China, and re-emergent powers like Russia. Thus, while Venezuelan media note that power is shifting within the global order from a declining West towards a strengthening East, the story remains the same: great powers immorally pursuing their interests only constrained by a fragile international community. Here agency is treasured and placed within power-differentials between week and strong states, understood as one's freedom to pursue their own cultural-political society. Nonetheless, Venezuela's inability to compete in global affairs, owing to its lack of material and now ideational resources place it as an object for foreign interference.

First and second image implications

Taken together, our four cases present varying levels of projections of an alternative future order. Their positioning along regional versus global powers appears to provide some difference regarding how these visions of the global order manifest. For China and Russia, these imaginings take larger, albeit differing forms. Although China claims its own political-economic model is unique to its self, nonetheless its depiction of the importance of broad international norms and rules related to international trade and diplomacy are argued to benefit all—even desired by others—marking Chinese visions the most global in nature. Russia's vision of a revised global order is the most ambitious with its suggestion that non-Western nations come to organize as a counterbalance to the unfair deployment of influence from the West; while possessing global ramifications, the target audience nonetheless appears smaller.

Iran and Venezuela appear regionally contained with their visions of the global order. Both nations draw on international norms but in doing so apply them more specifically to immediate dynamics affecting their regional area of concern. Thus, the vision of global order is primarily seen as placing normative restraints on nations possessing greater influence than themselves. This is not to say regional orders cannot influence global orders. Indeed, previous research argues the opposite (Pu, 2011; Acharaya, 2018). Furthermore, under Chávez, Venezuela did project regional narratives designed to influence the global order (Mijares, 2017) with Iran's theocratic revolution undoubtedly shifting global alignments. The difference then comes from Iran and Venezuela's current defensive and tenuously situated position: Iran facing significant international and regional efforts to contain it, with mounting pressures internally, while Venezuela is unable to provide even a basic level of political stability or economic development. Thus, when one's capacity to compete is limited by heightened threats to one's security, the degree to which future oriented and constructive-based narratives are discussed fall into abeyance. In other words, previous OS identities, narratives, and routines could provide some agency holding a nation together when facing significant threats but when left unadapted to current situations there is a trade for immediate security over more constructive, future oriented imaginations (Mitzen, 2006).

Therefore, our findings suggest that different OS beliefs can hold various capacities for agency influencing the global order based on their level of trust in the system to meet their needs. However, this is true too of the West led by the US. As the data demonstrates, these four nations, while presenting visions of global order counter to the West nonetheless appear largely fractured, even in competition with each other. For Russia, this is its need for recognition and prestige of itself as a global power to make up for disillusionment over its domestic economy and fears of cultural encroachment by the West. For China, it is its emphasis on economic innovation and trade to prevent it from falling into the middle-income trap. For Iran, it is its Islamic identity as defender of the Shia Crescent while diplomatically and economically isolated. And for Venezuela, it is preventing foreign intervention into its failed domestic political system while attempting to hold on to its Chavismo identity. For these four competitor nations, then, the driving factor remains domestic politics, which inhibits their ability to shape the global order; with four different foci situationally located related to their perceptions of their own abilities to compete in the global order and sense of continuity of self, such narrative visions are not easily shareable to others—perhaps reflective of the inherent rigidity of more authoritarian leaning states.

Thus, as counter narratives to the West, these visions do not achieve coalescence beyond their criticism of the US. This shows less of an international collective movement against the US-led *system*, perhaps even an affirmation of it if current international values are fairly applied. In other words, none of these nations narratively project enough influence to provide a sufficiently different alternative vision extendable to the entire globe, but instead call for revisions coming from within the current norms or rules. The values of the US-led order, then, still provide the most applicable vision of international order extendable across the globe. These findings support Acharya's (2018) claim that voice and representation matters most and Eilstrup-Sangiovanni and Hofmann's (2019) argument of not a profound or definitive crisis of the existing order, but one undergoing a transformation from within into a broader, more inclusive system of governance.

Agency, reflexivity, and change

In response to the evolving global order, and as the summaries of China, Russia, Iran, and Venezuela's depictions of their "self" demonstrate, all four nations draw upon their past to maintain a sense of continuity safeguarding their feelings of agency via their relations to others and routine participation in the global order as explained by early theorizations of OS. However, given the importance of agency in how global order is constructed (Acharya, 2018), it's worth further investigation regarding how these nations attempt to maintain and exert it.

Whereas previous OS research focused on agency as one's ability to maintain a continuous sense of self as the means to identify what actions to pursue (Mitzen, 2006; Giddens, 1991), more current studies have undertaken greater explication of what forms such agency could take. Recently, Berenskötter (2020) theorizes OS concerns beyond securitization to explore the extent to which reflexive actors can redefine themselves in new, and potentially more constructive manners. Specifically, he offers three notions of agency—muted, emancipatory, and creative constructive—with additional descriptions of radical agency. Although he calls for OS scholarship to explore more radical or revolutionary forms of agency, our study, perhaps optimistically, showcases that the four nations under analysis are not attempting a radical revision of themselves or their places in the global order in an attempt to overthrow the current system, but rather to make revisions from within the existing system. Thus, we describe our cases' conceptions of agency within Berenskötter's (2020) non-radical conceptions.

According to Berenskötter (2020), muted agency occurs when subjects are full of anxiety-stabilizing mechanisms they cannot or rather not question, sustaining one's existing mechanisms for managing anxiety. This notion feels agentic, but results in one acting out a role in a given script and thereby minimally creative. Emancipatory agency, however, is the realization of one having a choice, or the ability to act "otherwise." Emancipatory agency liberates one's sense of being through recognition of and confidence in its ability to transform one's being in the world. Creative-constitutive agency is a reaction to an event that undermines existing anxiety-stabilizing mechanisms and destabilizes conceptions of being in time. This then generates demands for the creation of new mechanisms to stabilize one's anxiety.

These three conceptions of agency are useful, but we argue overlap to varying degrees based upon our results. Specifically, in stepping back and comparing our four cases' different narrative imaginings regarding how their nation manages and adapts a sense of self in relation to an ontological *in*secure global landscape, we identify four different states of what we call agency actualization: constructive, reactionary, defensive, and collapsed. In doing so, we combine Berenskötter's (2020) typology with consideration of each nation's ability to actualize its identity to shape the global order.

The first, constructive is the most reflexive and demonstrates the greatest capacity to influence global norms, represented by the narratives of China. Here, Chinese narratives display the nation as enacting both emancipatory and creative-constructive agency. The first by China's balance and application of its multiple identities as a developing nation and one of economic strength and a great power but also one promising not to exercise such strength. In other words, China remains relatively unconstrained by the identity it projects at home and abroad based on the specific circumstances it finds itself in. The second comes from China's response to the leadership vacuum from the US's withdrawal and unwillingness to uphold international norms, to which China promises to support, in addition to its push towards embracing globalization and international trade, despite its destabilizing effects, in order to innovate its economy and ability to compete.

The second, reactionary, reflects Russian narratives combining muted and emancipatory forms of agency. In doing so, it is less reflexive—with Russia trapped in its biographical narratives of a strong, global power in opposition to the West, but still somewhat imaginative by adapting such identity towards its "rediscovery" of the Rus people and shifting its relations from the West to Eurasia. This narrative reapplication still manages significant international reshaping, marking it as relatively strong in agency onto global politics.

The third, defensive, combines muted and creative-constitutive agency as seen by Iranian narratives. Here Iran is placed into an inward, regional looking posture having to manage anxieties from US-led isolation and in response to immediate pressures on the state. Thus, Iran largely falls back on its autobiographical narratives to maintain a domestic sense of self and routine demonization of US actions. The pressures faced externally places additional obstacles on domestic political reform as further instability threatens to unravel its fragile political associations. Iranian narratives, then, have limited global sway.

The fourth, collapsed, describes a state of muted and *negative* creative-constitutive agency, illustrated in Venezuelan media narratives. Here Venezuelan society finds itself in such high levels of anxiety across international and domestic situations that it falls back to previous identities and autobiographical narratives. However, doing so marks a form of *negative* creative-constitutive agency in that it is a poor crisis response, to which new narratives of self are required, but are not created. Thus, the past sources of anxiety-stabilization result in only a minimum level of OS incapable of creating a strong enough sense of self for action but enough to inhibit a breaking or reimagining of new identities. Collapsed agency represents little capacity for action both at home and abroad.

In sum, when portending how the future global order might unfold, only Russian narratives mark a significant change in the global system. Nonetheless, even Russia, along with the other three cases incorporate values of the existing order within their narratives. Furthermore, whereas Chinese narratives have the greatest capacity for shaping global norms, they also support the current system the most. While each case's sense of self might be challenged or threatened by US behavior, such conflictual relations with the US enhances their sense of self through identification of the US as their chief competitor, lending some domestic legitimacy and identity stability. Additionally, US actions, perceived as self-serving or hypocritical further enables each country to claim moral leadership—an important element in state's OS foreign policy narratives (Steele, 2008), albeit in different ways: Russia as defender against the West, China as supporter of equitable trade and economic growth, Venezuela as standing against imperialists, and Iran as a moral and religious leader. The implication being that significant changing of the global order appears especially difficult as each nation's sense of trust and relations to other nations remain anchored in the current system's values, eschewing unilateralism in exchange for diplomacy. While nations are often portrayed as acting in opposition to such normative ideals, this behavior leads to signaling of such values, furthering the structuration of the current order, and providing some cognitive respite against an anarchical world; the construction of which we discuss in the next section.

Third image: Collective constitution of a fragile global system

While this study shares assumptions with constructivist concerns regarding the importance of norms and ideas in international politics, depictions from all four nations, to some extent, lend support towards realist's notions of an anarchical world. As Rumelili (2020) notes, anxiety is a central element driving Hobbesian individuals to egoism and power competition. However, it also serves as a constitutive condition. Here concerns for security, both physical and otherwise provides the potential for change while also motivating state behavior outside of security concerns including humanitarian actions. In this vein, our results suggest that anxiety over power differentials within a fragile global order constructed upon an anarchical system supports nations' affirmation and speech acts constituting the global order as one anchored in international norms and institutions. In other words, our four cases appear to see their pursuit of power as best operating largely within the international order, granting it some level of legitimacy.

When abstracting the narratives surrounding global competition from all four nations, the global system appears fragile but still offering constraints on international behavior. More importantly, its basic values remain supported, even called upon, when diagnosing inappropriate actions and the problems faced by the international community. Unsurprisingly, the US is ever present in these nations' description of global competition, to which they all hold severely negative views. Paradoxically though, the US represents one pillar of the global order though critiques leveled against it primarily take aim at its behavior being in contrast to the values it itself imbued in international institutions. Thus, our current international institutions represent the second pillar of the international order, the one holding up the system from falling into ill reputed power-based competition. By narrating US actions in contrast to international norms, the global order—as represented by its international institutions and values—remain important organizing anchors by which these four nations come to understand international relations broadly defined.

Despite some support for the international system, questions remain regarding its ability to provide all nations with the ability to succeed in operating within it opening up the potential for change. Here again predominate concerns are more so placed within the international system than outside; none of the four countries believe abandoning the international architecture is beneficial nor envision a new world order drastically different from the current, although Russia comes the closest to doing so. Thus the concerns are less about military application of power and more so about the consequences of the open, free flow of trade and information; that is, whether the system allows for their economic prosperity while safeguarding their sense of self as a cultural bound, unique socio-political entity.

Therefore, while global trade might offer significant benefits, it also leads to inequality within and between states. This economic dimension comes with cultural concerns as well as those over international media shaping people's imaginaries of what wealth looks like and alternatives for political governance and societal values. The latter of which can be seen as the driving force of Russian, Iranian, Venezuelan, and Chinese autobiographical narratives of who they are and what they stand for. Whether or not other nations want to emulate Western culture or values to varying levels matter less than the existence of them as alternatives. These alternatives create pressures for change as national leaders grapple with how to provide prosperity to their citizenry when confronted by globalization's disruptive forces demanding new notions of self, given that the past is no longer.

These challenges demonstrate the dynamic, interconnected challenges—both practical and symbolic—of third-image identity formation of the global system (Hom & Steele, 2020). Here the narratives circulated within Chinese, Russian, Iranian, and Venezuelan national media grapple with resisting consensus narratives regarding the efficacy of Western values, models of economics, and governance practices with the need to demonstrate how their own beliefs can still support their identities as capable of providing for their citizenry. Their narratives communicating how the international system works present the anxieties regarding US dominance, along with cultural and economic threats to themselves, as a result of to the competitive nature of globalization. But they also assuage such fears by depicting the morality of their own actions and conveying some belief in their ability to compete and overcome these challenges. Thus, as we argued in the introduction, the perceived ability for nations to compete in the global order influences how they come to see it as supportive or a hindrance. For those who have the economic and cultural resources to garner its benefits, their sense of self and views of the order are more supportive—like China. Those afraid of whether they possess sufficient resources are driven to find alternative means to maintain a sense of self, often directed against others, like Russia. Nonetheless, the shared belief that there should be an international system constraining state-power that provides multilateral institutions facilitating cooperation and trade defines the imperfect, but important constitutive creation of the international order.

Our four cases' concerns with the fragility of the current order and threats present within it as an imperfect system highlights the important distinction between fear and anxiety, implicating the nature of change within the future global order. A persistent criticism of ontological security (OS) research has been its focus on fear, specifically fear as motivating a resistance to change, leading to a status quo bias whereby actors lack the resources to conceptualize alternative possibilities (Rossdale, 2015; Lebow, 2016; Rumelili, 2015; Kinnvall & Mitzen, 2020). As Kinnvall and Mitzen (2020) explain, fear is more narrowly reflected in one's fight or flight responses whereas anxiety includes a broader range of emotions, such as excitement and anticipation as well as a variety of behaviors "from compulsive repetition, to acting out, to paralysis, to entrepreneurship" (p. 241). Our analysis of the competitive dynamics of global competition highlights this anxiety dimension of international politics as perceived within national media narratives. Chinese media best highlight the role of anxiety rather than fear in that their concerns over their ability to compete economically leads to adaptive identities. Their mix of optimism, that is capabilities, along with its stated vulnerabilities, places them in anxious anticipation regarding whether they will achieve their moderately prosperous society. Despite a trade war with the US, China still did not fall back on its anti-multilateralism narratives from the past but instead projected a greater leadership role in affirming the values of open trade; Russia, while worried about Western cultural encroachment and economic isolationism, fell back on previous identities but also exercised adaptability by envisioning a new Eurasian partnership. Even Iran, driven by concerns over concerted diplomatic action against it adapted, at first, by signing the Joint Comprehensive Plan of Action with the US, before then, once the US pulled out, stepped up its diplomatic overtures with the European Union (EU).

The difference, then, between fear and anxiety is important, especially when considering what the future global order looks like. Fear, like previous research suggests, most likely results in reaffirming past identities with the potential for greater conflict as shifts in the balance of power make past practices untenable. Mitigating such fears becomes essential to prevent a sharp revision of the global order, reflective of the international relations literature on power transitions. Anxiety, on the other hand, is both ever present and can provide motivation for change. As Arfi (2020) states, "to survive is to be anxious" (p. 291). As our study shows, US competitors are more so in a state of anxiety than fear, as all but Venezuela report greater capacity to compete than vulnerabilities. While their identities might pit themselves in opposition to the US, they remain capable, to various degrees, of reforming the international system through diplomatic endeavors to actualize a more constrained, multilateral order.

Importantly, anxiety is likely to increase. As Kissinger (2014) claimed, world order needs both commonly accepted rules as well as power to back them up when actors step outside appropriate behavior. Returning to Crick (2014) and Arendt (1972), power lies in the process by which political communities come together through communication towards concerted action. While our study focused on how this plays out within national media discourse, the four alternative, and perhaps competing, visions of global order identified suggests the international community has limited, but still some, capacity for cooperation. Thus, as US relative power declines greater uncertainty regarding how the international order hangs together will only grow. While one cannot escape anxiety, outright fear can be lessened. Healthy levels of anxiety could lead to a reaffirmation of global values and participation in the global order, if some trust remains in its ability to afford nations the capacity to successfully compete. If this trust disappears and space for alternative voices does not occur, various regionalized narratives will emerge to provide domestic cognitive stability to grapple with a less secure global landscape. If trust in the international system sufficiently declines, however, fear could overwhelm anxiety leading to insular, maladaptive identity changes, or retrenchment, resulting in a less robust and mutually constitutive global sensemaking.

Capacity for reflection and narrative trajectories

Living in an anxious world requires performative leaps of faith in the security of one's existence as the future is unknown (Arfi, 2020). Importantly, faith assumes some future. And like faith, the temporal nature of narratives provide a forward trajectory or resolution. While multiple narrative explanations always exist, their overlapping and repeated depiction of events and agents could form a sedimentation, even inertia—and like faith, be held stronger at times than others. While Arfi argues that both rigid and reflexive attachments require leaps of faith as individuals simultaneously secure a sense of being while moving towards the opposite—that is death, we contend that various levels of reflexivity remain important for states' narrative constructions of self as they, made up of societal collectives, can live on beyond their individuals. In this sense, rigid attachment can be a denial of change, even leading to state collapse if external events boil to crisis, whereas reflexivity can allow for growth while maintaining some continuity of the state into the future.

Thus, we can expect greater reflexivity when actors hold greater trust in their ability to compete in the global order, and the opposite as anxiety increases, especially if turning towards fear. As Krolikowski (2008) argues actors with stable basic trust systems have the cognitive space enabling rational deliberation, allowing them the capacity to learn to adapt, whereas those with little trust are unable to do so, falling on past practices. In this sense, we argue that less adaptive narrative forms rely more on essentialization practices, occurring when insecurity rises, whereas more transcendent narratives provide allow constructive, flexible imaginings possible when one believes in their ability to successfully compete in the global order.

Anxiety and essentialized identity narratives

Perhaps the easiest and most common means to understanding one's self is through definition of what one is not, or the construction of the "other." In the OS literature, this process occurs through the essentialization of identities (Kay, 2012; Skey, 2010; Steele, 2008). While such practices can form important social glues contributing to cooperative efforts, previous research suggests essentialized identities are more likely to produce hard attachment to past routines and relationships whereas more flexible characterizations of others allows for alternative visions of self (Krolikowski, 2008; Mitzen, 2006). Eberle's (2019) notion of fantasy narratives similarly provides black and white depictions, but not just related to identities but also resolutions to specific problems, or obstacles facing the subject from attaining their desired object. Like identity essentialization, fantasies hold political collectives together, but do so by providing an overarching mission of purpose fueled by desire. Fantasy narratives, while powerful, also pose significant risk if one fails to achieve its objective.

The results of our study suggests identity essentialization generally occurs most when feelings of angst regarding one's environment is highest. As the quantitative results showed, Iranian and Russian media were the most likely to signal deterrent messages, with Iran citing high levels of conflict and competitor nations and the most negative perspective of the US. Qualitatively, Iran and Russia appear most entrenched to their past identities as defined in opposition to the US. Both identities pose problems. For Russia, maintaining its anti-US/Western identity, while claiming great power status leads to foreign policy behavior symbolically affirming such ideations, but risks economic development and diplomatic isolation, furthering its insecure position to the West. Like Russia, Iran is stuck in its anti-US posturing while remaining committed to its antagonistic claim of Islamic leadership in the Middle East despite rising threats from Saudi Arabia, Israel, and the US. Nonetheless, both nations report greater competitive capabilities than vulnerabilities, and thus some elements of flexibility. Russia's essentialized notion of itself and the West is utilized to pursue an altered identity reclaiming its Eurasian roots. Iran's emphasis of itself as distinct from the US allows for further delineation between EU behavior and US actions; allowing Iran some ability to negotiate when the US takes a less confrontational approach and Iranian attempts at diplomatic alignment with the EU against the US.

The future of these two nations, however, is unclear. Russia's vision of a Eurasian cultural sphere marks its object of desire, painted clearly in opposition to the West. If obtained, it might garner enough confidence in the nation's ability to safely exist economically and culturally in a changing global order but furthers an oppositional positioning to the West, posing future challenges. If unobtained, the Russian state could repeat a similar fate as the Soviet Union—unable to compete economically as it detaches its economy from Western trade and innovation leading to domestic disillusionment confronted with a loss in international agency.

While Iran's narratives have a less clear object of desire, its rhetoric points to a state of regional strength capable of standing up against the US. More concretely included in this fantasy is its nuclear program and claims to religious leadership in the Middle East. But, as the fantasy narrative is less clear, so too is the extent of its communal attractiveness. Iranian domestic politics include debates over the efficacy of pursing nuclear capabilities, especially regarding what cost doing so will incur to basic economic growth (Chubin, 2010; Wintour, 2020; Nephew, 2016). Thus, if Iran's fundamentalist faction is unable to demonstrate some level of success in its pursuit of conflictual relations with the US, domestic dissatisfaction could lead to more progressive policies and identity revision. However, greater conflict with the US could also lead to fear resulting in retrenchment of its anti-US identity, further threatening its security, even resulting in war, as in the case in January 2020 (Ostovar, 2020). Managing a balance of its identity constructions is therefore crucial to the future Iranian state.

Venezuela offers a unique case in that its environment is the least secure as it was the only country to have more vulnerabilities cited than capabilities, as well as high levels of reported conflict escalation. In response it unreflexively falls back on its previous Chavismo identity. However the "others" in which it defines itself against have multiplied, becoming more ambiguous and abstracted to imperialist nations more generally with authoritarianism at home further mudding the fidelity of such narratives; instead of having one clear "other" it has Russia, China, the US, and perhaps even Nicolas Maduro. Thus, while still possessing essentialized notions of self and other, such constructions no longer hold the nation together, overwhelming anxieties over its ability to function inhibits new identities to form, even when confronted with a need for change. In terms of its fantasy narrative, then, we see the consequences of *failed* obtainment. Temporally, its object of desire, that is a socialist-democratic country leading Latin America in an alternative vision against the neoliberal economic order, has passed, leaving an unraveled society with little trust in itself or the world. Its future thus remains bleak, until a new source of trust emerges allowing for a revised sense of self.

China stands in contrast to all these three nations. As the only country with a positive view of the global order and with the greatest frequency of capacities to compete, it appears its relatively higher trust in the global system allows it greater adaptability of identities, resulting in a less essentialized view of itself and others. This does not mean that enemies are absent from Chinese narratives; instead they fall into the background allowing China itself to take center stage. Its self-identity is thus more multifaceted, with our results confirming Pu's (2019) analysis of China showing itself as both a developing nation and economically prosperous; both influential but also eschewing designs for hegemony. Likewise, the narratives present in Chinese media regarding others are broader and less polarizing; although critical of the US it includes concerns over policy direction with the US both as an adversary but also a partner depending on how its actions play into China's development goals. Other nations too are less defined in opposition to Chinese interests and instead viewed as potential partners for further economic growth. Thus, while possessing the desire to obtain a level of moderate economic prosperity, China's goals reflect less of Eberle's (2019) fantasy narratives and more so an acceptance of its fragile nature of self or "security of being" (Kinnvall et al., 2018).

Transcendent narratives

While the discussion above highlights the more rigid narrative visions from our four cases under analysis vis-à-vis their construction of others, it's important to note the environmental drivers by which these states in turn uniquely define themselves. As Subotić (2016) explains, embedded in narratives are answers regarding to what purpose is a community brought together. For our cases, the answers are intimately tied to each government's nondemocratic leanings and historical past. All four have turbulent pasts with the West. In response, all four have emerged with government systems in contrast to Western values. These alternative governance models specifically arose from the unstable conditions caused by Western preeminence, with their success, and in turn legitimacy, resulting from their ability to enact a new sense of national identity supported by defense of their borders and the provision of some economic growth and social stability. While not perfect systems, with instability remaining to various levels at different moments in time, fears of past inadequacy—and memories of societal chaos—maintain some cultural inertia against radical change. Indeed, all four nations' governments accentuate these fears thereby simultaneously reducing their citizenry's OS so that their populace becomes reliant upon their governments as the essential providers of it (see Krolikowski, 2008). The nation then becomes identified with the ruling party in power, most obviously seen by narratives of "China as the CCP, and the CCP as China;" as well as "Putin as Russia and Russia as Putin."

Global competition, then, exists beyond military consideration to include culture as a key battleground. While state level competition is one important dynamic, perceptions of domestic legitimacy are too. For these four nations, ensuring a continued sense of cultural identity remains tenuous as economic prosperity requires some degree of open borders inevitably ushering in competing Western values. They remain on the defensive until their alternative systems provide enough soft power, or attraction, relative to the West; or, conversely, until Western norms of democracy become sufficiently unattractive. Iran's green revolution, Russia's proposed decoupling with the West, and China's fears of Soviet collapse from perestroika and glasnost coupled with its China Dream narrative all highlight the very real perceptions regarding the consequences of cultural competition. Nonetheless, China's success in providing sustained economic growth despite an illiberal system of governance has symbolically come to be seen by many to point out how Western values are not the only pathway to growth. Likewise, perceptions in declining US and Western power coupled with disillusionment over the messiness of democracy has weakened Western hegemony. As economic globalization has brought new nations out of poverty, the belief in a viable multipolar world order has intensified, requiring new transcendent narratives of what the future global order comes to represent.

Competition does not necessarily portend conflict. Again, healthy levels of anxiety can produce change. However, if the global order fails to make space for others to participate on their own accords, albeit within mutually negotiated bounds—via a transcendent narrative of order, distrust in the system's affordance of others to provide some benefits to their populace could drive essentialized identities leading to conflict. Indeed, as all four nations examined in this study show their domestic national identities, and

OS, are defined in conflict with the US. Loss of trust and heightened anxiety giving rise to fear could place such anti-US identities at dangerous levels.

But what if the US adapted its relation vis-à-vis these nations? Theoretically, US cooperative overtures would disrupt the fidelity of Chinese, Russian, Iranian, and Venezuelan narratives, but not necessarily their coherence. While it is easy to think such a reset in relations could change things, our data suggests that this alone will not resolve the drivers of our four nations' OS constructions. Indeed, the US and Russia have reset their relations to little avail in the past; the Obama administration did much of the same with Iran. Likewise, US policymakers consistently discuss new means to positively engage with China. But, in each circumstance, trust remains in doubt as past memories and narratives of conflict still circulate. As each of these nations define their state as tied to their undemocratic system of governance, episodic claims of cooperation by the US fail to resolve its own underlining belief in democracy as universally worthy pursuit.

Thus, it appears that a peaceful evolution of the future global order will require new narratives moving beyond democratic values to include alternatives. Offering such a space will provide room for continued competition within more healthy boundaries. This is not to say that democratic principles could not eventually emerge; indeed, if such values are competitively successful others might gradually incorporate them. However, this is more peacefully possible if nations have enough trust in the international system and themselves so that reflexivity can occur. In contrast, forcibly applying such values might result in the opposite, as states feel threatened and fall back on past routines.

Conclusion

Though our data suggests that the future global order largely affirms its current international norms and values, it's important to recognize potential alternatives. As discussed above, the temporal nature of Venezuela's object of desire has come and gone, contributing to, we argue, its collapsed sense of agency, both at home and abroad. However, Russia and China's have not. Russia's current vision of a Eurasian cultural sphere distinct from the West and China's two centenary goals to achieve a moderately prosperous society and national rejuvenation hold important considerations to the future global order.

The specific nature of what a distinct Eurasian sphere will hold is unclear, especially the extent to which it will materialize. Russia's image of itself suggests such a project will not equally view others in the region as on the same level. Thus, the attractiveness or cohesion of such an alignment suggests limited impact on the future global order, including concerns over a new East vs West alignment. It is similarly unlikely that Russia will have the economic or technological resources to sustain such a grouping, let alone result in enough economic potential to curtail domestic concerns over Russia's economy. Instead, Russia will likely limp along, at times acting out, and continuing to critique the West to decrease its relative level of soft power attractiveness towards other partners.

China on the other hand, if able to continue its economic development, could surpass Russia's influence in the region, perhaps even becoming more of a competitor than ally. More importantly, though, when considering China's own vision of global power a crucial question emerges regarding what happens after 2049, the centenary of the founding of the CCP and the supposed date by which China is purported to have rejuvenated its strength. Currently, China sees the international order as necessary for its economic development. If, however, it is able to sustain domestic innovation and consumer-driven economic growth, whether such international institutions continue to be necessary could come in doubt, especially if the US is perceived as placing significant constraints on China's economy. At this point, or leading to it, depending on China's economic development and bilateral ties to other nations, the nation could begin a more ambitious project to reshape the global order more akin to its image.

Nonetheless, while Western audiences are quick to excite over fears of China's rise or Russian antagonism, their basis of OS remains fragile. While promising such ambitious projects might help hold their societies together now, if they fail while the West continues to succeed, the basis for both governments' legitimacy will be challenged. How they adapt will likely cause significant consternation, even chaos or further retrenchment in anti-Western essentialization practices making conflict dangerously more likely. How the world responds will play an important role too. If the US attempts to contain or isolate either nation, the situation could worsen. Whether the US or West possesses enough trust in their own systems to compete, and therefore the space for reflexivity and adaptation of their own imagined relations, will play an important role mitigating conflict and shaping the future global order.

References

Acharya, A. (2018). *Constructing global order: Agency and change in world politics.* Cambridge University Press.

Arendt, H. (1972). *Crises of the republic: Lying in politics; Civil disobedience; On violence; Thoughts on politics and revolution.* Harcourt Brace Jovanovich.

Arfi, B. (2020). Security qua existential surviving (while becoming otherwise) through performative leaps of faith. *International Theory.* 12(2), 291–305.

Berenskötter, F. (2020). Anxiety, time, and agency. *International Theory.* 12(2), 273–290.

Chubin, S. (2010, October). The politics of Iran's nuclear program. *The Iran primer.* https://iranprimer.usip.org/resource/politics-irans-nuclear-program.

Crick, N. (2014). *Rhetoric and power: The drama of classical Greece.* University of South Carolina Press.

Eberle, J. (2019). Narrative, desire, ontological security, transgression: Fantasy as a factor in international politics. *Journal of International Relations and Development*. 22(1), 243–268.

Eilstrup-Sangiovanni, M. & Hofmann, S. C. (2020). Of the contemporary global order, crisis, and change. *Journal of European Public Policy*. 27(7), 1077–1089.

Giddens, A. (1991). *Modernity and self-identity: Self and society in the late Modern Age*. Stanford University Press.

Hom, A. R. & Steele, B. J. (2020). Anxiety, time, and ontological security's third-image potential. *International Theory*. 12(2), 322–336.

Huntington, S. P. (1991). How countries democratize. *Political Science Quarterly*. 106(4), 579–616.

Huysmans, J. (1998). Security! What do you mean? From concept to thick signifier. *European Journal of International Relations*. 4(2), 226–255.

Kay, S. (2012). Ontological security and peace-building in Northern Ireland. *Contemporary Security Policy*. 33(2), 236–263.

Kinnvall, C., Manners, I., & Mitzen, J. (2018). Introduction to 2018 special issue of European Security: "Ontological (in)security in the European Union." *European Security*. 27(3), 249–265.

Kinnvall, C. & Mitzen, J. (2020). Anxiety, fear, and ontological security in world politics: Thinking with and beyond Giddens. *International Theory*. 12(2), 240–256.

Kissinger, H. (2014). *World Order*. Penguin Books.

Krolikowski, A. (2008). State personhood in ontological security theories of international relations and Chinese nationalism: A sceptical view. *Chinese Journal of International Politics*. 2(1), 109–133.

Lebow, R. N. (2016). *National identities and international relations*. Cambridge University Press.

Mijares, V. M. (2017). Soft balancing the titans: Venezuelan foreign-policy strategy toward the United States, China, and Russia. *Latin American Policy*. 8(2), 201–231.

Mitzen, J. (2006). Ontological security in world politics: State identity and the security dilemma. *European journal of international relations*. 12(3), 341–370.

Nephew, R. (2016). *What the nuclear deal means for moderates in Iranian politics*. Brookings Institute. February 16, 2016. www.brookings.edu/blog/markaz/2016/02/16/what-the-nuclear-deal-means-for-moderates-in-iranian-politics.

Ostovar, A. (2020). How did the U.S. get to the brink of war with Iran? *The Washington Post*. January 3, 2020. www.washingtonpost.com/politics/2020/01/03/how-did-us-get-brink-war-with-iran.

Pu, X. (2011). Socialisation as a two-way process: Emerging powers and the diffusion of international norms. *The Chinese Journal of International Politics*. 5(4), 341–367.

Pu, X. (2019). *Rebranding China: Contested status signaling in the changing global order*. Stanford University Press.

Rossdale, C. 2015. Enclosing critique: The limits of ontological security. *International Political Sociology*. 9(4), 369–386.

Rumelili, B. (2015). Identity and Desecuritization: The Pitfalls of Conflating Ontological and Physical Security. *Journal of International Relations and Development*. 18(1), 52–74.

Rumelili, B. (2020). Integrating anxiety into international relations theory: Hobbes, existentialism, and ontological security. *International Theory*. 12(2), 257–272.

Skey, M. (2010). 'A sense of where you belong in the world': National belonging, ontological security and the status of the ethnic majority in England. *Nations and Nationalism*. 16(4), 715–733.

Steele, B. J. (2008). *Ontological security in international relations: Self-identity and the IR state*. Routledge.

Subotić, J. (2016). Narrative, ontological security, and foreign policy change. *Foreign Policy Analysis*. 12(4), 610–627.

Wintour, P. (2020). Rise of Iran hardliners threatens nuclear diplomacy, Europe warned. *The Guardian*. June 24, 2020. www.theguardian.com/world/2020/jun/24/rise-of-iran-hardliners-threatens-nuclear-diplomacy-europe-warned.

Appendixes

Appendix A: Content Coding Schema

Table A.1

Quantitative Content Analysis Coding Schema

Category	*Code*	*Description*
Key Vulnerabilities: Stated weaknesses of the nation.	Diplomatic	Lack of diplomatic ties with power broker nations; international institutions-useful/effective or not; creation of new institutions.
	Information	Threats on cyber, AI, technology networks, propaganda or cultural information and nationalism.
	Military	Expressed military weakness: troops, equipment, infrastructure, balance of power.
	Economic	Sanctions, trade threats, trade espionage, economic growth-or weakness/decline; access to markets or institutions.
Necessary Capabilities: Stated capabilities seen as required to compete in the global order.	Diplomatic	Hosting summits, having representation in international forums, building of bilateral ties, requirement of international recognition.
	Information	AI, tech networks, cultural development; Note: informational capabilities under economic umbrella were not included here.
	Military	New weapons systems, military resources required for security in shifting global order, military alliances, hybrid warfare.
	Economic	Descriptive keys to economic growth: industries, strategies, alliances, innovation; benefits and participation in trade pacts; domestic or international driven economic growth.
Escalation Management		Conflict escalation is the process by which conflicts grow in severity over time. This category identifies mentions of ways to combat, thwart, or bypass conflict escalation.

Quantitative Content Analysis Coding Schema

Category	*Code*	*Description*
Legitimate Deterrence		The action of discouraging an action or event through instilling doubt or fear of the consequences, recognized as viable and legal in the eyes of the actor.
Competitors		Mentions of direct competitive challenging of the nation's interests in some critical capacity.
Alliances		Mentions of cooperative alliances, partners, treaties, trade and/or closeness between the nation and others.
Redlines		Statement that if actor x does y, military response will ensue.
National Perspectives: Stated viewpoints related to the functioning of the global order	Country's role in global order	Global order includes balance of power, global norms and rules, as well as references to global decision-making bodies comprising the bulk of nation state actors; this code requires a stated outline of the specific role of the host nation in shaping, contributing, or standing in contrast to it.
	Global order	Global order includes balance of power, global norms and rules, as well as references to global decision-making bodies; this code requires a direct statement on changes/shifts/maintenance/influence of global order.
	United States	Editorial type claim on the actions, values, or behavior of the United States.
	Western Europe	Editorial type claim on the actions, values, or behavior of Western Europe nations (as a bloc).

Each news article was also examined for the following elements: presence of a foreign media source citation, foreign political source direct quote, foreign government agency direct quote, foreign civil society (academic, industry professional, celebrity) direct quote.

Each news article was assessed by the following narrative components: Act (what happened, direction of action), Scene (when and where action occurred, including context or situation), Agent (who performed the action), Agency/Instrument (mechanism behind how the action itself was performed), Purpose (why the action occurred, toward what end was the action intended).

Appendix B: Media Sources

Table A2

Index of Media Sources Searched

China	Iran	Russia	Venezuela
163	*Al Alam News*	*Argumenty i Fakty*	*Correo del Orinoco*
Caixin	Alvefagh online	Gazeta.ru	*El Carabobeño*
Cankao Xiaoxi	FARS News Agency	*Izvestiya*	*El Nacional*
China Daily	*Iran Daily*	*Kommersant*	*El Universal*
China News Service	Iranian Students News Agency	*Komsomolskaya Pravda*	*El Viejo Topo*
China.com	Mehr News Agency	*Moskovskiy Komsomolez*	EntornoInteligente.com
Global Times	*Tehran Times*	*Nezavisimaya Gazeta*	Globovisión
People's Daily		RBK	La iguana TV
Xinhua News Agency		RIA Novosti	*La Nación*
		Rosbalt	*La Patilla*
		Rossiyskaya Gazeta	*La Verdad*
		Russia Today	*Panorama*
		TASS	*Rebelión*
		Trud	*Tal Cual*
		Vedomosti	unionradio.net
		Vesti.ru	

Appendix C: Key Terms

Table A3

Search Terms	
China	地缘政治竞争or全球竞争or国际比赛，全球秩序 or 国际秩序，国际影响力or 全球影响力or 地缘政治影响
Iran	النظام or المنافسة الجيوسياسية, النظام العالمي or مسابقة عالمية or مسابقة دولية سلطة دولي or الدولي, سلطة عالمي
Russia	геёпёлитическая кёнкуренция, глёбальная кёнкуренция, мирёвая кёнкуренция, междунарёдная кёнкуренция, глёбальный пёрядёк, междунарёдный пёрядёк, мирёвёй пёрядёк, глёбальнёе влияние, мирёвёе влияние, междунарёднёе влияние, геёпёлитическёе влияние
Venezuela	competencia global or Competicion internacional or competencia geopolítica, orden global or orden internacional, influencia global or influencia internacional or influencia geopolítica

Index

Note: **Bold** page numbers refer to tables.